Felix Mendelssol

# PASSION vs. DUTY

# HELEN MARTENS

# PASSION VERSUS DUTY
Copyright © 2012 by Helen Martens

ISBN: 978-1-77069-368-5

Printed in Canada

Word Alive Press
131 Cordite Road, Winnipeg, MB R3W 1S1
www.wordalivepress.ca

Library and Archives Canada Cataloguing in Publication

Martens, Helen
    Passion vs duty : Felix Mendelssohn / by Helen Martens.
Includes bibliographical references.
ISBN 978-1-77069-368-5

    1. Mendelssohn-Bartholdy, Felix, 1809-1847. 2. Composers--Germany--Biography. 3. Lind, Jenny, 1820-1887. I. Title. II. Title: Passion versus duty.
ML410.M5M37 2011          780.92          C2011-906315-8

# TABLE OF CONTENTS

*It is chiefly – perhaps only – in letters*
*that one gets the mother of pearl shimmer inside the oyster of fact.*

– Christopher Morley, 20th C American journalist, essayist and poet.

PASSION VERSUS DUTY IS THE STORY OF TWO OF THE MOST BRILLIANT AND BELOVED
musicians of the 19th century, Felix Mendelssohn Bartholdy and Jenny Lind,
told in the context of their families and friends, world events, and the music
and mores of the era. The first two chapters outline the early lives of Lind and
Mendelssohn; the last two are primarily about Lind. The intervening chapters
cover the same time period as in *Felix Mendelssohn: Out of the Depths of His
Heart,* but there is almost no exact duplication, and they include subtleties and
elucidations not found in the earlier book.

Both books, *Felix Mendelssohn: Out of the Depths of His Heart* and *Passion
Versus Duty,* were crafted in large part from thousands of autograph letters found
in dozens of libraries and archives in Austria, France, Germany, England, Poland,
Switzerland, the United States, Switzerland and Sweden. Many of the letters cited
in *Passion Versus Duty* have not been published before.[1]

None of Jenny Lind's letters to Mendelssohn have been located, and only three
autograph letters from Mendelssohn to Lind are known to be housed in public
libraries or archives.[2] All of Mendelssohn's letters to Lind were in the possession
of Mrs. Oliver Woods, Lind's great-granddaughter, until 1955, at which time she

was forced to have them sold by auction. However, many autograph letters of both protagonists' to and from their friends provided invaluable material for the story of Lind and Mendelssohn.

In their two-volume *Memoir of Madame Jenny Lind-Goldschmidt, 1820–1852*, Henry Scott Holland and William Smyth Rockstro appear to have included most of Mendelssohn's letters to Lind. However, the two authors, or Lind's husband, or all three, deliberately left out significant short sections, as the autograph letters proved.

In addition to the letters, two biographies about Lind, Joan Bulman's book *Jenny Lind; a Biography* and *Jenny Lind, die Schwedische Nachtigal* by Nils-Olof Franzén, proved to be valuable sources of information. The diary of Lind's companion Louise Johansson provided information not found elsewhere. Other helpful secondary sources included W. Porter Ware and Thaddeus C. Lockard Jr.'s *Lost Letters of Jenny Lind* and the published memoirs or correspondence, in German, of Mendelssohn's friends Eduard Devrient, Karl Klingemann, Emil Naumann, Elise Polko, and Julius Schubring; most of the memoirs include letters. L. Dahlgren's Swedish edition of letters, *Bref till A. Fr. Lindblad fran Mendelssohn, Dohrn, Almquist, Atterbom, Geijer, Fredrika Bremer, C. W. Boettiger och andra*, also proved to be useful.

Other sources for both Mendelssohn books include encyclopedias, biographies of Mendelssohn and Lind, and articles in nineteenth-century German, English, and French journals and newspapers, as well as auction catalogs, diaries, memoirs of Mendelssohn's friends, police files, and war and church records.

Unfortunately, some letters and diaries that might have shed more light on the Mendelssohn-Lind story were deliberately destroyed. These include large parts of Clara Schumann's diaries, all but one letter from Mendelssohn to his wife, and all the letters but one from Lind to the opera singer Julius Caesar Guenther. And almost all letters from Cécile Mendelssohn to her husband in the spring and summer of 1846 are missing.

---

All the letters were translated by the author. Most were not difficult to translate, but two words in Mendelssohn's last letter to Karl Klingemann initially stumped me. They appear at the end of two short sentences in both books.

The first short sentence translates easily to "I will stay at home, enjoy my family, and compose very diligently."

The first three words of the following short sentence, *Alles andere is vom*

PREFACE ix

*Uebel,* also are not problematic. They translate to "All else is" or "Everything else is." But the literal translation of *vom Uebel* is "of [or from the] evil," and the resultant "Everything else is from [the] evil" is, of course, unacceptable.

Fortunately, somehow I discovered that the colloquial *vom Uebel* means "no good." Thus I translated the second sentence as "All else is no good."[3]

Those two short sentences gave rise to a great many questions. Was he speaking in generalities, or did he have something specific in mind in the second short sentence? What might "all else" comprise?

Mendelssohn felt free to confide in Klingemann, but not by the written word, except sometimes to give hints. The friends had last spoken to each other in May 1847, and Mendelssohn wrote his last letter to Klingemann four months later. What might he have told his friend in May that could cause him to write "All else is no good"? Did he again, as in London in May, have the book of Ecclesiastes in mind?

This Old Testament book appears to have been one of the many books of the Bible that Mendelssohn knew well and contemplated in relationship to his life.[4] When Mendelssohn was asked in London in May 1847 which book of the Old Testament he prized the most, the composer picked up a Bible from the hall table and read the first verses of Ecclesiastes, presumably in the King James Version: "*Vanity of vanities, saith the Preacher, vanity of vanities; all is vanity. What profit hath a man of all his labour which he taketh under the sun? One generation passeth away, and another generation cometh: but the earth abideth for ever*" (Ecclesiastes 1:2–4). (The New International Version begins verse 2 with the words "*Meaningless! Meaningless!...Everything is meaningless.*")

The last chapter in the KJV reads,

*Remember now thy Creator in the days of thy youth, while the evil days come not, nor the years draw nigh, when thou shalt say, I have no pleasure in them...Let us hear the conclusion of the whole matter: Fear God, and keep his commandments: for this is the whole duty of man. For God shall bring every work into judgment, with every secret thing, whether it be good, or whether it be evil* (Ecclesiastes 12:1, 13-14).

Might Mendelssohn have regarded something in "all else" as evil? Might it have had anything to do with duty?

Since the beginning of 2009 much media attention has been given to Mendelssohn and Jenny Lind. In a rather long column for *The Independent,* Jessica Duchen mentioned a mysterious affidavit in the archive of the Mendelssohn Scholarship Foundation. It purportedly concerns an 1847 letter from the composer to the soprano that would have been deeply injurious to the reputations of both Lind and Mendelssohn.

Another journalist has claimed that Lind broke off a secret engagement to a Swedish prince in early October 1848, and Julia Fuller insisted that it has been publicly substantiated that Jenny Lind was romantically involved with Frederic Chopin in 1849. Still others claim that Julius Guenther and Claudius Harris were covers for the Swedish prince and Chopin. And some Mendelssohn aficionados have asked if Mendelssohn was the victim of "tempestuous, unrequited love" and if the Swedish Nightingale, soprano Jenny Lind, may have contributed to his early death.

The author does not address any of these claims in *Passion Versus Duty,* but careful reading of the text should allow readers to reach some of their own conclusions.

---

1. In 1980, when research for both books began, nothing was known about Delphine von Schauroth, other than that she was a fine pianist and that Mendelssohn dedicated his first piano concerto to her. It is not hyperbolic to say that before *Mendelssohn: Out of the Depths of His Heart* was published, almost all the material about Delphine von Schauroth was unknown to almost all readers.

2. The author has not checked since 2004 in libraries, archives, and auction catalogues for new acquisitions of autograph letters relating to Mendelssohn and Jenny Lind.

3. It seems plausible that the *vom Uebel* in *Erlöse uns vom Uebel* in the German Lord's Prayer ("Deliver us from evil") passed from the prayer to become the colloquial "no good."

4. At the beginning of his career Mendelssohn deplored the transitoriness of conducting and performing on the keyboard. In 1842 he ended a humorous letter with the words "So you see, Beckchen, all is vanity."

"Do you like to write letters?"

"There is nothing I like less. And *if* I wrote, I would merely say 'I am well and love you with all my heart.'"

This verbal exchange, followed by hearty laughter, took place in the elegant home of the sculptor Ludwig Wichmann and his wife, Amalia, in Berlin at the beginning of November 1845. The questioner was the "Swedish Nightingale" Jenny Lind; the respondent was Felix Mendelssohn, composer, brilliant keyboard artist, and orchestral conductor.

Lind had returned to Berlin at the end of October to star in twenty-six guest performances at the Royal Opera. Mendelssohn had left Leipzig a week earlier—after saying he would come home in two weeks—to conduct his incidental music for Sophocles' play *Oedipus* at the royal theater at Sanssouci in Potsdam on the 1st of November.

The performance of *Oedipus* took place as scheduled, on the 1st of November. But Mendelssohn did not leave Berlin three days later, as he had promised. Because he had heard only laudatory comments about Lind's singing, he had concluded that she must be unusually talented, so he decided to remain in Berlin to hear her sing the lead role in Bellini's opera *Norma*, on the 9th of November.

After the performance of *Norma*, Mendelssohn still did not leave Berlin. He remained to hear Lind sing the role of Donna Anna in Mozart's *Don Giovanni*. The next week he accompanied her at a court concert at Charlottenburg, the largest royal palace in Berlin. And throughout his sojourn in Berlin, he frequently attended the same social events as Lind did. On the 2nd of December he heard her sing the role of Agathe in Weber's *Der Freischuetz*.

Mendelssohn had been able to arrange for Lind to go to Leipzig, albeit with some difficulty. So on the 3rd of December, both he and Lind boarded the early train in Berlin and arrived in Leipzig in the afternoon, seven-and-a-half hours later. He had been gone for seven weeks less a day.

The next evening Lind sang in the weekly Gewandhaus concert. So many people thronged to hear her that not only the hall but also the entire vestibule of the Leipzig Gewandhaus was completely full, even though the price of a ticket had been boosted from twenty new groschen to one thaler and ten groschen. Many people had to stand.

Lind came on the stage on Mendelssohn's arm in a white satin gown, with white camellias in her blonde hair. She sang several operatic arias to the accompaniment of the Gewandhaus Orchestra, and two of Mendelssohn's little songs accompanied on the piano by the composer. The audience was so enchanted with the way she sang the love song "Leise zieht durch mein Gemüt" that she had to repeat it twice. Such a thing was unprecedented in the history of the Leipzig Gewandhaus concerts.

The next evening, when Lind sang in a benefit concert for the widows of orchestra members, the enthusiasm of the audience was even greater. An English music student, William S. Rockstro, who attended the concert later wrote, "Never before or since that memorable night have we heard Lind sing as superbly or Mendelssohn accompany as deliciously."

Before Lind embarked on the train in Leipzig on the morning after the second concert to return to Berlin, Mendelssohn presented her with a song he had written four years previously, "Ich hör ein Vöglein locken" ("I Hear a Little Bird Coaxing"). In this song a bird loudly and continuously courts his lady love, and his beloved replies with a million love songs; it ends with the beloved expressing anxiety and soft laments.

Despite his protestations about his dislike of writing letters, Mendelssohn composed a letter of over six hundred words to Jenny Lind only four days after bidding her farewell. It was not a business letter, not an invitation for her to sing, and not a reply to a letter; it was simply a friendly letter. He did not address her formally as *Mein hochgeehrtes* (highly honored) *Fräulein* or *Liebes Fräulein* Lind, but as *Mein liebes Fräulein* (my dear Fräulein). He began the letter by reminding her that she had asked him to write to her, perhaps in a year, and then asked her not to be offended that he was writing already. He recalled their conversations on their recent train trip from Berlin and the events during the four days she spent in Leipzig. And he continued in his breathless style, with little regard for syntax and punctuation, as he often did,

> The gas flames made exactly the same noise as if it was raining outside, not one single beautiful tone of yours there however and you were also not at the rehearsal—it seemed like the past in that I again *so vividly* felt your presence in that I felt my joy and gratitude just as clearly, just as fresh, perhaps even more purely and undisturbed and I could tell myself that it would never be otherwise.

There can be no doubt that, as Jenny Lind read the unwieldy sentence again and again, she grasped its meaning and it caused her heart to beat a little faster each time.

Mendelssohn then expressed his gratitude to her for many things, but, as he said, "especially for everything from Wednesday morning at 7 o'clock," when they had boarded the train in Berlin, "to Saturday at 1 o'clock," when they had parted in Leipzig. Toward the end of the letter he wrote, "My real reason for writing is to remind you of me."

Seven days later Lind posted a letter to Mendelssohn.

Only twelve days after writing his first letter to Lind, Mendelssohn penned another, much longer, letter to her. In addition, he spent many hours creating an album for her. On the hard cover he meticulously drew a decorated Christmas tree,[1] like the one at the Wichmann home, and a large window revealing a train outside; he copied five of his songs in the album.

Earlier that day he had composed two new songs. The first is about divine love, in which the poet asks the reader to take heart, neither suffer nor be fearful, and never give up hope, because God's mercy and goodness are great and always available.

The second is about human love:

There is no greater suffering than when two soul mates [or sweethearts—
*Herzen*] must part. The words "Farewell, farewell for evermore" have
such a sad ring…When I first felt that love might end, it felt as if the sun
disappeared during daylight hours.

He included the first song in the album, but not the second, and he posted
both the letter and the album so that Lind would receive them in Berlin on
Christmas Eve.

———————————

A mere two years later Jenny Lind mourned the loss of Mendelssohn. Almost
six weeks after his death she expressed some of her feelings to her friend in Berlin,
*Frau* Wichmann:

Stockholm, 15 December 1847
*Geliebte* [Beloved] Amalia,
One word from your Jenny, she has not yet become reasonable. She
is spending all her time mourning the friend whom she will never see
again, and she scarcely knows how to find consolation. O! what a blow,
Amalia! And what a fate hangs over us human beings! You see—he was
the only person to whom I felt myself so completely devoted! the only
person who brought fulfillment to my spirit, and almost as soon as I had
found him, I lost him again.

The next month she wrote to Charlotte Birch-Pfeiffer, actress, author, and
Lind's German coach:

The blow came when the loveliest and purest flower of my life was laid
in the grave…I have not even read your letter yet, I simply cannot do so
yet, for as soon as I hear or read a word about him, I am almost incapable
of carrying out the great duty I have freely taken on[2]…Oh, how I dream
of being high up in heaven, as the earth weighs so heavily on me. Oh
*Mutter, Mutter,*[3] I don't belong to this world. My heart no longer wants to
remain in my small breast. Oh, if I could only be in the only place in the
whole world where I could engulf myself in meditation. But the rolling
waves of the ocean separate me from his grave. That is where my music
lies—my poetry—my art—my purest happiness—*my lost happiness!*

In the following year she told John Ruskin[4] that it was "better not to have known him—the loss was too great."

Month after month Lind wrote about her grief to friends, male and female. But she did not communicate in any way with the young widow of Felix Mendelssohn until almost two years after his death, despite the fact that she had enjoyed her hospitality and played with her five small children in Leipzig.

---

1. Evergreen Christmas trees were common in Germany and Sweden at the time but unknown in other countries; Queen Victoria introduced them to England.
2. Lind performed in operas in Sweden to raise money for disadvantaged children.
3. It was common in Sweden and Germany at the time for young women to address older women friends as "Mutter" (mother) and older men friends as "Father."
4. John Ruskin, 1819–1900, was best known as the most important art critic of his era, but he was also a poet and an artist. Later in life his essays dealt more with complex explorations of the interconnection of cultural, social, and moral issues.

# o n e

JENNY LIND'S ENTRY INTO THE WORLD IN STOCKHOLM IN OCTOBER 1820 WAS anything but auspicious. The record of her birth is terse: "Parents unknown, mother, aged twenty-seven." At her baptism Jenny received the names Johanna and Maria.

Her mother, Anna Maria Fellborg, an austere, harsh, divorced mother of a nine-year-old daughter, provided for her family by keeping boarders and operating a day school for girls. Jenny's father, the twenty-two-year-old good-natured, gregarious, but indolent Niclas Jonas Lind, did little to fill the family coffers, and Jenny rarely saw him until after her fourteenth birthday. In fact, in the first four years of her life she lived with the family of an organist at a Lutheran church in Sollentuna, a village fifteen miles north of Stockholm. *Fru* Ferndal, the kindly wife of the organist, had time for Jenny as well as for her children. When Jenny was old enough, she romped in the countryside with the Ferndal children and enjoyed listening to the singing of birds.

In Sollentuna she heard her first instrumental and vocal music, the music of the church. From the time she was four years old, Jenny sang everything she heard. She sang, as she later said, "with every step and every jump [she] took."

When *Fru* Ferndal became terminally ill a few weeks after Jenny's fourth birthday, the child returned to Stockholm to live with her mother, grandmother, and half sister, Amalia, in a four-room apartment in the gray lower-class area of the city.

One day not much later, Jenny's gentle and devout grandmother, *Fru* Tengmark, heard someone pick out a tune on the spinet in the attic. She recognized it as a tune that soldiers had played as they marched past their apartment. Believing that Amalia must have come home from school, *Fru* Tengmark called her name. When she received no reply, she went up the stairs and discovered Jenny hiding under the spinet because her mother had forbidden her to touch the instrument. Later that day, *Fru* Tengmark told her daughter, "One day this child will be of great help to you."

Before Jenny was eight years old, her mother and Amalia moved to Linkoeping, a town 150 miles from Stockholm, where *Fru* Fellborg took a position as a governess. She left Jenny with the family of the caretaker on the first floor of the home for widows where Jenny's grandmother now lived.

One day soon after Jenny's ninth birthday, the maid of Mlle. Lundberg, a dancer at the Swedish Royal Theater, happened to walk past the widows' home. She stopped as soon as she heard someone singing at an open window at the home. After listening for a few minutes she hurried to tell Mlle. Lundberg, "Mamselle, you wouldn't believe what I just heard—I heard a mere child sing more beautifully to a cat than anyone I have ever heard."

The dancer was intrigued, and the next day she went to the widows' home and listened to Jenny sing again to her cat at the open window. When she enquired about the child's parents, she learned that her mother would soon return to Stockholm.

As soon as *Fru* Fellborg returned to Stockholm, Mlle. Lundberg went to see her and told her that Jenny must study to become a singer because of her beautiful voice.

*Fru* Fellborg shook her head. "Theaters are immoral, and actors are immoral."

Mlle. Lundberg countered, "But at least you must have her voice trained." However, Jenny's mother was unmoved.

As the next step, Mlle. Lundberg persuaded the music master at the Royal Opera School, Herr Croelius, to listen to Jenny sing. After he heard one song, he declared, with tears in his eyes, "The child is a genius."

When he told Count Puke, the head of the Royal Theater, that Jenny should enroll at their school, Puke replied, "We do not operate a crèche." Croelius thereupon responded that then he would teach her gratuitously.

When Mlle. Lundberg went to see Jenny's mother again, she asked her if she would let Jenny go to the Royal Opera School for an audition. *Fru* Fellborg merely shook her head.

"Don't you realize," Mlle. Lundberg argued, "that your daughter has an extraordinary voice and sings perfectly in tune? It would be a pity if her glorious gifts weren't developed. And at the royal theater school she would get the best training. If she becomes a student at our school, Jenny will receive a full education at the expense of the state. In addition to all the usual subjects, the curriculum at the royal theater school includes elocution, dancing and deportment, piano and singing and languages."

Mlle Lundberg asked *Fru* Fellborg to think about it and left.

The next time the dancer was able to speak to Jenny's mother, she asked if she had had enough time to think everything over carefully. Mlle. Lundberg now told her that Jenny could live at home and that she, Jenny's mother, would even be recompensed for her room and board expenses. "All we ask is that you give your daughter piano lessons and be a loving mother."

After that had sunk in, Mlle Lundberg noticed that *Fru* Fellborg seemed to waver. Finally Jenny's mother and grandmother reluctantly agreed to let Jenny have the audition. Herr Croelius made the arrangements and was able to persuade Count Puke to attend. As soon as he heard her, the count also wiped away tears as he said, "Let her enroll in the *école musicale* immediately."

Thus, at age nine, Jenny became the youngest pupil at the Stockholm Royal Theater School for spoken drama and opera. According to the contract they drew up, Jenny would remain with the Royal Opera until 1842. She made her stage debut in a speaking role shortly after her tenth birthday.

Croelius retired when Jenny was eleven years old, and at that time the intellectually and artistically stimulating court singer Isak Berg became her teacher. Before long Jenny sang duets with him at social events.

She had studied at the Royal Opera School for three years when a Swedish newspaper published an account of her progress:

Jenny's remarkable musical gift and its precocious development have made quite a sensation in the circle in which she has appeared…Her memory is as perfect as it is sure; her receptive powers as quick as they are profound. Everyone is thus both astonished and moved by her singing.

She can stand a trial of the most difficult *solfeggi*[1] and intricate phrases without being bewildered, and whatever turns the improvisation of her master takes, she follows, as if they were her own. There is every reason to expect that this young genius will eventually become an operatic artist of high rank if she does not ripen too prematurely.

Jenny's home life was so unpleasant that she ran away several times and pleaded with the director of the opera school to allow her to live in the school dormitory. The first time the authorities agreed that she was too young to live away from home but spoke to her mother. *Fru* Fellborg promised to improve.

When she ran away again at age fourteen, Jenny complained that her mother had given her no piano lessons and had treated her so badly that she would rather drown herself than go home.

Teenage dramatics? The school authorities decided to investigate. They called *Fru* Fellborg's former maid to the stand. She testified that after Jenny accidentally tipped over a carriage in a park one day, causing injury to one eye of the person sitting in the carriage, her mother beat her so hard with a yardstick and a broom that blood flowed from her mouth and nose and Amalia begged their mother not to kill her. Later Jenny was locked in a dark closet for several hours.

In further testimony, Gustava stated that at another time *Fru* Fellborg hurt Jenny so badly that she could not attend her classes or appear in a scheduled evening performance. She also testified that Jenny was always respectful and modest and that she had never seen her receive a piano lesson from her mother.

*Fru* Fellborg was ill on the day of Gustava's testimony, but the next day she denied everything. Nevertheless, as a result of the investigation, Jenny moved to the theater school dormitory, and for the first time in a decade she enjoyed a peaceful life.

The respite, however, was short-lived. One year later, *Fru* Fellborg went to court to regain custody of her daughter. At first the judge was unwilling to grant her custody. The lawyer for the school argued that Anna Maria Fellborg was not even Jenny's mother. But the lawyer of the midwife who had assisted at Jenny's delivery provided a written statement in which she testified that *Fru* Fellborg was, indeed, Jenny's mother.

During the long, drawn-out court case, Jenny's parents exchanged wedding vows; the judge ruled in their favor, and the theater was forced to pay court costs. And so, at age sixteen, Jenny reluctantly returned to her parents' home. Now her mother abused her less, but she was still far from being an ideal parent.

In the same year, Jenny completed her acting lessons; the next year her status at the theater school changed to that of a regular singer and actress. During the season she made ninety-two appearances on stage for an annual salary of 700 rix daler,[2] plus a bonus for each performance. The strain on her vocal chords was so severe that at the end of the season she could no longer sing. Fortunately, however, a few months later, while she sang a small part in an excerpt of *Robert of Normandie* that no one wanted, her voice returned.

During one of her singing lessons in the winter of 1838, Jenny did her best to satisfy her coach, Maria Charlotta Erichsen, in the role of Agathe in von Weber's opera *Der Freischütz*. When her effort evoked only dead silence, Jenny thought, *Am I that stupid and incompetent?* But then she noticed tears in Erichsen's eyes and heard her say, "My child, I have nothing more to teach you. Do as nature prompts you."

March 7, 1838, became a turning point in Jenny Lind's life. On that evening, at the age of seventeen-and-a-half, she made her first serious operatic debut as Agathe in *Der Freischütz*. Later she frequently remarked, "I got up that morning as one creature and went to bed another, for I had found my vocation."

In the 1838–39 season of the Stockholm Royal Opera, Jenny appeared seventy-three times in spoken dramas and nine times in *Der Freischütz*. Before she was nineteen years old, Jenny's annual salary was increased to the equivalent of ninety English pounds per annum.

Giacomo Meyerbeer,[3] one of the most popular composers of the era, came to Stockholm with his opera *Robert le diable* in 1839. However, he did not attend the performance in which Jenny sang the role of Alice in his opera for the first time that spring. That opera proved to be the breakthrough for Jenny, and she would sing the role seventy-three times during her short career.

However, it was her portrayal of Lucia in Gaetano Donizetti's *Lucia di Lammermoor* that so enraptured the Stockholm audiences that she sang the role twenty-eight times in one season.

That summer Jenny sang in her first concerts outside Stockholm, in Gothenburg. Someone in the press there referred to her as a nightingale, and the name stuck for the rest of her life.

Soon Jenny's fame spread. In July 1840, before she was twenty years old, a Leipzig music journal reported that she was creating a furor in Stockholm. At the same time the Swedish king, Carl Johan, conferred the title of court singer on her, and she was made a member of the Swedish Academy of Music. No one in the history of the Royal Opera had reached those heights so early in their career. Soon she mingled with members of the highest society.

It was also that fall that she heard Mendelssohn's *Songs Without Words* for the first time at the home of the composer Adolph Lindblad and his wife, Sophie.

In her 447th stage performance in the Royal Theater since her first spoken drama appearance, Jenny appeared for the first time in the lead role of Bellini's opera *Norma,* a role in which she would cause both furor and controversy.

The board of the Royal Opera hoped Jenny would remain with them indefinitely. However, the professor Eric Geijer, one of Jenny's great admirers, encouraged her to study with someone other than Herr Berg. And the Italian baritone Vincenzo Belletti, who had often been her singing partner, convinced her to go to Paris to study with Manuel Garcia. Garcia was generally regarded as one of the best singing teachers on the continent, if not the best. In order to raise money for her trip to Paris, Jenny made a round of concert tours in Sweden. And three thousand people each paid one rix daler to hear Jenny in her farewell concert in Stockholm in June.

Jenny arrived in Paris at the beginning of July 1841. She was totally devastated when Garcia uttered the dreadful words "*Mon enfant, vous n'avez plus de voix*" (My child, you no longer have a voice) and ordered her to sing no note for three months. However, Jenny spent the three months well by learning Italian, improving her French, and working on music theory, as well as singing on her own sometimes.

Subsequently Garcia helped her improve her vocal technique, especially her breathing. She composed cadenzas and fiorituras[4] that impressed Garcia so much that he copied them.

In the following spring Jenny received a letter from the Stockholm Royal Opera with the draft of a contract. At the same time Adolph Lindblad came to Paris. They discussed the conditions of the contract; Jenny asked for additional recompense; the Royal Opera agreed, and she signed the contract. She would sing for one or two years for the equivalent of £150 annually, plus costumes and a bonus for each performance.

As soon as Meyerbeer returned to Paris, Lindblad took Jenny to meet him so that the maestro could hear her privately. Meyerbeer was impressed with her vocal abilities but had no opportunity to see her act.

When she stepped on Swedish soil again, together with Adolph Lindblad, Jenny received a tumultuous reception from the crowd at the pier. In the following season she sang twelve times in each of nine months. Both of her costars, Vincenzo Belletti and Julius Caesar Guenther, would play important roles in her musical and personal life. And before long both would fall in love with her.

Jenny sang abroad for the first time—in Finland—in the summer of 1843 and immediately became everyone's darling there. And when she sang the part of Alice in *Robert of Normandie* in Copenhagen, Denmark, in the fall, the Lind fever swept through that city also.

In 1842 Meyerbeer had accepted the invitation of King Friedrich Wilhelm IV of Prussia to become the director of the Berlin Royal Opera. Two years later, after Hans Christian Andersen told him that Jenny could act as well as she sang, he invited her to sing the leading role in the opera he had been commissioned to compose. Thus in the summer of 1844 Jenny went to Dresden to learn the German language in preparation for her debut in Berlin.

On the 21st of October 1844, in Berlin, Jenny Lind met Felix Mendelssohn for the first time.

---

1. Solfeggi are textless vocal exercises.
2. Seven hundred rix daler was the equivalent of approximately sixty English pounds at the time.
3. Meyerbeer grew up in Berlin as Jakob Beer.
4. Cadenzas are free improvisatory sections, giving a soloist the opportunity to exhibit technical brilliance. Fiorituras, from the word *flower*, are embellishments.

# t w o

FELIX MENDELSSOHN'S EARLY LIFE WAS VIRTUALLY THE COMPLETE ANTITHESIS of Jenny Lind's. He was a member of one of the most prominent families in Berlin. His family—Abraham and Lea Mendelssohn and their four children, Fanny, Felix, Rebecka, and Paul—was knit together by great and genuine affection.

Felix's mother, Lea Salomon, was a granddaughter of the wealthy Prussian court banker Daniel Itzig. Itzig had been master of the mint under Frederick the Great and court banker for King Frederick William II from 1797. Itzig's family and grandchildren were the first Jews to receive full civic rights in Prussia—one of very few Jews to be given those benefits at the time.

Lea was fluent in German, French, and English and could read Italian and Greek. She began giving daily piano lessons to her oldest child, Fanny, from the age of four and to Felix, her second child, from the age of five.

Felix's father was the son of the famous philosopher Moses Mendelssohn. As a Jew, Abraham Mendelssohn had only two career options, as decreed by the Prussian government: medicine or banking. He said he had a third option, that of begging. Abraham chose to become a banker and became highly cultured at the same time. And with the considerable fortune Lea brought to the marriage, her husband managed to increase their finances significantly.

Abraham was proud of his children but, in true Prussian fashion, did not praise them face to face. When Felix was nine years old, Abraham's sister, Henriette, wrote to Lea from Paris, "The extraordinary talent of your children needs direction, not forcing. Papa Abraham, however, is insatiable, and the best appears only just good enough to him. I can imagine him…happy and content in his mind, but saying little."

Although Lea adored her brilliant children, she prevented friends from praising them, as far as she was able, so that they would not develop into what she termed "vain fools."

Felix attended a public school for four years before his father hired the best private tutors for his children. In addition to the regular school subjects, Felix enjoyed instruction in piano, violin, drawing, gymnastics, swimming, and painting. His mathematics teacher was amazed at his perspicuity in that field. At the age of ten he began attending the rehearsals of the Singakademie choir, the finest choir in Berlin, and the following year he became an official member. Soon thereafter he accompanied that choral group on the piano.

Felix made remarkable progress in his piano playing. However, unlike parents of other prodigies, Abraham and Lea did not allow him to be in the spotlight until, at age nine, he performed publicly for the first time, not as soloist but in a trio for two french horns and a pianoforte. He progressed equally well as a violinist, and when the whole family went to Paris in 1816, Felix and Fanny received lessons from the virtuoso violinist Pierre M. F. de Sales Baillot, as well as from Marie Bigot, a former piano student of Beethoven's. In the same year all four Mendelssohn children were secretly baptized in Berlin.[1]

Under Lea's supervision Felix learned the lesson of diligence. Often she called from the next room, "Felix, are you doing something?" She woke Fanny and Felix at five every morning except Sunday, and Felix formed the lifelong habit of composing all morning whenever he could.

Under the tutelage of Abraham's friend Carl Zelter, a former bricklayer and now a minor composer, the young prodigy developed just as rapidly in composition as in performance. At age eleven he had composed two operettas and a number of smaller choral and instrumental pieces. Lea wrote about him to her cousin in Vienna, Baroness Henriette von Pereira,

Felix wrote an opera in six weeks…You know that Zelter is not very sensitive and not very easily moved. So imagine how I felt; he sat next to Felix, his eyes moist all the way through…The humorous words were expressed well…Zelter said that the male quartet was worthy of Cimarosa,[2] and that the ensemble with choir and dance were as pleasant as they were original.

Despite his great and manifold talents, Felix remained modest and always asked his teacher how he could improve. And whenever and whatever he played, he played with all his heart. One observer wrote,

At the rehearsal of Handel's *Athalia,* Felix Mendelssohn, together with another young boy, played the viola in the orchestra. A lad, pretty as a picture, with noble, unforgettable shape of face, dark wavy curls, and the deep, large eyes of genius, quickly went to his viola. All eyes rested on him. There was nothing of posturing about him, nothing of a child prodigy; his modesty was surpassed only by his radiant appearance… (his) countenance reflected every stirring of his inner life in the liveliest expression in his features.[3]

The critic went on to say, "The register of songs, sonatas, symphonies, etudes, fugues, quartets, church compositions, operas, etc., already composed by Felix would, even by virtue of their number, outweigh those of many other older composers; how much more so in the worth of these compositions!"

When Felix was twelve years old, the composer Carl Maria von Weber and his pupil Julius Benedict called at the Mendelssohn home. Benedict played parts of Weber's new opera *Der Freischütz* on the piano, and Felix played some Bach fugues from memory for the two men but refused to play his own compositions. The next day Felix gave evidence of his astounding memory when he played the parts of the opera that Benedict had played the previous day.

Zelter was so proud of his star pupil that he took him to meet Germany's revered and greatest literary giant, Johann Wolfgang von Goethe, in Weimar in the fall of 1821. Before they went, he described him to Goethe:

Felix is a nice, good looking boy, lively and obedient. He is talented and diligent but lacking in patience and a calm spirit. Although he is the son of a Jew, he is no Jew. The father did not have his sons circumcised, and brings them up properly. It would really be *eppes Rores*[4] if a son of a Jew should become an artist.

On the way to Weimar, Zelter and Felix stopped in Leipzig for three days. Felix was delighted to see where his beloved Sebastian Bach had lived and worked and to hear the St. Thomas choir sing in the stunningly beautiful Gothic-style St. Paul's Church. Every day he worked at his opera from seven until twelve in the morning.

Abraham and Felix arrived at the Elefanten Hotel in Weimar on the 2nd of November. Everyone in the town who heard Felix play the piano was astonished by his sight-reading ability and his performance, from memory, of many compositions by the great composers.

After Felix returned from Weimar, Lea reported to her cousin Baroness Pereira,

> Felix is back ten times as lively as before. On the first day he was like a volcano, overflowing with good humor. He lived with Goethe for 16 days. Zelter cannot stop talking about the sensation he made in Weimar…The rascal had the audacity to improvise in the presence of Hummel.[5]

Abraham's sister, Henriette, responded to Lea's report about the visit to Weimar:

> How beautiful it must have been to observe his frank and familiar intercourse with Goethe, the poet king. The constant dream of our youth—the delight of living near Goethe—has been fulfilled in Felix, and Abraham's continual humming as a youth has ripened into the extraordinary talent of his son. I thank God that he has granted you the happiness to see the day that our poor mother hardly anticipated when she was impatient with your continuous singing, *lieber* Abraham—of the choruses from Schulz's[6] *Athalie*—and used to exclaim, "How sick I am of *tout l'univers.*"

Beginning in July 1822, the whole Mendelssohn family, Lea's two cousins, and a tutor spent four months traveling throughout Germany and Switzerland. In Germany Felix met and played for the leading music directors in numerous cities. In Switzerland, while the rest of the family reveled in the beauties of nature, Felix composed in the mornings and played on church organs. He completed *Die beiden Neffen* (The Two Nephews), a comic opera with some spoken dialogue, as well as some smaller compositions.

Before returning to Berlin in November, the Mendelssohn family stopped in Weimar again. Afterwards Lea sent another report to Baroness Pereira:

> Goethe behaved in a benevolent, mellow, friendly, yes, fatherly way toward Felix. He said to Felix, "You are my David; my bad dreams will disappear with your playing." Felix, who is normally very indifferent to praise, is proud of Goethe's.

Abraham and Lea opened their home at Neue Promenadenstrasse 7 for Sunday musical matinees for the first time after they returned to Berlin. Both Fanny and Felix performed on the piano, and Felix conducted his own compositions, assisted by singers from the Royal Opera.

The larger public heard Felix perform for the first time when he was thirteen years old. A small, short-lived Berlin journal, *Iris,* devoted a large part of a long review of the concert to him in January 1823:

> Last month the not yet fourteen-year-old son of the respected banker…gave evidence of his surprisingly premature musical genius as pianist in Mad. Milder's[7] annual concert…This critic has followed the progress of, and been delighted by other *Wunderkinder* who have arrived at their virtuosity by sound beatings, but Felix plays Bach reverently on his instrument; wittily in naive, lively Haydn; with youthful bright fire in Cramer's studies, and lingers with deeply felt tenderness in Gluck's and Mozart's soulful melodies…His playing has unbelievable volubility, rich elasticity of touch, and polished tones…The musical spirit of the remarkable boy suffuses the greatest compositions with unbelievable ease…His compositions are in the same rank as those of the great composers.

The year 1823 was significant in other ways for Felix. At Pentecost he completed his eleventh symphony, and in December, spurred on by his mother, he published his C-minor piano quartet.

At the Singakademie, the director, Carl Zelter, introduced the choir to many of the choral sections of Johann Sebastian Bach's *St. Matthew Passion.* Felix became so enamored with these selections that he requested a copy of the entire Passion as a Christmas present. Because it had never yet been printed—it was written in 1729—his grandmother or great aunt paid to have the entire oratorio copied from a copy, and Felix received the Christmas gift he desired.

On Felix's fifteenth birthday he received a promotion of sorts: at the first orchestra rehearsal of his singspiel *Die Beiden Neffen,* Zelter took Felix's hand and said, "*Mein lieber Sohn,* from this day you are no longer an apprentice; from this day you are a journeyman. I make you a *Gesellen* in the name of Mozart, Haydn and the old Bach." Then he hugged and kissed his prize pupil.

Later that year Zelter wrote to Goethe, "Felix is a well rooted tree, healthy, more and more his own person…[He is] strong and swims against the stream."

In the same year a virtuoso pianist and composer, Ignaz Moscheles, described his first meeting with the Mendelssohn family:

This is a family the likes of which I have never known. Felix, a boy of fifteen, is a phenomenon…already a mature artist!…Both parents are far from overrating their children's talents; in fact, they are anxious about Felix's future and wonder if his gift will prove to be sufficient to lead to a noble and truly great career. Would he not, like so many other brilliant children, suddenly fall? I stated my conscientious conviction that Felix would ultimately become a great master, that I did not have the slightest doubt of his genius; but I had to repeat my opinion over and over before they believed me.

Felix had decided at an early age that he wanted to earn his living by composing, but Abraham was still not convinced that his son could succeed in that endeavor. To settle the matter, Abraham took him to Paris in 1825 to consult with Luigi Cherubini, composer and director of the Paris conservatory, about his son's future. Felix brought manuscript copies of some of his compositions and his published piano quartet. Cherubini listened to several of the lad's compositions and told Abraham that his son would do well. That decided it; Abraham relented. The Parisians were amazed that the taciturn Cherubini complimented Felix publicly.

Circumstances improved even more for Felix when he returned to Berlin from Paris and the family moved into their renovated palatial home at Leipzigerstrasse 3. One of the buildings on the seven-acre estate had a hall that could seat over two hundred people, and there Felix was able to play or conduct his compositions almost as soon as he completed them; his father paid for the best Royal Opera singers and instrumentalists. The Mendelssohn Sunday-after-church musicale became the most important event of its kind in Berlin. Poets, singers, composers, and visiting dignitaries attended; in fact, anyone could attend, gratis.

Felix was only sixteen years old when he completed his first masterpiece, a string octet. And the next summer, he composed a second masterpiece, the *Midsummer Night's Dream Overture.* An English composer, George Macfarren, opined that there was more that was "new in the overture than in any other ever produced."

At the time Lea wrote to Henriette von Pereira again:

What pleases me extraordinarily much is that with all his abilities [Felix] has a devout mind, as completely clear as he is in his thinking about the outward forms of religion. Already when he was a child, he began no piece without the letters LegG...As he always has been a foe of ostentatiousness, only I and Fanny knew the true meaning, that it meant *Lass es gelingen, Gott* [Let it succeed, God]. Isn't that touching?

Felix was unaccustomed to rejection and negative critiques, even though he was aware that he might experience one or both sooner or later. But the youth was not really prepared for the comments in the press after a performance, in 1827, of his opera *Die Hochzeit des Camacho* at the Royal Opera, attended by the cream of society. One critic referred to him as "a rich man's son." Another wrote of the performance of the opera as "a Mendelssohn family event." Still another said he would suspend judgment until he heard the opera again; yet, without going into details, he said the opera could be improved. The most hurtful comment was about Felix's "overrated reputation."[8]

At age eighteen, Felix published his first book of solo songs. Two years later, in March 1829, he stunned the members of the Singakademie and the Berlin public when he conducted, as a benefit, the first performance of J. S. Bach's *St. Matthew Passion* since the composer had conducted it a century earlier. Felix accompanied it from memory at the dress rehearsal and conducted it from memory at the performance. But if it had not been for Eduard Devrient, a singer at the Royal Berlin opera, Felix would almost certainly not have conducted the masterpiece at that time.

Devrient and a number of Felix's friends had met informally for some time in Felix's spacious room to sing parts of the Passion that winter. They agreed that the Passion was the greatest German composition. After one meeting, Devrient decided that it must be publicly performed and that Felix must conduct it. Felix's parents and Fanny enthusiastically supported Devrient's plan, but Abraham did not want to antagonize Zelter, the Singakademie director.

Several days later, twenty-seven-year-old Eduard Devrient and nineteen-year-old Felix went to Zelter's office on the main floor of the Singakademie. Before they knocked, Felix said, "Listen, if he becomes rough, I'll leave. I can't squabble with him."

"He'll definitely become rough, but I'll take care of the squabbling."

They knocked, and Zelter loudly called to them to enter. He was seated at his old piano, enveloped in tobacco smoke. His thick white mane was combed back, manuscript paper lay in front of him, and in his hand he held a swan feather. As the two young men entered, he turned his coarse, homely, yet imposing face toward them and said in a friendly manner, "What do we have here? Two such lovely young people here so early in the morning. To what do I owe the honor? Here, come, sit down."

After they were seated, Devrient reminded Zelter that it was he who had introduced them to the *St. Matthew Passion*. He then told him that a number of their friends had sung many parts of it and that now they wanted to introduce it to the people of Berlin. He hesitated before adding, "If you give us permission… and support us in our endeavor with the help of the Singakademie."

"Yes," and Zelter raised his chin and his voice as he did when he had something important to say, "if that were only possible. It would take a St. Thomas choir and the kind which Sebastian Bach had as cantor." He argued even more loudly, "If all the difficulties could be removed, all four Bach Passions would already have been performed."

His face had become red; he got up and strode up and down the room. The young men also got up, and Felix pulled at Devrient's coat; he felt that the matter had been settled. But Devrient persisted. "Felix and I recognize that there are difficulties, but we believe they can be overcome, and we would like to make the attempt."

Next he appealed to Zelter's pride. "It's because of *you* that the Singakademie choir is already familiar with Bach, and because you were such a capable teacher, the choir members will be able to learn the work. It was you who introduced Felix to the great composition…And I believe that Felix's and my enthusiasm will be contagious."

As Zelter became angrier and angrier and continued to mutter his opposition, Felix pulled at Devrient's coat and headed for the door again. Finally the old man exploded. "You expect me to patiently listen to you. Quite other folk than you have tried to do what you want to do. And then a couple of *Rotznasen*[9] act as if it's child's play."

Devrient bit his tongue so as not to laugh. Felix had his hand on the doorknob; the color was drained from his face, and he motioned for them to leave. Undaunted, Devrient continued with his arguments. "Despite our youth we are not that inexperienced, and you have entrusted us with many difficult works. It is precisely the young people who would risk the venture...Would it not be gratifying to you that two of your students undertook the task?"

When Zelter no longer blustered, Devrient continued. "We want to at least try to see if it's possible to learn the masterpiece, and we would like your permission and support, Herr Professor. If it turns out to be impossible, we can abandon our plan without disgrace."

Zelter stopped his pacing. "How do you plan to do it?...First you have to consult the board, which must give their consent—yes, and there are women among them—you will not so easily find them in agreement."

Devrient countered, "The female members of the board have been singing parts of the Passion at the Mendelssohn home and are in agreement. And I hope to achieve permission to use the Singakademie hall and the agreement of its members to participate."

"*Ja, ja,* the members," Zelter shouted again, "that's where the misery will begin. One day ten members will attend, and the next day, twenty will remain away."

All three burst out laughing at Zelter's joke. Felix then timorously explained how he planned to rehearse and how the orchestra would be constituted with the help of Eduard Rietz, his friend and violin teacher.

Finally Zelter relented. "Well then, I won't oppose you—and will even help where I can. Go then, in the name of God, and we'll see what happens."

As soon as they were outside, Felix called Devrient a "damned arch Jesuit," to which Devrient responded, "All to the glory of God and Sebastian Bach, Felix."[10]

All the tickets for the first performance of the Passion on the 11th of March were sold one day after the announcement, and a thousand people were turned away. The Singakademie was filled in fifteen minutes. The opera director tried to stop a second performance, but after Felix and Devrient appealed to the crown prince, two more performances were scheduled, the second on Bach's birthday, the 21st of March. Again some of the best singers from the Royal Opera waived their fees.

One month after the overwhelming success of the first performance of the *St. Matthew Passion,* Felix went to London to become acquainted with English music. The pianist Ignaz Moscheles persuaded him to bring along some of his compositions so that the people of London could become acquainted with them. The London audience and critics were enthusiastic about his symphony opus 1, and when he played Weber's difficult *Konzertstück* from memory, the audience was thunderstruck. To top it off, Felix received a commission to write an opera for a London opera house.

Soon he became the darling of many homes and received invitations to aristocratic balls and to the homes of a number of prominent English families.

At the end of the music season he went on a four-week trip to Scotland and the islands with his friend Karl Klingemann, a Hannoverian diplomat. There he received inspiration for his *Scotch Symphony* and the *Hebrides Overture.*

When Felix returned to London, he began composing an operetta for his parents' twenty-fifth wedding anniversary, and he almost completed it on his way back to Berlin. Two Berlin Royal Opera singers, Felix's sisters, and Fanny's husband studied their parts as soon as Felix returned to Berlin. And on the 26th of December, he conducted his *Hemkehr aus der Fremde* (Return from Foreign Lands). When his tone-deaf brother-in-law began singing his monotone part off-pitch, Felix doubled over with laughter at the podium.

In the spring of 1830, Felix began a three-year music learning trip throughout Europe. He stopped in Leipzig, Weimar, Munich, Vienna, Florence, Rome, Naples, Paris, and London. He was feted everywhere; he met all the greatest composers and conductors; he astounded audiences everywhere with his piano playing and conducting.

After he returned to Berlin, Felix allowed his family to persuade him to let his name stand as a candidate for the position of director of the Singakademie.[11] He had at one time hoped to succeed Zelter but found the process used to choose the director most unsettling. He did nothing to further his candidacy.

After months of agonized waiting, Rungenhagen received almost twice as many votes as Felix did. Although he had not really wanted the position, Felix was devastated by the rejection and the gossip—especially the comment that it would be strange to have a "Jewish boy" conduct a choir whose mission it was to promote Christian music.

In the following spring Felix conducted the most important choral festival in Europe, the Lower Rhine Music Festival, in Duesseldorf. Then and there the city offered him the position of city music director. Although he would much rather have remained free to travel for a few more years, Felix signed a contract for at least two years; that is what his papa wished him to do.

In 1835 his fame was so great that publishers vied with each other to publish his compositions. Also, at the beginning of that year Felix received at least six job offers. After much hesitation and unenthusiastically, he accepted the invitation of the city of Leipzig to become the director of the Gewandhaus Orchestra. The most compelling reason for his decision was the city's proximity to his family in Berlin. Only a few days after his arrival in Leipzig, he realized that it was a good decision.

Felix received many honors. Two German kings wished to have his services. Friedrich Wilhelm IV of Prussia prevailed upon him to come to Berlin, but each time Mendelssohn asked to be released after one season. King Friedrich August of Saxony revered him as a musician and as a man but had to be content with occasional performances at his court. And Queen Victoria of England invited him to play for her at Buckingham Palace.

He conducted the Lower Rhine Music Festival, held alternately in Aachen, Cologne, and Duesseldorf, a total of seven times. He went to England ten times to conduct and play. Countless cities from far and near, including New York City, invited him to perform.

In 1844, at the age of thirty-five, he was invited to conduct the London Philharmonic Society orchestra for the entire season.

In October of that year he first met Jenny Lind.

---

1. The children's baptism was kept secret from Lea's mother, who had disowned her son Jacob when he was baptized in 1799. In 1822, Dr. Anton Kirchner, one of the best minds in the theological world of his time, who turned down the position of court preacher to work with the poor and disadvantaged, instructed and baptized Abraham and Lea in Frankfurt.
2. Domenico Cimarosa was one of the 18th century's great masters of comic opera.
3. According to Felix's contemporaries, no painter ever captured the liveliness of his face. His brother was not pleased with the most well-known portrait by Magnus for that reason.
4. *Eppes rores* is Yiddish for "something unusual."
5. Johann Nepomuk Hummel, 1778–1837, pianist and composer, was famous for his improvisations and as author of a piano method, the first rational treatment of fingering.
6. Johann A. Peter Schulz, 1747–1800, was a leading 18th century Berlin composer, primarily of songs.
7. This refers to Anna Milder, later Milder-Hauptmann, 1785–1838. Beethoven wrote the part of Leonore in *Fidelio* for her.
8. The Edinburgh correspondent for *Harmonicon* opined that there were "striking and original ideas" in the opera and that parts were like "perfect miracles that would do honor to any composer whatsoever."
9. *Rotznasen* means cheeky brats, literally translated "snot-nosed ones."
10. The account of the young men's meeting with Zelter is based on Devrient's book *Meine Erinnerungen an Felix Mendelssohn Bartholdy und Seine Briefe an mich.*
11. Zelter had died in the winter of 1832.

# t h r e e

FEWER THAN TEN YEARS BEFORE FELIX MENDELSSOHN BARTHOLDY WROTE HIS first letter to Jenny Lind, he met his future wife in May of 1836.

At the beginning of September Felix was settled in an apartment in Reichels Garten, one of the two loveliest areas of Leipzig. He informed his parents about his new abode:

> It's across from the St. Thomas Church, 200 steps from the Hotel Bavière, where I eat my noon meals, 300 from the Gewandhaus, and 400 steps from the whole of Leipzig. It is excessively expensive,[1] but is so very nice and comfortable, with large windows that close tightly, very elegant curtains, whitish wall covering, a red sofa and a large stove, that I take pleasure in it anew every morning, and I even get value for my money, as I'm in a good composing mood because of it, and it makes me diligent, so that in the three days that I've been living in it, I have already composed a number of things…
>
> My reception here has pleased me beyond all expectation; if it continues, I'll have a most pleasant winter…Believe it or not, I get up at 7 every

morning and am at work at 8…I got used to getting up early and will continue this habit now with the help of the barber who comes to shave me at 7.

Mendelssohn soon established a good working relationship with the board members of the Gewandhaus Orchestra and developed a close personal relationship with one of them, the lawyer Konrad Schleinitz.

Before Mendelssohn's first orchestra rehearsal, the chairman of the Gewandhaus board, Dr. Doerrien, ceremoniously introduced him to the members of the orchestra. Two weeks later the maestro conducted his first subscription concert. He reported only briefly about the evening to his parents: "The audience was very pleased with the concert on the fourth of October; they and the musicians were attentive; fifty ladies were turned away."

He sent another report to his parents about the second subscription concert. "Yesterday I played the G-minor [concerto] to the immense jubilation of the Leipzigers; they made such a racket after the first solo passage of the last movement that I had to laugh."

The weekly Gewandhaus Symphony subscription concerts soon became so popular that the hall could not accommodate everyone.

Before long, Felix rhapsodized to his parents about the Leipzig prima donna Henriette Grabau.[2] He told a friend that because of her, he wished to do nothing but compose songs.

---

Felix had endured more than two difficult, sometimes agonizing, years, making it difficult, and sometimes impossible, for him to compose.[3] He had begun working on the oratorio *Paulus*[4] three years earlier and knew that his father was anxious that he complete it. In November he wrote to him, "You think I won't finish *Paulus;* I will, and hope to bring the complete score to Berlin on the 18th of December."

However, it did not happen that way. On the 19th of November his father suddenly died. Felix's grief was so profound that his family was alarmed. He wrote to his pastor friends, thus to Albert Baur,

The thought that recurred in my mind more than all others every night was that I might not survive my loss because I so entirely clung to my father, or rather still cling to him, that I don't know how I can now spend my life, for not only must I deplore the loss of a father (a sorrow which of all others from my childhood I always thought the most acute), but also that of my best and most perfect friend during the last few years, and my instructor in art and in life.

And to Pastor Julius Schubring he wrote that he must now work diligently to complete *Paulus* and imagine his father taking part in it. He expressed confidence that God would "reveal to [him] what [he] must do next."

He spent the Christmas season with his family at Leipzigerstrasse in Berlin without the normal revelry. There he concluded that the only way to continue with his life and achieve peace of mind was to live out his father's wishes that he finish his oratorio and write an opera, have a secure position, and get married. His sister Fanny encouraged him, "Felix, I'm convinced that it would be good for you to get married; it would provide a new outlet for your emotions."

Felix replied that he was going to Frankfurt to conduct Johann Schelble's[5] choir in the summer, and that "on the Rhine" he would "look around" for a wife. All of Felix's three siblings were happily married by this time, his older sister Fanny for five years, his younger sister Rebecka for three, and twenty-two-year-old Paul for eight months. Felix was almost twenty-seven years old.

As Felix prepared to return to Leipzig at the end of December, Rebecka's two-year-old son, Walter, asked his mother, with tears in his eyes, "But *Mama*, who will make pancakes for me in the morning when *Onkel* Felix isn't here any more?"

Lea Mendelssohn shared her husband's wish that Felix get married and was not content to wait until her darling went to Frankfurt. Soon afterward, at the end of January 1836, she wrote to Felix's old friend, now his concertmaster, Ferdinand David,

> Among the young women who are kindly disposed to Felix, can you not find one with whom one would wish him to form a closer relationship? It's no wonder that Mother Claudia[6] thinks there aren't many girls good enough for him. But what do you think?…Do look about at the daughters of the land, and don't forget to draw his attention to them.

It so happened that some of Felix's new Leipzig friends, Friedrich Schlemmer and members of the Phillip Schunck family, had relatives in Frankfurt, and they wrote to ask members of the large patrician Souchay family to invite

Mendelssohn to call on them when he came to Frankfurt. Several members duly sent invitations to Felix. One of the Souchay granddaughters, Cécile Jeanrenaud, wondered, "After all that our relatives have written about the amiability of the composer, might I have too idealized an image of the man?"

Felix was still despondent about the death of his father when he called at the large, elegant Souchay home in Frankfurt on the 4th of May. He was invited to the Souchay home several times in the first two days. The eighteen-year-old granddaughter was pleased to discover that Felix Mendelssohn was an animated young man. "Much earlier," she later confessed, "I wasn't able to imagine him other than as a most stiff, horrible old man who would give no man his due, and who wore a little velvet cap on his head while he played boring fugues."

Two days after his arrival in Frankfurt, Felix left for Duesseldorf to conduct the premiere of his oratorio *Paulus* at the annual choral festival. Fanny, Paul Mendelssohn, and his new bride also went, and all three sang in their brother's oratorio.

Because his doctor had ordered him to go to a seacoast for the sake of his health, Felix and Wilhelm von Schadow—his former landlord and director of the Duesseldorf Art Academy—enthusiastically made plans to go to the Dutch coast together after Felix completed his six-week conducting stint in Frankfurt.

While Mendelssohn was in Duesseldorf, Cécile Jeanrenaud wrote to Cornelia Schunck in Leipzig,

> I forgot the main thing—Herr Mendelssohn—but what can I tell you that you don't know? That he is very amiable. That his playing, which Fritz [Schlemmer] had described in detail, pleased us to an extraordinary degree. You know all that, but I won't tell you that he is very enchanted with both of you[7] because you would become vain.

When he returned to Frankfurt from Duesseldorf, Felix lived in part of Johann Schelble's lovely, spacious home, where he had the large music room and library all to himself. From the corner window of the music room he had a lovely view of the Main River. When not admiring the view, he revised his oratorio.

Felix had been back in Frankfurt for eight days when he wrote a long letter to his mother, with many of the details she so longed to read. Toward the end of the letter he made a brief comment about the Jeanrenaud sisters:

Frankfurt, 14 June 1836

…I also know a nice [*nette*] Souchay family, relatives of Schuncks, with two such lovely granddaughters that I count the evenings until I can go there to cheer myself up, play the piano, let them sing for me, etc., etc. When I'm not with them, I'm gray and sad.

However, he confided to his aunt, Dorothea Schlegel,[8] who lived in Frankfurt, "I can't stand Mme. Souchay; she acts like a damned aristocrat and tyrant; but I like Mme. Jeanrenaud and her two daughters and most other members of the large family."

A few hours before Lea Mendelssohn received her son's letter about the beautiful granddaughters, she posted a letter to Karl Klingemann, a family friend in London. She complained that she had not received "a syllable" from Felix for almost four weeks and was "dreadfully tormented" that he would write "only a few lines out of a sense of duty and out of pity."

---

At the home of a friend, the pianist Ferdinand Hiller, Felix met the most popular operatic composer of the era, Giacomo Rossini. He wrote to Klingemann,

Frankfurt, 20 June 1836

*Lieber Freund,*

Forgive me that I haven't written for a long time; as you said to me some time ago, it's my fate not to be able to escape a hectic existence so easily…Yesterday I went to Hiller's place, and who should be sitting there? Rossini, big and fat, in the most glorious mood. I really know few men who can be as witty and amusing…The rascal kept us laughing the whole time. I promised him that the St. Cecilia Society would sing the *B-minor mass* and several other works of Sebastian Bach. Rossini admiring Sebastian Bach! That is something. However, he thinks "different countries, different customs" and chooses to howl with the wolves. He says he is fascinated with Germany, and once he gets the list of wines at the Rhine hotel in the evening, the waiter has to show him the way to his room, or he would never manage to find it. He tells the most ludicrous and amusing tales about Paris and all the musicians there…and that he has the utmost respect for all the men of the present day—so that you might believe him if you did not see his clever satyr's face. But intellect, liveliness and wit sparkle in all his features and in every word, and whoever does not consider him a genius only has to hear him expatiating once in order to change his opinion.

Near the end of the letter he mentioned the Jeanrenaud sisters:

By the way, there are two very lovely granddaughters in the home, who help to paint us all in sky blue or rosy hues and who spread an aura of well-being over everyone around them—but the people themselves are also really amiable, and I believe I was a bear not to want to see that for such a long time.

Finally he made a request: "A propos, O send me a poem! I need it so badly! If possible, a love poem. Or rather a couple! I'll set them to music immediately."

---

Schelble had trained the members of the St. Cecilia Society to sing J. S. Bach's compositions splendidly. At one performance, Felix conducted one of his father's favorite Bach cantatas, *Gottes Zeit ist die Beste Zeit* (God's Time Is the Best Time), in his memory.

On the 20th of June the younger Souchay granddaughter, Cécile, returned from a two-week visit with relatives in Heidelberg. Her sister, blonde Julie Jeanrenaud, at age nineteen was vivacious and fun loving; her sister was quiet. Neither girl was an outstanding musician, but both were very attractive. Everyone commented on Cécile's striking dark blue eyes and long black eyelashes.

Three days after Cécile returned to Frankfurt, Mme. Jeanrenaud sent an invitation to Felix. "If you really wish to spend a little time with us, I would be happy to see you *after church* tomorrow, or in the afternoon, if you have no special plans." She signed the note "Your true and faithful friend." Not only did Felix have no other "special plans," he was anxious to spend time with the widowed Mme. Jeanrenaud and her two daughters.

Much of the conversation that Sunday afternoon was between him and the still attractive, youthful-appearing Mme. Jeanrenaud. But he and her younger daughter both enjoyed drawing, and they spent part of the afternoon at the large window, sketching the scene on the Main River.

When the six weeks in Frankfurt were drawing to a close, Felix had serious second thoughts about going to Holland and asked his doctor if it was really necessary for him to go to the seacoast. Doctor Clarus replied that he needed the clean sea air to recover fully. Thereupon Felix wrote to his mother,

> I'm planning to leave Frankfurt to go to den Haag, but it will only be a four-week endurance test. Instead of returning directly to Leipzig at the end of August, I'll go up the Rhine again, because I would very much like to see a few people and also a very beautiful girl before I go back to my winter quarters at the beginning of September.

"A very beautiful girl." Had Felix made up his mind in less than six weeks which of the two lovely sisters he favored? He wrote no more about her to his mother at the time, but he was less taciturn when he spoke about her to his friend Hiller. Thus Hiller wrote,

> Felix's calls at the home of *Frau* Jeanrenaud became ever more frequent, but he behaved in such a reserved manner towards his chosen one that for several weeks she did not regard Mendelssohn's visits as having any relationship to her, but believed he came on account of her mother, who was highly attractive…Although Felix spoke little to her at first, he spoke all the more about her when she wasn't present. In my room and on long walks he raved about her loveliness, charm and beauty and naturalness…With delightful openness and naturalness he spoke about all the good qualities of the beloved girl, often with the greatest joviality, half in jest, then again in a most heartfelt manner, never in a sentimental or pathetic or burning passionate manner. But it was clear how serious he was about the matter.

Hiller also noted that some members of the Frankfurt high society made comments to the effect that genius, culture, fame, amiability, and fortune were hardly enough for a young man to dare to seek to win the hand of a member of a prominent patrician family. Julie Jeanrenaud had other reservations about Mendelssohn; she regarded him as that disreputable being known as a "traveling musician."

Lea Mendelssohn was captivated by the thoughts of the beautiful girl, whom Felix had not yet named, but at first wrote to Felix only about marriage in general:

Berlin, 19 July 1836

…A propos the finances, or not à propos, don't you, you twenty-seven-year-old, ever want to take a wife? I wish you would look for a pretty, good, and cheerful wife, and don't worry about the means for a decent establishment…You don't need to use your savings but will receive a marriage portion, as well as furnishings from me. And it shall also approach your style of living and desires, *lieber* Junge. You have too affectionate a nature not to be happy as head of a family…Although immediately after my dreadful anxiety during Beckchen's miscarriage I decided not to persuade you, I cannot neglect to tell you how happy it would make me to see you spin new life threads. But then, my shining butterfly, you must be constant…Most young women today are too inept at having healthy children, and Father always believed this to be the actual purpose of marriage. Beauty is a divine bonus; health, the necessary element of life.

The next day Lea asked Felix's concertmaster, Ferdinand David, to enquire of Schuncks or Schlemmer about the Souchays and expressed the wish that her son seriously consider marriage.

On the same day, "with calculated diplomacy, and expressing fearful concern,"[9] Felix wrote a note to Mme. Jeanrenaud, timorously asking if he could draw Sachsenhausen[10] and scolding about Mme. de Stael's[11] renown.

The next day Felix expressed his regret to Klingemann that he had not sent poems, and he praised both beautiful nieces: "I have never before known such lovely girls, and only when I converse with Hiller or with the beautiful granddaughters in the evenings do I enjoy a sense of well-being and have a few happy hours again, the first in a long time."

In the meantime, Lea sought out everyone who had come from Frankfurt, had visited Frankfurt, or merely knew people in Frankfurt and enquired discreetly about the members of the Souchay family.

Two days before he reluctantly left for Holland with Schadow, Felix revealed somewhat more about his feelings for "the girl and her family" to his mother:

Frankfurt, July 24, 1836

…I would give anything to stay in Frankfurt the entire time with the lovely girl and her family about whom I have already written to you. It was there that I experienced the first happy days of this year and again felt freer and happier than I had been for a long time.

He described M. and Mme. Souchay as being somewhat snobbish and unappealing at first but meted out only praise to three members of the extended family, Mme. Jeanrenaud and her two daughters.

He wrote quite differently to his younger sister, Rebecka, on the same day. She was at Franzensbad, Bohemia, the finest health resort in Europe, with her son, Walter, and a maid:

*Mein liebes* Beckchen…I am going through a strange period. Never before in my life have I been so terribly in love, and I don't know what to do. The day after tomorrow I am supposed to leave for Scheveningen, but I feel as if it will cost me my life; in any case I'll come back here before I go to Leipzig, to at least see this absolutely lovely girl once more, but I have no idea what she thinks of me, and I don't know what to do. But one thing is certain: it is owing to her that I have had the first really happy hours this year and that it is only now that I have become more relaxed…You see, now you know a secret which you must tell no one, but in order that you will set an example for the rest of the world as being someone who can remain quiet, I will tell you absolutely no more…O Beckchen, what shall I do? This is my mood all day, I can't compose or write letters or play the piano—I can only sketch a little…I directed the St. Cecilia Society for the last time on Wednesday, and four members brought me a travel *necessaire* in the name of the society, which would be more suitable for a prince in disguise than for a musician; it is a *non plus ultra* of splendor and elegance, but I will use it anyway. On top are the words Felix Mendelssohn Bartholdy—Cecilia—which pleases me quite well.

Felix had formulated his modus operandi regarding his chosen one before he received a highly disturbing letter. The chairman of the Gewandhaus orchestra board instructed him to return to Leipzig at the end of August to resume his duties. So three hours before he left for Holland, Felix penned a frantic letter to Konrad Schleinitz:

Frankfurt, July 26, 1836
I have to leave today; that is becoming dreadfully difficult; if I didn't have such unspeakable respect for Clarus I really wouldn't do it…Moreover, I have to come back here after the great sea bathing and remain *at least* a

week, and I am to bathe for four weeks, and Doerrien wrote that I had
to be in Leipzig at the end of August. But that is *absolutely impossible*
and not even right at the beginning of September, and if you only knew
*how* impossible it is, you wouldn't be enraged about it. I don't know
how you will put the argument to Chairman Doerrien, but be my friend
and practice some dissembling, and either keep it from him entirely or
inform him very gently.

He did not explain why he could not return in August.

Six days after he arrived in Holland, Felix wrote to Frankfurt—not to one of
the beautiful nieces, but to Hiller. He mentioned Mlle. Jeanrenaud once: "Tell
Mlle. J. that here in my room there is only a copper etching of *la ville de Toulon,*
which causes me to always think of her as a *Toulonne.*"

Two days later he wrote to Lea that he and the "lovely girl" hardly knew each
other, but if it were possible that something serious might develop, he wished to
have her permission to marry. And then for the first time, near the end of the
letter, he named his chosen one, eighteen-year-old Cécile Jeanrenaud.

When Mendelssohn still had no reply from Schleinitz, he sent him a second
frantic letter. This time he said that it was now absolutely clear to him that he
would not be able to return to Leipzig before the 10th of September:

Den Haag, 9 August 1836
…It would be invaluable to me for a hundred reasons if I could remain
until the 15th. Just believe me and if at all possible do what you can to
not make my presence in Leipzig necessary before the 15th. I'll explain
all the important reasons which make me wish this so very urgently, by
word of mouth.

The next day he pleaded with Ferdinand David to induce Schleinitz to answer
his letter. Again he gave no reasons why he must spend some time in Frankfurt:

My life here is quite miserable. My Frankfurt friends haven't written
a word. My main pleasures are a little drawing and eating and
complaining…And I'm making one enemy after another, for when the
sea bathers come and begin to talk about music, I snap at them ferociously
or become so miserable that they are shocked and leave. O Haag, O
Holland, O bathing machines. If only I were going up the Rhine again,

where there are German-speaking and wine-drinking people who don't chew tobacco, don't speak a *Platt* dialect, and are very kind.

As soon as the four weeks in Holland came to an end, Felix traveled the quickest way, by steamer, up the Rhine River toward Frankfurt. However, because he had hurt his foot, he stopped for a few days at the summer home of his uncle Joseph Mendelssohn near Coblenz. There he finally received a reply from Schleinitz, and he argued in response,

> Perhaps it will be possible for me to be in Leipzig before the 15th of September, but of course I might have to stay a few days longer, which will not occur, of course, except for the most urgent necessity…As the first concert will be only on the 2nd of October, I will definitely be in Leipzig fourteen days before that time, and certainly with body and soul, as you say.

Felix returned to Frankfurt in the evening of the last day of August. He was still there on the 18th of September. That day he posted another letter to Schleinitz, and without any explanation for his state of mind he signed it "Your very happy Felix Mendelssohn Bartholdy."

---

1. His lodgings cost 20 thaler per month; his annual salary was 600 thaler.
2. Henriette Grabau was four years older than Mendelssohn.
3. Readers can learn a great deal about the two difficult years by reading (or rereading) *Felix Mendelssohn: Out of the Depths of His Heart.*
4. *Paulus* was Felix's first oratorio; he completed it in 1836. In 1834 Felix and friends had played and sung many parts of the oratorio for his father.
5. Johann Schelble, 1789–1837, was a singer and founder of the St. Cecilia Society in Frankfurt. He was a Bach admirer before the Bach revival.
6. Claudia is the over-fond mother in Gotthold Lessing's play *Emilia Galotti.*
7. Cornelia Schunck and her sister, both near Cécile's age, were cousins of Cécile's mother.
8. Dorothea Schlegel, Abraham Mendelssohn's older sister, was the widow of the German poet Friedrich Schlegel.
9. The letter was thus characterized by Mendelssohn's younger daughter in a letter to Hiller in 1877.
10. Sachsenhausen is a part of Frankfurt.
11. Germaine de Stael, 1766–1817, a Swiss-born woman of letters who espoused German Romanticism, led a complicated and unconventional love life. Because she antagonized Napoleon with one of her books, she fled first to Russia, then to England.

# f o u r

BETWEEN FELIX'S DEPARTURE AND RETURN TO FRANKFURT THERE HAD BEEN A flurry of letters. In reply to Felix's long letter to Rebecka about his feelings for the "lovely girl," she immediately replied with an equally long letter from the elegant health resort in Bohemia:

Franzensbad, 28 July (1836)

What shall I write to you, *lieber* Felix, are there any words? Would to God I could be with you for a little while now. You see, I am beside myself as if it were already decided that you want to make yourself and us happy. And I am stuck here now.

Forget about the sea resort, it can be of no benefit to you in your agitated state. Remain in Frankfurt regardless of whether you are calm or agitated…But I must see to it that I pull myself together. The ray of hope that shines from the letter I just received has put me in such an agitated state that my hand is trembling, but I had to write immediately, as I couldn't throw my arms around you. But I want to hear more…It's a good thing it's evening and that no more mail will come today. Perhaps

I'll be somewhat more reasonable tomorrow. For today, good night. May God bless you and your undertakings.

2 hours later

You'll believe I have taken leave of my senses that I am so beside myself just because you said you were in love…I read between the lines that this love will have great consequences in your life…God grant that she is clever enough to appreciate your love and to return it. She has already won my heart since you say she gave you some happy hours…

But, sweetheart, write again soon! Don't leave us in suspense. You wouldn't believe how bad my nerves are. That's not the right thing for a health resort! Write me a real love letter about her, how she looks, speaks, walks, stands, if she is musical, and also write that I am still your dear sister and can make all my old claims on your affection. I won't give that up for any loved ones in the world, just as you have retained your special place along with true maternal love in my affection. It isn't true that true love makes love for the rest of the world grow cold; in fact, the opposite is true.

But I adjure you, write immediately—not even my husband shall know of the existence of this letter—and tell me everything. Give me the pleasure of your confidence for all that I have suffered, especially since Father's death…

Perhaps your fate is already sealed, and I, who love you as much as only your fiancée can love you, know nothing. And what if this letter should come too late? No, heaven preserve us! I won't believe it. I am so inclined to look at the dark side, but with your letters I can entertain happy revelations…

Now you have been told to write soon. "All right" is enough. God grant that you can write that. Listen! If my hopes should be dashed, God forbid, and you don't want to hear anything more about it, send me an empty envelope, and all will be buried in forgetfulness. But it won't develop that way. I will count every minute until your next letter. Don't make me wait a second longer than necessary…

What plans I have already made for you, and then discarded in these 2 hours! And in between I get cold shivers thinking that perhaps nothing will come of it! God knows you can't be more agitated than I am.

Rebecka still could not stop. She asked if his decision at Christmas in Berlin to "again live for and through a person" had "magnified his love in his imagination," or did he "love the girl for her own sake?" She then advised him, "You ask two times, 'What shall I do?' Do you really love her? Proceed! Amen."

---

At the beginning of July Adolph Lindblad[1] came from Sweden to visit Felix in Frankfurt; from there he went to Berlin to visit old friends. And of course he went to the hospitable home at Leipzigerstrasse 3. And of course Lea plied him with questions. Consequently she intimated in a letter to Felix that he, Felix, was engaged to be married. Fanny also wrote to him as if it were quite definite that she would soon have a new sister-in-law and that she would be very disappointed if that would *again* not come to pass.

Felix responded quickly to Rebecka's long letter:

Den Haag, 6 August 1836
*All right!*[2]
I received your dear letter a minute ago, *mein liebes Schwesterlein*, and I have to write again to thank you for it. Above are the words "All right," which I very much wanted you to read again, and it is also true.
How good you are that my little letter agitated you and made you happy; I hardly know what I wrote to you, but it was the truth in any case.
You want me to write more and everything, but I've already done that, and nothing at all has happened since then, and I am sitting in Haag and cursing the seacoast and all Dutchmen…As soon as the 24th of August arrives, I'll go to Frankfurt again, God willing, and will stay there until about the middle of September and then I'll write again, perhaps happy and good things, but everything is very indefinite and hazy, and I still have no idea how the Frankfurt letters will read; as of now I know no more than what is in your letter.

Felix then pleaded with his sister not to be "agitated, fearful, or alarmed" on his account; he expressed the hope that they would "always remain the same to one another forever" and promised he would love her with all his heart as long as he lived. He forbade her and Paul to come to Frankfurt until everything was clarified. At the end he mentioned the letter from his mother:

This is my first letter from this cursed Haag, but isn't it strange, I had written a letter to Mother, not like the one to you, only in general terms, barely mentioning the dear, lovely girl. Nonetheless, yesterday I received a letter from Mother which is almost like yours, and Fanny wrote like that too, and I don't know how they could have gleaned that from my letter. I will have to answer that one today also, but it will be very difficult. You wrote that my fate may already be decided, and of my declaration—and I haven't thought about that at all yet…But when I return and get to know her better, I'll see whether or not she will be my wife…

I wish I could write you a better letter for your dear, kind one. But one thing is certain, I feel more in love than ever before in my life; no other intelligent thought comes into my head—I can't make music at all—that is a serious sign…

And now I will reply to your letter point by point: How does she look? Very, very nice [*gar sehr schön*]. Speak? German and much French, because she is the daughter of a French Pastor Jeanrenaud…Musical? No, not at all; that is precisely the best. But she can draw, but I attach no significance to that. Whether your letter is coming at a bad time? Would I send you an empty envelope? Oh *mein Schwesterlein*, don't think I would do that…

Write again soon…All right! Lebewohl!

Dein Felix MB

Regardless of the Gewandhaus board's directive, Felix Mendelssohn's mind was made up; he would remain in Frankfurt until he had accomplished his purpose—or at least tried. When he took leave of a friend in Rotterdam he thought, *The next time we meet, you will see me either with Cécile or as a "totally lost person."*

…….

Without divulging the contents of her letter from her brother, Rebecka sent a short letter to her mother:

Franzensbad, 6 August 1836

…Mother and Fanny, you have written two divine letters. If I were generous I would send them back to you so that you would have something nice to read. But Mother, dear Mother, calm your sixteen-year-old-heart that gives you no rest because Felix is in love. Can Dr. W.

not prescribe a potion for your youthful disposition? But it is also *agitant* for a sister's soul, and if only we knew something definite! But he will have picked someone appropriate; the man has taste!

Three days later, mindful of his mother's history of severe heart palpitations, Felix pleaded with her to remain calm. And that is when he first named the "very beautiful, lovely" girl and asked his mother for permission to marry, even though everything was "very uncertain." He wished, he said, to go through the matter as coolly as he had always managed to do in the past whenever he needed to make quick decisions in his life.

Finally he made a request: "I really hope that you'll tell no one of this matter, least of all anyone in Frankfurt; it could spoil everything for me. *Liebe Mutter*, answer this letter immediately."

Lea Mendelssohn wept tears of gratitude as she read Felix's expression of filial devotion and replied,

Don't neglect to tell me what you know about her and her family; in the meantime, the curious *Mama* has not been idle in discreet research. I let her relative, *Frau* Benecke,[3] give me information in the most natural way; and quite coincidentally, when we were talking of railroads not long ago, a gentleman from Hamburg told me he had traveled on one that had been newly opened in England…with a very pleasant family, Souchay, seven years ago, when Mme. Jeanrenaud was so fearful that she traveled in a carriage alongside the train; the daughters, of course, were too small to be noticed by him, but as unsatisfying as it was, I occupied myself with that information all evening.

After Felix had been in Holland for two weeks, he wrote a long letter to Mme. Jeanrenaud:

Haag, 13 August 1836
*Hochgeehrte Frau* [Greatly honored lady],
Will you be angry that I dare to direct these lines to you without first having asked for your permission? You laughed once when I told you of my fear of being a burden, and now it's even much worse…don't attribute that to my persistence. Often enough I resolved the opposite, and despite that, I cannot refrain from doing so. Every day I recall the

happy time and every happy hour which your kindness afforded me, and I must repeat my thanks; if you find this boring, read no further, put aside the letter and don't give it another thought. But I still had to write to you.

Felix mentioned Cécile only once: "I get the greatest pleasure from sketching or painting in my...gray book, into which I have pasted the stinging nettle from Fräulein Cécile." He declared that he had distanced himself from acquaintances and social events and could hardly wait for the end of the month. Three days later Mme. Jeanrenaud replied with an equally long letter. She did not mention Cécile.

Only one week after first writing to Mme. Jeanrenaud, Felix wrote her another long, carefully composed letter. This time he also avoided mentioning Cécile. But surprisingly, this great admirer of Bach and composer of many fugues and fugal compositions strongly disavowed counterpoint and fugues:

Haag (Sunday, 20 August 1836)
...But now I am going to complain about a word in your dear letter, a very terrible, dreadful word, for you say that I am a learned person. But people call those musicians "learned" to whose music they don't want to listen, which is made up of nothing but four-part writing and counterpoint and fugues, and in which music sounds really confused and muddled, that is called "learned."

While Felix was already en route to Frankfurt from Holland, Lea wrote to him again:

Berlin, 29 August 1836
...You know how longingly I wait for news from you, and thus don't need to advise you to tell me about your plans as quickly as possible...
I have heard only gratifying, good and favorable comments and wish you happiness and blessing. Through *Frau* Benecke I heard that you intend to take a little trip with the family; it's amid flowers and birdsongs, in woods and fields, that it is easiest and sweetest to convey nice secrets, and so I hope that it may be as a lovely omen that the mother, who is described to me as very pleasant and youthfully well preserved, has agreed to such an excursion (or motivated it).

Felix returned to Frankfurt on the 31st of August. A week later, he timorously spoke to Mme. Jeanrenaud of his intentions, and she encouraged him. On the 9th of September, precisely one month after Felix had asked his mother for permission to marry, he went to meet Mme. Jeanrenaud and her two daughters in the woods at Kronthal. He found Cécile by herself, gathering chestnuts. After that meeting, Felix briefly relayed the latest news to his mother:

*Liebe Mutter*!

At this moment as I again enter my room, I cannot do otherwise than to write to you that I have just become engaged to Cécile Jeanrenaud. My head is dizzy from what I have experienced today, it is already late at night, I don't know what else to say, but I had to tell you. I feel so rich and happy.

Tomorrow, if I possibly can, I'll write you a detailed letter, and probably my dear fiancée will, too. Your letter is lying here; I opened it to see whether you are all well but couldn't read it. Farewell, and always remain close to me. Dein Felix.

P.S. The family thinks it desirable not to announce it for some time; so I beg you, don't tell anyone.

He sent a much longer account of his engagement to Rebecka:

Frankfurt am Main, September 13, 1836

O Beckchen, I am engaged, and you don't know anything about it!…I would have written to you immediately on the 9th, as I did to Mother… but the following day I couldn't write a letter, not even to you. It is only now that I have regained my senses and have an inkling of how very, very happy I am.

O Beckchen, when you will see this Cécile, who is sitting beside me and writing to Mother, when you will have seen her and talked with her, you will know how I feel and that I cannot write letters now!

Next Monday I have to go back to Leipzig, and I won't come back here until Christmas. Then we will ride about and make 3,000 calls, which will be quite an adventure. But it is a secret until now (the 50 or 60 people who already know will perhaps be discreet), and that's why I'm telling you…that I am totally and completely engaged and happy.

I would never have believed that I would be able to thank God for such days as these last happy ones. But when twilight comes, I seat myself next to the two sisters on the sofa…and we talk about all the good and bad times of the past year and of the coming year and are glad that we can enjoy it, and I sit between the two and tell them it's the second time that I can chat between two sisters like this, that I would never have thought that this could happen again, and you must know what the names of the two sisters are:

Julie Jeanrenaud

Cécile Jeanrenaud [in their own hands]…

Farewell, *mein sehr liebes Schwesterlein*, never stop loving me, and remain close to me and rejoice in my happiness. Greet Dirichlet, tell him everything, and *Auf Wiedersehen* in Leipzig.

*Dein* Felix

Before she received the letter, Rebecka wrote to Felix from Munich, deploring the fact that she knew nothing. From there she left for Leipzig, as she had planned, in order to visit with Felix for a few days.

In the meantime Felix reported to his mother that he was very happy and that the members of Cécile's large extended family were "lively, good people, who enjoyed each other, and lived together, also really quarreled," just like their own family.

---

1. Lindblad had studied composition, together with Felix Mendelssohn, with Carl Zelter in Berlin in 1826–27. He was known as the Swedish Schubert.
2. Both Rebecka and Felix used the English words "All right."
3. *Frau* Benecke was the former Emmeline Schunck, Mme. Jeanrenaud's cousin, who had married Dr. Victor Benecke in 1836 and now lived in Berlin.

# five

Nine days after her betrothal, Cécile wrote her second letter to her future mother-in-law:

Frankfurt, 18 September 1836

Honorable and beloved mother of him to whom I am bound with all my heart, or may I already say *Meine liebe Mutter*, please do me the honor of looking at these lines, they are to tell you of my happiness, of my gratitude, and to entreat you, whom I must thank for all this, for your love!

If you knew all the bliss I have felt through your son these days, and which, I believe, will remain all my life, you would forgive this agitated letter, but it is pervaded with gratitude and contains fewer words than feelings. But please enfold me in your heart, and with the prayers for your dear son also send prayers to heaven for me; they will not be rejected; yes, in your goodness, pray for your Cécile! I need so much forbearance and wish it from your whole family, and of course I send my dearest wishes and greetings to my dear sisters and relatives.

*Leben Sie wohl,* and be assured of the most faithful and loving feelings of your daughter,
Cécile Jeanrenaud

Felix added a few sentences to the letter:

Now Cécile wants me to ask your forgiveness for having written the way she did; she had wanted to say something entirely different! But I think that whatever she says and does is fine and right...I know you will love her as soon as you see and speak with her for just one moment.

The next day Felix left for Leipzig to begin his second year as director of the Gewandhaus Orchestra. Two days later Cécile responded to a letter from Felix's older sister, Fanny:

Even though Felix often said you would really love me when you got to know me, I always thought you would find much to criticize in me; but now that you accept me as your sister with so much love and have put an end to all my doubts about your affection, I cannot do otherwise than thank you for that...It took only *fourteen days to change me completely,* so that every thought that is not about him seems strange. I was used to seeing him come into the drawing room every morning, and to accompanying him to the door every evening; now all I have is the memories of all the happiness I enjoyed...
I have a letter from Felix lying here in which he tells me that he still loves me! And I can't reply quickly enough that my whole soul belongs to him!

As soon as Rebecka stepped into Felix's dwelling at Reichels Garten in Leipzig on the 23rd of September, she wrapped her arms around him and said, "Felix, you look wonderful. Now you are again the happy man I knew in earlier days."
On her way to Berlin, Lea's cousin, Marianne Saaling, called on Felix and Rebecka. As soon as she arrived, she went to Leipzigerstrasse 3 to report about her visit. Subsequently, Lea wrote to Felix and Rebecka:

Berlin, 27 September 1836
...Marianne Saaling brought me the longed-for news about your well-being, *liebe Kinder!...Mein* Felixchen, how happy I am about your

good humor, that you are looking so well; she assures me that you are more than in love, full of expectation for the happiness that lies before you.

I must immediately add here that according to all I hear and see, you have made a splendid choice. *Frau* Schlegel[1] has written such an exact and lovely description of your Cécile that I believe I can picture her with my lively imagination…

Yesterday morning we received most pleasant, dear letters from Cécile and her mother. But it moved me as much as it delighted me; the letter was a kind of biography, which described her as a most lovely woman. That is no wonder, of course, as we are already of one heart and mind in our love for Felix.[2]

On the same day, Rebecka received a diffident letter from Cécile:

*Liebe Schwester*,

…You are very vivid in my mind, and I love you as if I had known you for a long time already, but I would so much like to see you, if only you won't be shocked at me, an ignorant, untalented girl. When, every day and always, I hear from people, again and again, about the intellect, talents and kindness of your family, I become more and more anxious, and I imagine that you won't be satisfied with me, and I have nothing other than my boundless love for Felix, which completely dominates me, and I know he will become angry if by chance he should read this, but I don't care, that's the way it is, and you must know that I still cannot comprehend what it is that makes him love me.

Rebecka had been in Leipzig for a week when she wrote to her husband that she would be home in a few days. Felix asked what she had written, took the letter from her, tore it into many pieces, and said, "Beckchen, you are staying at least two weeks. We have so dreadfully much to talk about, and I need you to pour tea for my guests." Beckchen stayed for three weeks.

She and Felix wrote a double letter to Klingemann with the news that Mme. Souchay had commanded be kept secret until Christmas:

Leipzig, October 7 1836

…Since it concerns him the most, Felix can himself write the main item of news, which is very old, and which you have known a long time already, which is, nevertheless, a great secret, and is in all the papers, although we, too, are all moved by it, and it is only since the engagement that we believe that joy and hope have been renewed in him.

My brother must give you the details regarding the name of his fiancée and her appearance; unfortunately, none of us know her, but we hear only the best and loveliest things about her from everyone; and Felix is overjoyed, happy and content; after his departure at Christmas, I had never hoped to see him this way again…

O Klingemann, how shall I begin? Perhaps you're angry that I didn't write to you about Cécile Jeanrenaud a long time ago already, and that she is my fiancée…But at first it was to be a secret, then I had to leave to come here. Now I have discovered that the whole world has discovered it, and now I feel ashamed…O write again soon and tell me that you are and will remain my friend, that you share my happiness, which is really greater than even I can comprehend. My whole life has taken on such a bright, happy hue again…

*Dein* Felix

After Rebecka returned to Berlin, she assured Felix that he need have no fears about Lea. "Mother is so much in love with you and Cécile that her spelling and other errors, if there were any, have evoked no negative responses from her."

In fact, without having met Cécile, based solely on her and Felix's letters and what other people reported about her, Lea wrote to Mme. Jeanrenaud, "Cécile is an angel, and I find her innocence and naiveté delightful." And from Hamburg, Felix's brother, Paul, heartily welcomed Cécile into the family by letter.

When Felix's *Onkel* Joseph and *Tante* Hinny Mendelssohn heard about Felix's engagement, they could not resist traveling from Horchheim to Frankfurt to see the one whom Felix had chosen. After they returned to Berlin, Rebecka reported to her brother about their and *Frau* Joseph Mendelssohn's lady companion's impressions of Cécile:

(Berlin) Thursday, October 13, 1836
…I've already talked to *Tante* Hinny and Lenchen; they are mad about our Cécile, and also say that a person forgets her beauty through the enchantingly lovely expression on her face; they couldn't get over their

astonishment at the eyes. *Tante* said the expression was one of pleading for love; they were amazed at her childlike, trusting being…

They are also very taken with Lilly and Julie. Taken by herself, Julie would be a very pretty girl, but in Cécile's presence they could not take their eyes off her, says the patriarch.

Alexander Mendelssohn also met Cécile, and after he met Felix in Leipzig later, he informed Klingemann, "I have never seen [Felix] in such a happy mood. It was obvious that his deepest feelings were those of happiness. But his fiancée is a most charming girl; although I saw her for only a few hours, it became clear to me why she is able to charm him so greatly."

Just as Lea Mendelssohn had sought others' opinions of Cécile, Mme. Jeanrenaud asked Professor Edouard Deodati[3] what he thought of her future son-in-law. She received this reply:

Felix Mendelssohn has the greatest affection for his family; he is a good son and good brother, and will be a good husband. He belongs to one of the finest families in Germany and his heart is of the same quality as his spirit. Ever since I met him in 1831 I have taken a lively interest in his life and career with sincere affection.

Meanwhile, still not entirely certain that his mother would fully accept Cécile, Felix sent her another lovely description of his fiancée:

Leipzig, 11 October 1836

…You cannot really imagine this innocent, childlike nature and her great kindness and goodness of heart in the midst of great and much elegance. I love her so much that I still can hardly believe that she is my fiancée.

She has written that Phillip Veit[4] will really make the sketch that Fanny requested…and then you will see how lovely, how good and beautiful Cécile is, but that isn't the most important. If at the same time you would hear her good, deep voice and see her refined, shy, yet firm character drawn in it too, that would be good. But one cannot imagine it; even I, who know her well, cannot. It's impossible, and I'm longing for Christmas, when I'll see her again.

Write again very soon, and tell me that you love her, and will love her.

That will make me happy all over again; and Cécile wrote and told me how happy it makes her when I write her your kind words.

Felix wrote regularly to both Cécile and Mme. Jeanrenaud. The draft of the first letter to his future mother-in-law from Leipzig in the fall of 1836 begins with overlong birthday wishes.

He asked Mme. Jeanrenaud to also think of him on her birthday, and when she looked at Cécile she should think of the happy person who owed all his happiness to her. As he did in all his letters to her during the period of his engagement, he expressed his anxiety:

It's precisely on this day I am so very anxious about my dear fiancée and I don't know how I shall survive these three months. I think that being occupied is the best remedy to overcome such a feeling of sadness, and so the many things I have found to do here are not unwelcome.

But if only I could see Cécile again; I always try to visualize her, how she looks, speaks, how her voice sounds when she says this or that, and I get so upset that I cannot clearly do this with exactly the person to whom I cling with all my heart…I don't understand how that can be, but I tried so hard all day today, and I cannot precisely visualize her features and don't know exactly how it sounds when she says "Felix" to me.

I also must not write in too melancholy a vein, or you won't be pleased— but how can I be other than melancholy, when I am at Reichels Garten and not at the Fahrthor, and have to go to see Councilor Rochlitz at 10, and not Cécile, and this evening when…I sit at my Hotel de Bavière… and am glad when I can leave, go home and dream undisturbed of the Fahrthor, of all of you and my dear fiancée.

Two weeks later he sent an urgent plea to Mme. Jeanrenaud:

*Liebe Mama*,

I have a request that is so important to me that I cannot wait until I'm calm and would write a better letter. Cécile's yesterday's letter closes with the words that you thought she wrote to me too often now, and now you know my whole request. O *liebe, liebe Mama*, don't say that! And don't believe it. You see, with that you take away my greatest and only pleasure I have here…

I know you're happy when I'm happy, that you're pleased when I can enjoy one more happy moment in my life, and you tell me so yourself in your dear letter, that you still love me...so let me enjoy the greatest happiness I can have here as often as possible until Christmas...If you would only see that on the day that I expect a letter, I can think only about that, and that on the other days, I read and reread the last letter until I know it from memory.

He reminded her that she knew how high-strung he was. At the end he became even more maudlin: "If I have to wait another day without a letter from her, I don't know how I can get through that day with the expectation and all the anxious thoughts that go through my head...there are moments when I could die of impatience."

In his next letter he responded to her chiding and promised to try to obey her and rid himself of the flaws of impatience, tenseness, and fearfulness but said that it was "so difficult." He tried to explain his shortcomings as being in part his nature, in part a result of the long separation from his family on his three-year music trip and getting used to strangers. To top it all off, he expressed self-doubts:

I have even been impatient and have not even trusted myself and, as a result, have given myself very bad times...I feared I wasn't good enough and didn't accomplish enough, that I had no real talent in my subject, and other negative thoughts like that. But the greater part of all these bouts of ill humor disappeared through Cécile's mere *Ja*, which made me well again; since I know that she loves me, I can truly love myself.

He assured Mme. Jeanrenaud that he would heed her admonitions about looking after his health, that he would "take walks, go to bed before 11, and not compose anything late in the evening." But keeping busy, he insisted, was good for his health.

Soon after Fanny received another letter from Cécile,[5] she apprised her brother of it:

October 19, 1836
I have received the dearest possible letter from Cécile. If I were as unselfish as Mother, I would send it to you, but I shall take good care

not to do that; you wouldn't send it back to me. At my request she wrote the whole account of your acquaintance and engagement with such an adorable naïveté and simplicity that one must love her with all one's heart. Everyone showers us with so much praise of her that I'm finally beginning to be truly annoyed that I don't know her.

And Lea was so charmed by Cécile's letter that she wrote to Mme. Jeanrenaud in the best Berlin enthusiasm-and-flattery style on the following day:

How very good of you and your dear, dear daughters, best Mme. Jeanrenaud, to write in such a kind and detailed way, and how could you possibly manage…to preserve their charming naïveté and childlike simplicity in the midst of all the luxury and all the associations in the social milieu?
Both Cécile's and Julie's letters moved, gladdened and delighted me, and if I haven't yet especially thanked the lovely Julie for her letter, I did feel the charm and pleasantness of her joking, through which her pain of the separation shone through…I have always had a passion for cheerful, lively people, and enjoyed Julie's joking mood immensely. She must not be angry at my Felix that he will carry off her Cécile. I can at least assure her that he was unbelievably happy to be with both sisters…
How indescribably amiable Cécile appears in her account to Fanny, which we read with tears and laughter; feelings and expression of such innocence can seldom be found, and they so completely reveal the soul of this angel! Thank God that Felix's star allowed him to find her! For he, too, I may say, has a most capital heart, and it makes me particularly happy that Cécile wrote to me once that she was far more impressed by his goodness than by his talent…
My younger daughter…has told me so many edifying, good and favorable things about his state of being, health and contentment in Leipzig that one could wish for no more. My sister-in-law has sketched the most charming picture of you and your daughters, best Mme. Jeanrenaud… which brought sweet tears to my eyes.[6]

Despite such affirming letters, Cécile still harbored doubts. In one letter to Felix she wrote that it would be better if his mother didn't see her before the wedding, as she might forbid him to marry her. When Felix informed his mother about the letter, he said, "The nicest thing about her statement is that she was even very serious about it."

In November Mme. Jeanrenaud reminded Felix that he and Cécile would be calling on many relatives during the Christmas season and that he should bring his calling cards. His response was far from enthusiastic:

> Naturally, I have the greatest desire to get to know everyone related to you and everyone close to you, but when I think of the list that I saw just before I left Frankfurt, and when I thought about the five days that these calls are to take up, and about the mere ten days I will be with you at Christmas, then I would like to ask and beg if it would not be possible to cancel some?

Near the end of the letter Felix wrote that he had been so busy that it was forgivable if he was somewhat unsociable and if he was somewhat shabby, for she would surely find him thus.

Felix arrived at the Fahrthor eight days before Christmas, truly looking somewhat shabby. However, his ruse did not work. Mme. Jeanrenaud immediately sent for a tailor to make him a new coat for their many calls.

On Christmas Eve Felix presented his fiancée with a priceless gift, an album with autograph copies of short compositions by Mozart, Beethoven, and some contemporary composers; some of Felix's watercolors; autograph letters by Goethe and other luminaries of the literary world; and some songs by Fanny, decorated with vignettes by her husband.

In a long letter on the 28th of December, Rebecka thanked Cécile for the "four-handed" letter she had received and complimented her on the "charming" vignettes she had drawn.

One day after Felix returned to Leipzig, he wrote to Fanny,

> O Fanny, what a Christmas I had. I have never had one like it and never will have another; the happiest, most wonderful days, when living and breathing give one new pleasure and gratitude…When I went to bed before midnight last New Year's Eve, feeling sad, and heard the clock strike twelve, little did I think with what gratitude I would experience the last hours of the next year and with what hope I look to the new year. Then I thanked God for all the goodness, and I know you feel the same and share my happiness.

He assured his mother that it was firm that he and Cécile would come to Berlin for a while in summer. But first they would spend some time in Frankfurt after the wedding trip—Mme. Jeanrenaud had insisted that they do so.

At the end of January Mme. Jeanrenaud and her daughter Julie went to Leipzig in order to look for living quarters for Felix and Cécile. Lea advised her son to discuss bedroom furniture and bedding with Mme. Schunck, but he told his mother that he could not possibly do that.

His friends in Leipzig were anxious to invite the young couple to social gatherings, but Mme. Jeanrenaud extracted the promise from both that they would attend no parties. So Felix dutifully refused all invitations.

Although Lea intensely disliked traveling, particularly in winter, she was determined to meet Cécile and her mother. Therefore she decided to make the whole-day trip to Leipzig by carriage with a dual purpose: to hear *Paulus* and to meet Cécile. Felix believed that Leipzig did not proffer the best conditions for their first meeting because he would be busy with rehearsals. So he suggested that he and Cécile and her mother travel to Berlin, even though Mme. Jeanrenaud resolutely opposed the idea. After much cajoling, he persuaded her to agree to his plan, but each time they planned to leave, either Cécile or her mother felt unwell.

In preparation for the Sunday that Lea expected the couple and Mme. Jeanrenaud, Lea reserved a loge for an opera at the Royal Theater, and she and her daughters prepared special gifts for Cécile and her mother. Ten times on that Sunday they went into the carefully arranged room. They sat at the table in a state of agitation when, instead of the couple and Mme. Jeanrenaud, a letter arrived.

When Lea heard that Cécile and her mother planned to leave before the performance of *Paulus,* she wrote an angry letter to Mme. Jeanrenaud and complained to her son Paul:

Berlin, 2 March 1837
…Cécile will leave Leipzig tomorrow at the latest without hearing *Paulus.* That being so, she need not marry an artist like Felix. They don't write if the purpose of the trip, to find lodgings, has been accomplished. What great *Duselei* [stupidity]!

Mme. Jeanrenaud, on the other hand, was fearful on two counts. She was apprehensive about meeting Lea and afraid that Mme. Souchay would be angry if she stayed longer.

A few hours after Lea mailed her letter to Mme. Jeanrenaud, she received word from Felix that the Schuncks had persuaded Mme. Jeanrenaud to remain in Leipzig until after the performance of *Paulus*. The next day Lea asked Mme. Jeanrenaud to forgive her for her "rude letter."

Lea sent suggestions to Felix about his upcoming marriage and lifestyle:

We all think it would be wise if you got married without much fuss; your parents also spent the first winter in two rooms, and how often your father spoke of this outwardly limited yet happy time. *Mais que la volonté de Mme. Jeanrenaud soit faite!* [But may the will of Mme. Jeanrenaud be done!]

Cécile participated in the rehearsals of *Paulus* and let Fanny know how they affected her:

Sitting in the midst of the singers I could hear everything they said. You can't imagine how strange it seemed to me the first time I saw Felix conduct. He looks just marvelous up there on his throne; and when the people clapped, I became red again and again, as if it was meant for me. Unfortunately I can hardly ever sing, for I have had a *grippe* since Mother had it…That is now like a thorn in the flesh for my mother, that I can't present myself in the most advantageous way to my mother-in-law, and that they could perhaps think I am sickly. But it is more fear on my part that I won't please her in other ways.

Lea went to Leipzig for a week and stayed at the Hotel de Bavière, where Cécile and her mother went to greet her. Cécile noted that when they met, both Felix and Mme. Jeanrenaud regarded each other with "penetrating looks."

Lea attended the performance of *Paulus* in the magnificent St. Paul's Church on the 17th of March and returned to Berlin content. Soon thereafter she reported to Klingemann again: "I saw Felix in Leipzig in all the bliss of an engaged man, and of the kind that pleased me greatly, because it was not the usual languishing, dreamy kind; rather, it endowed him with double the cheerfulness, energy and elasticity."

---

Felix, Cécile, and Mme. Jeanrenaud left for Frankfurt by carriage on the

24th of March. No member of Felix's immediate family went to Frankfurt for the wedding. Both of Felix's sisters were expecting, and because both had suffered miscarriages before, they wanted to take no risks. Paul was working at his uncle's bank in Hamburg, and Lea would not travel the long distance by carriage alone in winter.

On their wedding day *Frau* Schlegel gave Felix the letter his mother had sent for the couple:

These few words shall express only wishes, *liebe Kinder!* for the loveliest, most important day of your lives. You will be so busy and occupied that every diversion from the main thought might seem unwelcome to you. But you still have two mothers, and the words of blessing of those who are absent must not be wanting. And so may happiness and health and contentment go with you, as they have until the present, and may your love grow ever stronger and richer!...

Give greetings to your honored grandparents, siblings, and the esteemed man who will unite your hearts; name me as the tender mother of the one to whom they are all entrusting their child.

And so may spring, heaven, love, blessedness, happiness, joy and success in every undertaking go with you throughout the loveliest, richest inner life, and may you remain devoted and faithful to the friends and relatives who are absent. May we hope that the blessed fathers know about and bless your union.

At eleven o'clock on Tuesday morning, the 28th of March, Cécile and Felix spoke their wedding vows in a ceremony in the French language in the French Reformed church where Cécile's father had served. Pastor Appia chose Psalm 92 as the wedding text. It exhorts the reader to praise God with all manner of stringed instruments.

When they arrived at the Souchay mansion for the reception and wedding meal, the newlyweds were greeted by a choir led by Felix's friend Ferdinand Hiller.

At 5:30 the coachman arrived at the Souchay residence with the handsome new blue and brown carriage Felix had purchased for the honeymoon. A crowd of well-wishers surrounded the couple as Felix helped Cécile into the carriage. Before he closed the carriage door, Felix called out, "*Auf Wiedersehen*. God willing, we'll see you again in a month."

Then in glorious weather Felix and Cécile left for their first stopover in Mainz, not far from Frankfurt. Felix described their wedding night lodgings at the Rheinischer Hof as "the most elegant, most comfortable two rooms one could wish for, with a view towards the Rhine."

---

1. Dorothea Mendelssohn Schlegel's letter has not been located.
2. Cécile's and her mother's letters have not been found.
3. Felix had become acquainted with the Swiss professor Edouard Deodati in Rome in the winter of 1830–31 and briefly met him again in Geneva in August 1831.
4. Felix's cousin Phillip Veit, son of Dorothea Schlegel and her first husband, Simon Veit, was an artist.
5. Cécile's letter to Fanny has not been found.
6. *Frau* Schlegel's letter has not been located.

# six

ON THE MORNING AFTER HIS WEDDING, FELIX DELIVERED SOME OF HIS COMPOSI-tions to a music publishing firm in Mainz before he and his bride traveled along the Rhine to Worms. Early the next morning Felix wrote to his mother-in-law:

> *Liebe Mama,*
>
> I must write to you after two days, you may or may not want to read it, but I must tell you how happy these days, this whole time since our departure from Frankfurt has been, how blissful it has been; I would like to thank you again that you have given your beloved Cécile to be my beloved Cécile, who is my whole life now, and my joy in it, to whom I am grateful for everything, all my happiness. O *liebe Mama*, I cannot describe them to you, these two blissful days; some day I will try to do it verbally, as it is impossible to do it in writing.

After breakfast he and Cécile slogged through mud and rain to visit the cathedral and the church where Martin Luther is pictured standing in front of the Reichstag (Diet) in 1521.

Even on his honeymoon Felix could not be idle. While he worked on some organ preludes in the mornings, Cécile began to write in their honeymoon diary. In the first entry she described their morning in Mainz and the carriage ride along the Rhine to Worms and expressed her displeasure that they had ended up in a dark inn and a cold room.

When they left Worms the next morning, the sun soon shone brightly again, coaxing buds to burst everywhere.

The couple remained at their next stop, Speyer, for almost a week. In inclement weather, Cécile sketched and Felix composed. In good weather they wandered about the old Roman ruins and spent hours in and around the splendid four-towered, two-domed Romanesque cathedral. There they sat on benches and admired the views: the embanked river encircling small islands, the Rhine, and the famous *Bergstrasse* (mountain road) stretching to Heidelberg.

Both Cécile and Felix were amused that Madame Jeanrenaud had extracted the promise from them that each write a "secret letter" four days after their wedding, but both kept their promises. Thus Felix wrote,

> With every passing hour of these four happy, happy days, I have learned to know my dear Cécile better and to love her more. I thought it wasn't possible, and yet I feel such a calm happiness and have a blissful feeling that I could never have imagined before. But she is also absolutely too good.

On the same day, Cécile and Felix prepared separate letters for Lea Mendelssohn. Cécile began by saying that she could never thank her enough for her great happiness, that all her hopes had been surpassed, and that Felix was too good for her. Felix's letter is almost identical to the one he wrote to his mother-in-law.

Rebecka responded in her unique way to their letters:

> I was very glad to learn that you still have such an exceedingly happy marriage after four days. But patience, the actual test of love is still coming, when Felix has to dress very quickly before he goes to a rehearsal, and a button is missing from his shirt…It could also happen that Cécile is preparing a soup with dumplings fit for a connoisseur, and Felix makes her wait and quickly composes an oratorio, and the dumplings become as hard as rocks. But that will hardly be the case, as Felix is always hungry.

But such tests will come, and then one learns whether or not the characters are compatible. But I have no fears.

Five days after the wedding, Fanny suffered another miscarriage, but Cécile and Felix did not receive the news until they arrived at their final honeymoon destination ten days later.

Cécile continued to write in their diary, and soon both she and Felix added illustrations. She wrote about the art galleries and churches they visited, the organs on which Felix played, their walks, the natural beauty, the weather, her toothache, food and drink, and other mundane matters. On April 7 she wrote, "Blinded already upon awakening, the snow on the rooftops. Two decisions: the first, difficult, not to continue on the trip; the other, easy, 'To stay in bed.'"

From Speyer the happy couple continued to travel along the Rhine until they crossed the river to Strasbourg, France. The next day Felix got up while Cécile was still sleeping and then "dragged" her out to admire the magnificent cathedral—so the young bride wrote. In the evening they went to a vaudeville show, *L'amoureux de la reine* (The Loves of the Queen), but "fled" after the first act.

One evening Cécile wrote that Felix teased her that she was born in France and that she went to their room "beside herself."

Felix began a birthday letter to Rebecka by rhapsodizing about the cathedral and its "glorious" Silbermann organ:

Strasbourg, April 11, 1837
You know the cathedral; it's the most beautiful in the world; it has a see-through tower, like lace, with the light blue sky showing through the dark brown of the whole building, the stained glass windows and the slim columns and countless statues and all the art.

He then criticized the Frenchmen in Strasbourg for their "frivolous conversations," for behaving "in their 1830s free-and-easy style as if they were still adolescents, and trying to deny the old elegant Frenchmen." He found the mixture disagreeable and said he looked forward to the German border.

Both newlyweds wrote numerous letters to friends and relatives during their honeymoon, and especially long ones to Mme. Jeanrenaud in reply to her expressions of anxiety and fearfulness. From her daughter's letters she deduced that Felix was not attentive or knowledgeable enough to be able to help Cécile when she had a toothache and that the walks the pair took were too strenuous. She even accused her daughter of not loving her. Cécile and Felix did their best to allay her fears.

Fifteen days after their wedding, the couple arrived in Freiburg im Breisgau, a particularly lovely area on the Rhine at the edge of the Black Forest, surrounded by several mountain chains. The last snow was still on the mountains, but the first green of spring was appearing in the valley round about the city. Towns and villages were visible as far as the eye could see, and rushing mountain streams were visible everywhere.

The couple took lodgings in the finest hotel in the city, the Zähringer Hof. It was around the corner from the splendid 15th century Gothic cathedral whose tower soars almost four hundred feet toward the sky. The proprietor of the hotel sent a piano to the couple's quarters, and Felix began composing parts of Psalm 42. The translator rendered its beginning thus: "As the hart longs for the running streams, so pants my soul after Thee, O God."

Cécile mended her husband's clothes and darned his socks while Felix diligently composed in the mornings. He prepared a third book of *Songs Without Words* for publication and sent it to London and Mainz, asking for twenty-four louis d'or as payment, almost enough to buy a horse.

While the couple was in Freiburg, Rebecka vented some of her frustrations to Klingemann:

Berlin, April 18, 1837
…We have received wonderful letters four days and a week after the wedding. It's uncertain if the bad people will come to Berlin, so it's almost certain they won't come. You will probably meet her before we do. Don't write about her, I don't want to hear any more about the dark blue eyes before I see them. But she must really be delightful. I can't imagine anything more appealing than her letters, although they would not exactly be suitable for publication. But there is such sincerity and naiveté in them that one has to immediately love her.

Four weeks after their wedding, Felix and Cécile had their first big quarrel, and Cécile faithfully recorded the details. It began with Felix turning around several times on an outing to the Suggen Valley to look at a farmer's beautiful daughter:

All it took were some nonchalant looks and offhand comments to cause me to become totally obdurate, melancholy and jealous by the time we arrived at the inn at the entrance to the valley. We walked up the mountain…where Felix complained about pain, but where I behaved very badly.

After some time I began to blink my eyes, without Felix being able to discover why. In the meantime it began to rain; we sat down in the doorway of the house, as mute as two fishes; we went up, but nothing helped.—Felix's pleas, his anger, only made me more mute and stupid; I did nothing but cry, tormenting him and myself.

In the meantime, the horses had been harnessed. We drove home, first in a lovely sunset, then in a downpour, and only then did we become ourselves. I told Felix about my unreasonable thoughts, and he again became sweet and loving toward me. Firm resolve, never again to be morose without being able to give my husband the reason. Felix played very beautifully for me all evening, all my favorite pieces.

Felix added to the diary entry, "Don't be angry at me, *liebe* Cécile." He did not say that he would stop turning around to admire pretty girls.

Felix and Cécile remained in the Freiburg area until the beginning of May. From there they traveled south to *Basler Land* before heading north. On their return journey to Frankfurt they traveled via the Black Forest Bergstrasse through orchards that were now in full bloom.

They stopped in Heidelberg, a city famous for its castle ruins and the leading German university of the nineteenth century. There, for the first time on their honeymoon, they met people who were not innkeepers, concierges, coachmen, waiters, or hotel personnel. In Heidelberg they presented themselves as a married couple to two widowed sisters of Cécile's grandmother and their children and grandchildren.

More than six weeks after their wedding, Felix and Cécile arrived at the Souchay home at the Fahrthor. There Cécile visited with relatives and friends while Felix spent his mornings in a little back room with a piano and continued composing parts of Psalm 42.

Cécile had been married for precisely two months when she made a pregnant comment in a letter to Lea: "I have seldom seen Felix as happy as he has been these last days, and it shows in his face; everyone says that he looks so blooming and well, and *Tante* Schlegel says that she has never known him this way in his entire life."

Felix echoed those sentiments the next day:

*Liebe Mutter,*
...I could hardly be enjoying myself more, when I experience as much
as I do now...I hardly need to tell you how they have passed, all too
happy; I would never have been able to imagine that I would ever be so
happy...It is such a lovely time in my life and art that I never know how
to thank God enough; no end of new musical ideas...have come to me,
and I make an impression with all of them...
Someday I'll write about the happy days with my wife, whom I love
even far more now than I would ever have believed possible, whom I
find more amiable every day, and with all those pleasant, jolly people
here—it's too much happiness.

Felix then delicately explained his great buoyancy by saying no more than
that he had wanted to write "the news" several weeks previously but that Cécile
had not wished it. Lea responded quickly, and just as delicately:

Berlin, 12 June 1837
May God be praised forever, my Felix, you are such a child of fortune to
be able to experience the hopes and blessing of marriage with the utmost
speed, for whose best development I am sending heartiest good wishes
and prayers to heaven.
I am very, very happy to have seen Cécile and to have concluded from
her appearance that one can have the best expectations in this regard...
Her size as well as her build, her color, her teeth, are certainly all salutary
signs that the desirable conditions will hold. God bless you and her and
your progeny *in spé!*...
It makes me deeply happy that you thank me for the gift of life, because
it proves to me how fortunate you feel, and how far removed you are
from the misanthropic bad temper and ingratitude of base natures who
do not believe that parents have the right to foist an unwanted existence
upon them without having given them the freedom to agree to it.

To his also newly married concertmaster, Ferdinand David, Felix wrote,
"The smartest move we've made in our whole lives is that we've abandoned
the Holy Order of Bachelors. I, at least, know with certainty that I wouldn't

exchange these last two months with any year of my former life for any price."

Despite his solemn promise to go to Berlin in the summer, Felix and Cécile spent six weeks at the Souchay mansion, and then Cécile, Mme. Jeanrenaud, Julie, and he went to Bingen on the Rhine, southwest of Frankfurt. From their balcony in the Weißer Roß (White Horse) Inn they could see the Niederwald woods, castle ruins, the Johannisberg, and the town of Ruedesheim on the other side of Ehrenfels.[1]

Felix was fascinated by the famous *Mäusethurm* (Mouse Tower) on an island in the middle of the Rhine, named after the legendary 10th century Bishop Hatto of Mainz. One version of the legend has it that during a famine, Hatto herded all the poor people of Mainz into a huge barn and set it on fire. When he was subsequently pursued by hordes of mice, Hatto fled to the island, but the mice pursued him there too and ate the hapless bishop. Felix made a drawing of Hatto being pursued by the mice.

From Bingen the newlyweds sent a merry letter to Rebecka on the 24th of July:

*Liebes* Beckchen…Very early this morning I went across the Rhine in a canoe, first to a little island rock, on which a crazy court advisor from Frankfurt had his heart and brain buried (the stomach is buried in the Johannisberg in accordance with his will), then I went to my *Mäusethurm,* where there is a glorious beach, and swam. As reassurance for Mother, the water was only up to my chest…then I went to the Ehrenfels ruins, about which I could write several symphonies…Then I came home again and woke up Cécile. Then we had breakfast, then a big Bingen cherry cake and a lovely bouquet with nice little verses in it appeared, because today is the anniversary of our renowned window drawing in Frankfurt, then I finished a big chunk of my piano concerto…

Felix is busy with his notes, is sitting across from me and trilling with his fingers, writing, singing, blowing the trumpet and flute all at once, then he goes up and down the room with his staff paper, beats time or plays the bass fiddle with his arm. His piano concerto is giving him a great deal of trouble, but I'm sure it will turn out very well…We will soon leave and travel down the Rhine; then it will be only three weeks until Felix leaves. O Beckchen, wail for me then.

Felix composed both mornings and afternoons now, because he hoped to play a new piano concerto in Birmingham in less than two months. He informed Schleinitz that the adagio and last movement were finished, "but only God [knew] the first now—or maybe even the devil."

After celebrating Joseph Mendelssohn's sixty-seventh birthday in Horchheim, the three women and Felix traveled north to Duesseldorf to visit Felix's many friends.

Finally, on the 25th of August, Felix boarded a steamboat to travel down the Rhine to Holland, and Cécile and her mother and sister left for Frankfurt by carriage. Cécile did not accompany her husband to England because "under the circumstances," her *maman* said—and Lea concurred—"it would not be wise for her to make the long voyage."

Five days after Felix arrived at Klingemann's apartment at 4 Hobart Place in Pimlico, he wrote to his mother about meeting his old friend:

> Today I feel quite at home again in London. Klingemann is living so delightfully…and he has such a good old John Bull servant and *desto* cook, and he has such a nice grand piano that it is inestimable to be living with him here, and as he says, to take in all of London…I enjoy being with Klingemann in the early hours most, when we talk, make music and think about all of you so much, and yet I hardly need to tell you that I am counting the hours when I'll be in Germany with my Cécile again.

On the 13th of September Felix traveled to Birmingham. The festival began six days later in the city's town hall, which was constructed in the style of ancient Greek temples. A week later Felix's doting *mama* wrote to Cécile:

> Now, at exactly 11 a.m., our Felix is standing at the conductor's podium, high above the orchestra for all to see, and is conducting his *Paulus*. I didn't want to neglect to write to you, his beloved Cécile, at precisely this moment, to let you know of my interest. It is moving to be able to know how our greatly beloved is occupied across the sea and to be able to approximately assess the sensations.
>
> If he is well and has good news from you, Felix will be happy and content, and will be in that heightened excitable state of mind that is so becoming to him, and which makes his eyes shine so, and that gives him such good color, with a clear consciousness of his abilities, and that he

will please a public which is so favorably inclined toward him…May his good star continue to light his path in the future! There will be no dearth of good wishes on our part, *liebe Tochter*.

In his review of the festival for *The Musical World*, Henry Gauntlett, lawyer and organist, highlighted Mendelssohn's organ improvisation:

His extempore playing is very diversified—the soft movements full of tenderness and expression, exquisitely beautiful, impassioned and yet so regular and methodical that they appear the productions of long thought and meditation…

In his loud preludes there is an endless variety of new ideas, totally different from those usually in vogue, and the pedal passages so novel and independent, so solemn and impressive, so grand and dignified as to take his auditors quite by surprise.

His last performance…on a subject given him at the moment, was the most extraordinary of his efforts. The theme was followed with an intensity and ardor surpassing belief, but in the eagerness of pursuit was never deprived of its dignity or importance. There were no wild eccentricities, no excursive digressions, no ineffective displays of erudition.

Mendelssohn often crouched over the keys while he improvised, bringing his head almost level with his fingers; and at times an amused smile illuminated his face, as if expressing satisfaction with what his agile fingers could do. Now and then this was accompanied by a slight nasal snort of excitement.

Two weeks after the festival, Felix returned to Frankfurt, and on the first of October, he and Cécile arrived in Leipzig. Four hours later he began conducting the first concert of the season.

In a letter to his mother he mentioned how gratified he was that his oratorio was so enthusiastically received and, more importantly, that he had recognized that he need not write "fashionable or popular music." He also expressed his pleasure about the splendid offers he had received from England. "They" wanted to give him 1,000 guineas for a few performances of his oratorio without his selling the manuscript, and a big publishing company wanted to get a libretto by Planché,[2] and then buy the opera, etc.…

Mme. Schunck had rented a suite of three large rooms on the *parterre* of a building in one of the loveliest areas in Leipzig for the newlyweds. She had

tastefully arranged Felix's furniture and other belongings and hired a maid for
Cécile. The young couple had lived there for four days when Felix wrote to
Lea,

> How nicely Cécile occupies herself as my housewife, how nicely she
> talks to the paperhanger, the cabinetmaker and the mason and maid,
> briefly and *to the purpose*...and how she *verhutschelt* [spoils] me (so she
> says), and how very good it tasted at noon today, the first time that we
> ate all alone at home. The whole day and every hour is a celebration...
> now every day is a succession of joys and pleasure, and now I love life
> again only because I have my Cécile...I have lost many Thaler in our
> new living quarters.

On the same day he wrote to Klingemann,

> How extraordinarily pleasant it is to be at home in the evening, calm and
> happy and not alone; you would have to see that, *lieber* Klingemann, it
> can't be described...Yesterday I had my first noon meal at home, and
> food has never tasted better in my whole life; I gorged myself like a
> rhinoceros, and Cécile even tried to persuade me to eat more. I can
> imagine that you're laughing, but come and see, and then decide if I am
> not too happy, and if I should not have to write you about it.

Meanwhile, from Berlin Fanny complained to Cécile, "It's very annoying
that in the book of fate it states that not only are we not living together, but that
Felix should have a wife for eight months already. I have to tell you that when
someone now comes and talks to me about your beauty and your eyes, I'll snap
at him."

The Woringen family[3] was in Berlin at the time and persuaded Fanny to travel
to Leipzig with her husband and son. And so in the middle of October, Fanny
finally met Cécile. Because all three Hensels became ill, they remained in Leipzig
for two weeks. Fanny subsequently described her sister-in-law to Klingemann as
"an amiable, childlike, lively, refreshing, always-the-same and cheerful being,"
who loved Felix with "an inexpressible love."

Others echoed what Felix and his family expressed about Cécile. One
friend, Eduard Devrient, mentioned one less glowing characteristic: "Although
intellectually weak, Cécile was one of those sweet feminine creatures whose quiet

and childlike being, whose mere presence must have a pleasant and calming effect on every person."

---

1. The most scenic part of the Rhine extends from Bingen to Koblenz; it includes the treacherous Loreley rock.
2. James Robinson Planché, 1796–1880, was an English author and librettist.
3. The Woringens were a distinguished and musical Duesseldorf family whom Felix and Abraham had first met in 1833.

# seven

AT THE SAME TIME THAT FELIX EXULTED IN HIS HAPPY MARRIAGE, HE WROTE LESS enthusiastically about his career. When his brother, Paul, complained about what he called his "humdrum, secure and harmonious existence," Felix responded, "And I long for a calmer life and am disturbed by what people call recognition." He believed his real mission was to compose and to leave the task of performing to others. However, as an afterthought he wrote, "But it seems that this may not be granted to me, and I would be ungrateful if I were dissatisfied with life the way it is."

Felix also wrote to Hiller about his professional life: "I have never had the public occupy themselves with me as much. But there is something so—how shall I say it—fleeting, vanishing about it all, and which irritates and depresses me, rather than uplifts me."

---

In one of her many letters to Felix and Cécile in the late fall, Mme. Jeanrenaud expressed her displeasure: Cécile and Felix were entertaining far too much— guests even for breakfast! It was all far too strenuous for her daughter! Because in her childlike way Cécile was often perfectly open in her letters, Felix had to expend much energy to pacify the over-anxious *maman*. His response to Mme. Jeanrenaud's concerns, comprising more than a thousand words, began thus:

4 November 1837
*Liebe Mama,*
…Since I didn't answer your first letter which was so kind and good, it is just punishment that I have to answer your second letter, which is, to be sure, a little angry…I would so much like to dissipate all your motherly concerns with these lines to tell you, thank God, that until now there is absolutely no basis for any fears, and I hope you will believe this, as you know how dreadfully anxious I am when anything is wrong with Cécile.

He responded to Mme. Jeanrenaud's concerns, point by point. First he pointed out that he did not receive callers before eleven o'clock and that Cécile did not see them. "She always remains in her negligee until 11, at which time the maid combs her hair and helps her put on, say, her Scottish dress, as she did today."

He admitted that Fanny had been at their home all day, every day, for two weeks, but that had been the exception to the rule. "Now the previous regimen has been reinstated with all severity," he added.

About the "many callers" he wrote that they did "torment" him and fray his nerves, but as long as he held a public position, he could not refuse to see them.

He assured her that Dr. Clarus often came to the house and recommended all the things she recommended: "a moderate amount of exercise every day, going to bed early, a massage every evening, lying down for half an hour after a meal, etc., etc." He begged his mother-in-law to trust him, and he expressed regret that he couldn't let Cécile read her letter because of the part about her cousin's miscarriages and premature deliveries, because, he said, she already had "the most melancholy thoughts" about those things.

Two weeks before Christmas Felix and Cécile moved to a new, larger third-floor apartment in Lurgensteins Garten. The building was across from the Thomasschule where J. S. Bach had been cantor for twenty-seven years. Their abode faced south, affording them a pleasant view of fields and woods. Toward the west they could see a water mill; to the north, the city promenade and towers. Felix was pleased to be able to inform Julie Jeanrenaud about the move: "Last

Saturday we moved. Cécile was absolutely blissful because she was out of the old apartment, which she couldn't stand, and into this one which she likes very much."

---

At age seventeen, in Stockholm in 1837, Jenny Lind had almost lost her voice from overexertion, when suddenly in the last act of *Robert of Normandy*, while singing a small role, her voice returned.

---

Felix did not carry out his earlier plan to spend Christmas in Berlin; he wanted, as he said, to be "as cautious as possible." And on February 7, 1838, the progeny *in spé* about whom Felix had delicately written to Lea seven months earlier appeared in the person of the healthy little Carl Wolfgang Paul Mendelssohn Bartholdy. Felix expressed his profound gratitude for the birth of his son. Cécile ruefully remarked that Lea would not be pleased about a fourth grandson, because she had so hoped for a granddaughter.

Mme. Jeanrenaud and Julie had come to Leipzig before the child's birth and remained until six weeks after his birth. Despite the fact that Cécile complained that she was starving, Mme. Jeanrenaud did not allow her to be given meat for the first few days. Nor did she allow her to engage in strenuous activities, such as writing letters, during the six-week childbed.

Sometimes Cécile gave little Carl to her husband to hold, because, as she put it, "He is comically awkward when he holds him, and I like putting him into such a predicament."

In the seventh of his daily bulletins about the little newcomer, Felix wrote to Lea, "I enjoy his grunting [*Knurren*] and am a happy *Mensch*. Furthermore, it's a real pleasure to see joy such as Mme. Jeanrenaud's, who glows and beams and carries on the work of the household, everything very clean and in order."

When his son was three weeks old, Felix described him for Rebecka:

I'm to describe my son? Well, what do I know? He's round and red and has a turned up nose (like Cécile) and eyes like mine (so the people say, up to this point I see only peepholes), and he's screaming wildly at the moment and kicking with hands and feet and screaming more all the time and he sticks both fists into his little mouth until Cécile wakes up, as she did just now, and takes him to her (as she did just now) and then he's immediately as quiet as a mouse and drinks ravenously and thereupon falls asleep immediately. Then Cécile scratches him on the cheek with her finger so that he'll wake up, but he doesn't wake up, but snores a little in contralto, then Cécile says, "See how nicely he breathes," but if I snore, she says, "What dreadful sounds you make." When he wakes up again, he drinks oatmeal slime and is usually changed then…

He has hair on his head, ash blond like Cécile's, and large hands that he flexes on the bedspread. He's most intelligent in the morning when he is bathed like a young dog, and the least so at night when he regularly complains two times during the night until Cécile wakes up…He very much likes to be carried about, and screams less then, but when I take him he screams more.

Lea and her daughters praised Cécile for her exemplary childbed, and Felix continually found new ways of expressing his admiration for his wife. Thus he wrote to Rebecka, "No one in the whole world would have been able to invent Cécile; she is more refreshing and pleasant than anyone in the world…I read Voss's translation of 'Nausikaa'[1] to her, and had to read the whole canto to her because she took so much childish delight in all the details."

Paul and Albertine, Mme. Jeanrenaud, and Cécile's uncle Phillip Schunck stood as godparents at the christening service at the end of March. Felix informed his mother about the event:

We were all so happy, and everything was so lovely and successful that I was completely confused, and am writing somewhat moved…The meditation by Pastor Blass was one of the best I have heard on such occasions, very simple and serious, and without all airs and sentimentality, and the little one was so quiet and calm, and Cécile was so moved that her eyes sometimes wanted to overflow…Dr. Clarus proposed the toast to little Carl, and half an hour ago the people left, Pauls also, to the hotel to change their clothes and then come here to eat.

He described Paul and Albertine as being "balm for [his] soul" and the nanny who arrived after Mme. Jeanrenaud and Julie returned to Frankfurt as "dreadfully ugly."

---

Felix had promised to conduct the Lower Rhine festival in Cologne in spring and knew that Cécile desired with all her heart to go to Frankfurt with him. But he and Cécile had already been married for more than a year, and two of his siblings still had not met her. If they both went to the Rhine, his family argued, Mme. Jeanrenaud would do her best to keep them there for the entire summer. So in April Felix went to Berlin for the first time since the Christmas after his father's funeral in 1835.

A few days after his arrival with wife and child, Felix kept his promise to Mme. Jeanrenaud that he would write to her as soon as they arrived in Berlin. She and other members of the Souchay clan still were not certain that the Mendelssohns would completely accept Cécile.

You can imagine with what joy we were welcomed here, and how happy my mother, siblings and in-laws are to have Cécile with them. They already have made great plans regarding how they want to show her Berlin, and yesterday, as a good beginning, we were already at the theater. The grandeur of the building and stage and the fine orchestra and everything delighted Cécile, and I have never had a more enjoyable evening in the theater.

Many of Cécile's letters to her mother are brief—very brief, in fact—but from Berlin she wrote at greater length about Felix's relatives, but not in the way that Lea consistently wrote about Cécile and her family:

Jeudi, 30 Avril 1838
*Chère maman,*
…When one is with her often, my mother-in-law is not at all as *terrible* [French] as I had thought…my sister-in-law is very amiable, although not very pretty…Her younger sister is very pleasant but also no beauty. She has charming children, the little one is especially pretty…Everything in Frankfurt is a hundred times better than here.

And on a subsequent Thursday she wrote,

Jeudi
…I don't find the renown of Berlin at all well founded; they pressure me terribly to eat…They also give me a great many compliments here,

more than I have ever received in my life. I am pleased about that for the sake of my mother-in-law. They also always admire my wardrobe, which you used to criticize…My younger sister-in-law is not at all the way you think of her; she appears to me to be very good [*bien bonne*], but not as talented as her sister.

After Felix and his family had been in Berlin for a month, he left for Cologne to conduct the Lower Rhine Choral Festival. It was a resounding success, and Felix returned to Berlin on schedule. From there he wrote a second letter to Mme. Jeanrenaud. He described Cécile as "the darling of all [his] acquaintances and of [his] whole family," who "enchanted" his mother and sisters, who praised everything she said and did. At the end he expressed his astonishment that they accepted her so soon and so completely.

On the 3rd of March 1838, at the age of seventeen-and-a-half, Jenny Lind made her operatic debut in Weber's opera *Freischütz* and realized that she could have a successful career in the world of opera.

Felix and Cécile spent more than four months in the stately mansion at Leipzigerstrasse 3 with its vast, beautiful gardens and walkways. Besides a private park, the seven-acre estate boasted a huge garden, from which the gardener brought baskets of vegetables and fruit of all kinds as soon as possible to the cooks of each of the three kitchens: Lea's, Fanny's, and Rebecka's.

Between visits to relatives, Felix composed, and Cécile painted in oil. Felix reported to Mme. Jeanrenaud about her artistic endeavors:

The little picture that she completed in four days is so very lovely, such a perfect landscape that I cannot admire it enough. I am somewhat partisan, as you know, but all the others have the same opinion, and my mother and my brother-in-law came a few times every day to admire it…She is now doing another larger landscape, and it too is becoming very good.

Felix, Cécile and Carlchen left Leipzigerstrasse 3 for their much less spacious quarters earlier than planned, because a measles epidemic broke out in Berlin.

---

In the 1838–39 concert season Mendelssohn continued to be innovative in his weekly symphony programs in Leipzig. He conducted numerous compositions by Johann Sebastian Bach that had never before been performed in the Gewandhaus.

---

At least once each week Lea wrote long letters to Leipzig; this to Cécile at the beginning of October:

How glad I was to see your dear handwriting again, my Cécile. You were critical of it, but I find it very good and more legible than usual…
Felix was the most beautiful child you can imagine. But his beauty only developed in his fourth year, and in addition to the most wonderful coloring, the most glorious curls, he also got his remarkable expression of his spirit, mind and liveliness. My Carlchen will also become beautiful and good and lovely, whichever of his parents he may resemble. I have such a passion for the angel that my Marie always flatters me and talks to me about his beauty day and night.

Because Fanny also longed to receive news about little Carl, Cécile obliged when the child was eleven months old:

Leipzig, 11 January 1839
Carl is really a dear droll child, and Felix has a great deal of fun with him. But just think, the boy loves music to an amazing degree; he hears Felix playing through two rooms, and crawls to the door right away and tries to get out. When I finally carry him over he is very happy. But then Felix sends me away again, not because it bothers him, but because he maintains that it's unhealthy and bad for his nerves. Did you ever hear of such a thing? This method has an advantage: I won't have to blame only myself if one day the boy will not be the most stupid person in the world regarding music, which I am actually expecting.

Almost precisely on the second anniversary of Felix and Cécile's wedding day, Lea posted another effusive letter about Cécile to Mme. Jeanrenaud:

Berlin, 29 March 1839

My nephew Alexander with his two sons stayed in Leipzig for a few days, and they are so delighted with Cécile, her hospitality and her boundless goodness, kindness and beauty, that they poured out streams of eloquent praise until I was moved to tears by all they told me about all three, whose hub is our Cécile.

I have written to you a number of times that of all the blessings Felix has received from heaven, none has had such a lovely influence as the great fortune to find a Cécile. All my children, all my friends and acquaintances are of one opinion on this, and I cannot describe how much I adore this angel ever since she was here last summer. She has grown very close to my heart, and I'm so happy that Carlchen resembles her, and it seems that there is also a spiritual resemblance.

---

Because he regarded the pleasure of conducting as too ephemeral, Mendelssohn initially refused the invitation from the Duesseldorf Lower Rhine Festival committee to direct the festival in 1839. But Cécile wanted to go to Frankfurt and exerted quiet pressure until he agreed to go.

The critics wrote laudatory reviews about the festival, in particular about the performance of Handel's *Messiah* and Clara Novello's beautiful, bell-like voice. Yet Mendelssohn still maintained that the whole festival was "too great an effort for the results." And he wrote to Schleinitz, "Novello and Fassmann[2] didn't beat or scratch each other; they did everything else."

---

Back in Leipzig, on the 2nd of October 1839, Felix became the father of a second child, Marie Helene Pauline. He sent daily bulletins about her, the first to his mother, one-and-one-half hours after her birth. He informed her that although Cécile has suffered great pain for a short while, which had frightened him very much, she and the child were doing well. At eleven that morning, he continued, Cécile had not wanted to cancel the guests she had invited for dinner,[3] and Marie was born that afternoon at five. About the child he wrote, "[She] is now screaming wildly and has black hair and blue eyes and drinks *Fenchel* tea[4] and behaves quite well for her age. I don't know how I can thank God enough that all has gone so well, and I am absolutely confused, and am writing a confused letter."

Five days later he wrote to his mother again:

Mme. Jeanrenaud maintains that we manage the household as if Cécile were a princess: two doctors in the morning, then two nurses, then daily bulletins. But I maintain that it's run as in Kirghis,[5] where the husband also goes to bed when a woman gives birth. I still haven't recovered from the fear of last Wednesday and am miserable, and my hair is falling out dreadfully, and there is no decent thought in my head, and I have to sleep in the afternoons to recover from the childbed.

When the child was two weeks old, he described her for his mother as looking "more like a person than a little frog."

On the same day Felix thanked Mme. Jeanrenaud: "My whole happiness is predicated on Cécile. 1,000 thanks that you brought her into being, and that she has become so good, so lovely, so unique."

---

In the fall of 1839 while Jenny Lind's parents were at the opera, Louise Johansson[6] packed most of her and Jenny's things and took them to the home of Jenny's well-to-do *Tante* Lona. The next morning when Louise announced she was moving out, an argument ensued, after which both she and Jenny went to stay with *Tante* Lona. A few weeks later Jenny begged her dearest friends, Adolph Lindblad, "the Swedish Schubert," and his wife, Sophie, to let her move into a small room next to Sophie's. The couple heartily welcomed her to their spacious apartment in Bonde Palace. The Lindblad home was a center of cultural life, and there Jenny heard Mendelssohn's *Songs Without Words* for the piano for the first time.

---

1. Presumably "Nausikaa" is part of Homer's eighth century B.C. epic poem *Ulysses*.
2. Novello, 1818–1908, was an English soprano. Auguste von Fassmann, 1811–1872, was an opera singer in Munich.
3. Dinner at the Mendelssohn household was normally at 2 p.m.
4. *Fenchel* tea is sassafras tea.
5. Kirghis, originally part of the Soviet Union, is a country northeast of the Caspian Sea.
6. Louise Johansson, 1810–1894, was an out-of-wedlock child of a well-to-do man who brought her to board with and be educated by *Fru* Fellborg. Instead, *Fru* Fellborg used her as a maid, and when the father inquired how she was progressing, she told him she was "too stupid to learn."

# eight

IN 1840 JENNY LIND MET THREE MEN WHO WOULD PROVE TO BE IMPORTANT IN her life. At the literary salon of Malla Silfverstolpe,[1] Lindblad's wealthy patroness in Uppsala, Jenny met Jakob Josephson, a twenty-one-year-old aspiring Swedish composer, and Professor Erik Geijer, an elderly Swedish historian, philosopher, poet, amateur composer, and professor at Uppsala University. The third man was the Danish fairy tale author Hans Christian Andersen.

Having heard about Jenny's musical success, Andersen had made her a courtesy call when he and Lind stayed in the same hotel in Copenhagen. At this initial meeting she responded coolly to the coarse featured, ungainly thirty-eight-year-old man, and he commented afterwards, "She's just an ordinary woman."

In the same year another man caused turmoil for Jenny. Adolph Lindblad, husband and father of three children, had become so enamored with the young singer that his wife offered to give him a divorce. Jenny was so horrified at the thought of the breakup of a family she dearly loved that she left Bonde Palace. Lindblad expressed his adoration of Jenny and his spiritual conflict in verse.

Mendelssohn went to England in the fall of 1840 to conduct in Birmingham and London.

During his four-week absence, Cécile expressed her longing for her husband again and again; thus at the end of September,

> Never in my life have I felt such impatience, joy and longing as I have since I received your last letter from London. I'm not calm for one moment and believe that I would become ill if I didn't soon see you. Only God knows what will become of me on account of my amorousness.

---

The next winter, on the 18th of January 1841, when Carl was not quite three years old and Marie not yet sixteen months, Paul Felix Abraham became the fifth member of the Mendelssohn Bartholdy household.

---

Mendelssohn had been in a state of turmoil since the fall of 1840. He was happy in his position as conductor of the Gewandhaus orchestra and felt comfortable with the people in Leipzig. But the new king of Prussia, Wilhelm Friedrich IV, one of the most culturally enlightened monarchs of the era, ardently wished that he become head of a music section at the Berlin Academy. The composer wavered for months before heeding his king's call in the summer of 1841.

Lea was ecstatic when she learned that her son would come to Berlin. Cécile was decidedly less enthusiastic about the prospect of the move and expressed her feelings to Sophie Horsley:

> I can't say that our time in Berlin was pleasant for me. Felix was very out of sorts, and so I also could not be happy. But I'm very glad that the indefiniteness is over and that we are going to Berlin for a year. I'm particularly glad for my mother-in-law, although I fear that the separation from her darling will be doubly difficult after having enjoyed his company for a year, and it's a firm resolve of mine that Berlin will not be our abiding place.

Doubting that he would be in Berlin longer than one year, Felix rented an apartment for only six months. A few days before he and his family moved, his mother expressed her joy: "Nothing is more welcome to me, *Ihr lieben Leutchen,* than to gather with you under my roof and at my table, and of course have the blessed hope that this will be my portion for a long time…You will be indulged… *Addio carissimi! a rividerci in gioja e pace!"*

At the end of July the little family moved to Berlin, and Felix reveled in the company of his mother and siblings once more. However, he had been in Berlin less than two weeks when he believed that he could have few expectations regarding the musical life and the reorganization of a conservatory or an arts section of an academy of arts.

The king asked Mendelssohn to provide incidental music for *Antigone*,[2] the first of several ancient Greek plays he wished to have performed at court. The composer was deeply moved by the play and composed the music quickly and enthusiastically. After a few rehearsals with the men's choir, he expressed genuine pleasure to his Leipzig concertmaster:

> The chorus parts are so genuinely musical, each so different from the others, that one could wish for nothing finer to compose…They have chosen the best voices from the choir and added the best solo singers…
> It gives me great pleasure to see the furious *animo* with which they all participate; they make such a racket in the Bacchus chorus that one's hair stands on end.

The premiere, for invited guests only, took place at the end of October in the magnificent "new palace" at Sanssouci in Potsdam. Fanny noted in her diary that the endeavor created a great sensation. Mendelssohn exulted in a letter to David and Schleinitz; Cécile wrote to her mother, "It was a *jour de fête* for my mother-in-law—and I have never seen her more alert."

Mendelssohn had written to Ferdinand David that although no one could be in such good hands as he in Berlin, he didn't feel at home. Eight days later he reported to his concertmaster that the acting, singing, and orchestral playing in the performance of *Antigone* were superb and had made a tremendous impression. But then the mood in his letter changed:

> I am already quite anxious to hear all the criticism, and how I should have done it if I were a privy councilor, and how they would have imagined the choruses…They can do nothing but flatter and fawn or pompously criticize, no natural feeling, no honest impression…I knew beforehand that I could not improve [the orchestra]; it is only another

proof of it. You have no idea of the crawling servility of these high-brow people. Both usually go together; and I haven't found more than four in the forty with whom I would like to make music.

To Rietz he complained about his situation in Berlin as well. But after rereading the letter, he asked forgiveness for his "boring, critical, Berlin-smart-alecky" (*Berlinisch-klug*) letter.

He also sent some of his thoughts about the Berlin position to the Duesseldorf landscape artist Johann Schirmer. He mentioned that "everyone, without exception, [was] so kind and respectful to [him] without [his] deserving it" that he should feel obligated to remain in Berlin for that reason alone. But he continued by stating that he had only a strong desire to leave Berlin again. The state of art there, he said, was "deplorable, deteriorated, and the deterioration so well established" that he didn't know if anything could be done about it.

Soon afterward, at the beginning of 1842, Mendelssohn told Devrient, but not his mother or the king, that he would not remain in Berlin. Devrient tried his best to encourage him to stay.

---

While her husband was in Leipzig in November, Cécile often sent news about the children. In one letter she related an account of three-year-old Carl:

Yesterday Hanne [one of the maids] said, "Did you dream about Papa again?" Carl, "Oh, yes." I asked him, "What did you dream?" "I saw Papa in *seep,* he sat at the writing desk." "What was he doing?" Carl, "Writing." "What did he say to you?" "Absolutely nothing."

In February Mendelssohn traveled to Leipzig again, this time to conduct the premiere of his *Scotch Symphony* and the Leipzig premiere of *Antigone* in a benefit concert. Cécile wrote to her husband almost every day; in almost every letter she expressed her longing to see him again, as she did on the 27th of February: "I have 'travel fever' in all my bones. But what can one do, a paltry woman cannot travel alone, and the others don't have husbands in distant lands."

---

Jenny Lind had realized that in order to further her career she must seek the best vocal teacher she could find. Professor Geijer was probably the most influential in her thinking. Already in 1839 he had written to his wife, "It's too bad that she clings only to Berg's manner of singing, but that will disappear with better training." And one of her singing partners, Belletti, advised her to go to Paris to study with Manuel Garcia.

She should have rested her voice in the summer of 1840 but embarked on a concert tour throughout the province in order to raise money. It turned out to be like a triumphal procession in town after town. Her reputation as an unsullied singer increased the admiration of the people.

In the 1840–41 season she sang her great roles, Alice in *Roberto,* Agathe in *Freischuetz,* and Pamina in *The Magic Flute.* She sang in her first Bellini opera, *La straniera,* and finally in his *Norma* in the spring.

Before she left for Paris she gave a concert in Stockholm, where 3,000 people each paid a rix daler to hear her sing. Soon thereafter she left, arriving in Paris on the 12th of July. At her audition Garcia told her that she no longer had a voice and that she must not sing a note for three months. Much later she told Mendelssohn that that moment was the worst time in her life. After six weeks, Garcia gave her two lessons per week for ten rix daler per lesson. Most importantly, Garcia corrected her breathing. Twenty-five years later, however, she maintained that she had learned little from Garcia—that she had learned much more from birdsongs.

Garcia also taught another Swedish singer, named Henriette Nissen. She and Jenny became friends and often sang together. To Malla Silfverstolpe Jenny wrote, "If only I had a voice like Nissen and could sing like she sings; but I am grateful for what has been given to me. I have more than many others." Garcia is reported to have said that a singer with Nissen's voice and Jenny's expressive power would constitute perfection.

After months of Manuel Garcia's coaching, Jenny said she believed her vocal powers had improved greatly; yet in the spring of 1842 she wrote to her father, "What would I do if I came home without having an engagement? Perhaps I may have to sit in Djurgard's Common with a little money box in front of me, gathering pennies while I sing. But perhaps they haven't entirely forgotten me."

She also wrote to Sophie Lindblad about some of her fears:

Something you wrote in your letter gave me a fright. You say that if I come home without having appeared here in public, they will nevertheless say that I wasn't up to it, regardless of how well I sing. Oh dear, what will I do then? Then it's probably best if I look for a position as a nanny, as it is a very difficult matter to appear in public here. On the stage it would be out of the question, and in the concert room I am at my weakest. One must have admirers (or lovers [*amangers*]) here and if I were inclined to have them, then it would probably be possible, but that I will not do.

Lindblad, who had come to Paris in the summer at the behest of the Swedish Royal Opera, agreed with Lind's assessment: "The greatest stage reputations in Paris are only won through sacrificing honor and reputation, but even Parisian salons are closed to courtesans."

Upon Lindblad's urging, Jenny renewed her contract with the Royal Opera, committing herself to sing for one or two years at the equivalent of £150 per annum, plus costumes and bonuses for each performance.

Lindblad took her to meet and sing for one of the most celebrated composers, Giacomo Meyerbeer. He was impressed by her singing but had no opportunity to see her act.

Two weeks later Lindblad and Jenny returned to Stockholm. She was greatly relieved that she received a tumultuous welcome from the crowd waiting for her at the pier.

———————————

Before Mendelssohn left Berlin, he spoke to a court councilor in Berlin about his position. The councilor told him to be patient; they would soon finalize plans. The composer responded that he would not remain in Berlin if "no serious efforts were made." The councilor told him there were too many difficulties regarding the conservatory, but they had "other plans" for which they wished him to remain in Berlin. Mendelssohn summed up the situation for Klingemann:

I have the choice of remaining in Berlin for the rest of my life in complete freedom, and to compose whatever I want, but to receive a salary while performing no public duties. But I don't believe I am able to decide to do that, and wouldn't feel comfortable if I did, at least for the time being. Or I will return to Leipzig where I know what I must do, and where I can accomplish what they want me to do. I hope the king will come to terms with my decision, as I don't wish to hurt him.

But if you consider that my mother has been happy all this time to have me with the family again, and that I have to separate myself from her again, you will probably realize that it's becoming difficult and bitter for me. But art, and where it thrives, must again remain the main thing, difficult or not. That is my answer and it sounds bad.

After he returned to Leipzig in the spring, Mendelssohn informed his mother that he might remain in Berlin "for a longer period of time." Not convinced, Lea wrote to her darling, "I tremble when I think that perhaps you will not come back."

---

Mendelssohn co-planned and conducted the Lower Rhine Festival once more in the spring of 1842. And once again, while Felix was at the festival in Düsseldorf, Cécile lived at the home of her grandmother and mother in Frankfurt.

In May Cécile left her children with her mother and accompanied her husband to England for the first time. They stayed with her Benecke relatives in Denmark Hill on the outskirts of London. In London Mendelssohn participated in a benefit concert for the victims of the eight-day Hamburg fire, which netted five hundred pounds clear profit. And he received his second invitation to Buckingham Palace to play for Queen Victoria and Prince Albert. He described the visit for his mother:

> The Prince of Gotha came in, and we five proceeded through the corridors and rooms to the queen's sitting room, where, next to the piano, stood an enormous, heavy rocking horse and two great bird cages and pictures on the walls, and beautifully bound books lay on the tables, and music on the piano…
>
> I rummaged about a little among the music and found my first set of songs. So, naturally I begged her to choose one of those…and which did she choose? Fanny's song, "Schöner und schöner" ["Lovelier and Lovelier"][3] and sang it beautifully in tune, in strict time, and with very nice expression. Then she sang "Laß Dich nur nichts"…It was wonderful, but I didn't praise her too much…I improvised very well on a chorale and *Schnitter* and added songs the queen had sung; they were very attentive. If Dirichlet says that I'm an aristocrat, I swear I'm more radical than ever.

During his hectic schedule in London, Mendelssohn found little time to compose. One day, however, when he remained at home alone in Denmark Hill, he composed a song without words, known as "Spring Song." It would become one of his most popular pieces in that genre; Clara Schumann would have to play it three times in succession at a concert in Moscow.

In a letter to Felix in June, Lea expressed her great pride that he had received a decoration from King Friedrich Wilhelm. She also informed Mme. Jeanrenaud about the honor:

> We mothers are just not stoical enough not to experience a surge of joy about such things, particularly since the idea that science and art are connected to the memory of Frederick the Great...It also pleases us that there are to be only 30 knights, as such decorations have become commonplace in other places.

The highlight for Felix in 1842 was not the knighthood but a trip to Switzerland with Cécile and Paul and his wife, Albertine. From Iverdon on Lake Neufchatel, Cécile wrote to Fanny, "Wherever your famous brother goes, he is followed by crowds of people and events, which don't affect him at all (he's so used to it), but which often leave his much more stupid [*dumm*] wife confused."

In Switzerland, Felix received a letter from Mme. Jeanrenaud in which she expressed her anger over what she perceived to be her other son-in-law's lack of concern for her daughter Julie's health. She was not subtle but less vociferous when she commented in the same letter, "Your wife has really become a little thin."

So from beautiful Unterseen, Felix composed another effusive account to his mother-in-law about Cécile's well-being.

From Unterseen, the Mendelssohn party went to Interlaken in south-central Switzerland. As the name implies, it lies between lakes—Lake Brienz and Lake Thun. There, in the heart of the Alps, they had a magnificent view of the Jungfrau, the highest peak in Europe, at more than 13,600 feet. From the Jungfraujoch, altitude 11,333 feet, they admired the spectacular panorama. They could see where the Aletsch Glacier, on the south side of the Jungfrau, began on the plateau.

As they hiked along mule tracks, they caught the scent of alpine flowers and spicy herbs everywhere. Felix was not displeased that the only music they heard was the faint sounds of the cow and goat bells in the grazing areas or that the only artworks they saw were Felix's watercolors of the mountains and Cécile's oil paintings of alpine flowers.

From Interlaken Felix apologized to his mother:

18 August 1842
How gladly I would write that I would remain in Berlin! But the whole matter has again taken such strange turns that I become totally confused when I want to think about what I am to do…Don't be angry about the long period of indecision; I can't help it.

After a glorious month in Interlaken, Lucerne, and Zurich, a time almost totally devoid of stress, totally free of correspondence, business matters, and the public, Felix left refreshed. But now he had to deal with the thorny problem. Dr. A. J. Becher, one of a number of friends from whom Mendelssohn had solicited opinions about his situation in Berlin, was blunt:

What do I think of Meyerbeer replacing Spontini as director of the Royal Opera, and you as director of the Berlin conservatory? I'm not happy about the former, and am highly indignant…the appearance of Felix Mendelssohn Bartholdy under Meyerbeer is an outrage. Except for that, I would have said, "Stay." A great man must have a great sphere of effective influence.

As part of a long reply, Mendelssohn wrote,

Frankfurt, 10 September 1842
I fear it's the king, and he alone, who truly wishes to see me firmly settled in Berlin, but as he is (as perhaps, several others) supported therein by no one, he is unable to make his intentions prevail, despite the fact that he is king and has more intelligence and spirit than all the rest of the gentlemen there, but I had no desire to be publicly inactive.

He found it almost unbelievable, he continued, that during the entire year no one had spoken of the conservatory or the academy "or of any of the great matters," but that the whole world knew that he was receiving the princely sum of 3,000 thaler per annum from the king.

Mendelssohn returned to Berlin with his family at the end of September, and a month later he had a long audience with the king. He declined the offer of head of Protestant church music for the nation and requested to be released. The king gave him the freedom to go where he chose. Felix chose to return to Leipzig but promised the king's councilors that he would return to Berlin as soon as someone could "clearly and definitely" tell him how he should serve the king.

Now the most difficult task was to inform his family of his decision. After he gave them the news, his mother and Fanny wept all day. Cécile also could not refrain from crying, and in a rare show of impertinence she wrote to her mother:

> Your last letter was short and contained nothing but questions. I think I had already told you all I know about this matter in my last letter. You and my mother-in-law are one of a kind, as you both rack your brains with suppositions. She also always thinks that Felix has secrets...I'm impatient to go to find my cozy place [*coin chaud*] before the winter, and how and why I must be in Berlin and not in Leipzig upsets me at the moment. As I have always been very happy when I was with Felix, I hope to be so, wherever that will be.

King Friedrich Wilhelm and Mendelssohn reached a verbal agreement at the beginning of November regarding his return to Berlin in 1843. Thereupon Felix returned to Leipzig with the children. Fanny had a sixteen-hour nosebleed after he left. Cécile, in an advanced state of pregnancy, stayed with her mother-in-law for another week before joining her family.

Mendelssohn described his situation in a long letter to Klingemann:

> Leipzig, 23 November 1842
> ...I could no longer put up with the state of uncertainty in Berlin; nothing was certain there except that I received such and a sum of money, and that alone should not constitute the career of a musician. It depressed me more and more every day, and I requested that they should either say that I should do nothing...or they should specify what I should do. The answer again was that there would be enough for me to do, so I wrote Herr von Massow and asked him to arrange an audience with the king so that I could personally thank him and ask him for my release...

I finally had to talk to Mother about it…I would not have believed that it would affect her as terribly as it did. You know how calm Mother usually is, and how seldom she really lets us know her deepest feelings, and so it was two or three times more painful to me that I should give her such a bad time. And yet I could not do otherwise…So on the following day I went to the king with Massow…what he had in mind…was a small choir of some thirty excellent singers, and a little orchestra whose duty it would be to provide music for Sundays and festivals, and to perform oratorios and the like, and I would conduct this "instrument" and compose for it, etc. Two days later I wrote to the king and told him that after what he had said to me, I could no longer leave his service but would be willing to serve him with all my powers all my life.

Lea penned a long letter to Felix at the beginning of December, to which he responded immediately. He recalled that it was his father's birthday on that very day. "Today is the day of lovely, glorious, unforgettable memories. Think of me today also, as I will think of you and him all my life."

One day after Lea received the letter, Felix received the news that his mother was ill, and he hurried to Berlin, only to find that she had already died. Usually the epitome of equanimity, Cécile wrote to Felix,

Leipzig, 13 December (Postmark 14 December 1842)
*Mein lieber* Felix,
My aunt has just been here to bring me the sad news for which I should have been prepared, but which shook me more than almost anything has in my life. So you did not find her alive any more, your dear, good mother, and my hopes were in vain; God grant that you will be more steadfast than I was when I received the news…
Here, far away, I have a boundless longing to see her dear face (which smiled at me so often) once more, to kiss the dear hand that offered me only goodness and love. The gratitude which I was never able to show her weighs on me like a ton of bricks, and I will need time to get hold of myself even outwardly. So don't hurry back to me; I can be of no comfort to you now. My in-laws will have to excuse me; I cannot be consoled. The children are well…The innocent little ones plague me with their questions. Carl can't understand it, he says, "But don't you

know how *Großmama* enjoyed it when we made such a din with Ernst?[4]
Now her whole room must be completely dark."

Fanny ended an account of her mother's death to Cécile,

You're right when you say you have lost a true friend; it is totally
indescribable how much she loved you. She certainly hardly loved either
of her daughters more. She would have done anything for you, just as
you deserve…God grant that we may remain bound together in love
and in remembrance of our beloved parents.

---

1. Malla Silfverstolpe said that she loved Adolf Lindblad "more than anyone," that he was "the most
   lovable man on earth."
2. Antigone, in Sophocles' play, is the daughter of Oedipus. His son Laius kills him, whereupon his
   wife Jocasta kills herself, whereupon their sons kill each other in the battle for the throne. Their
   uncle Creon, king of Thebes, forbids the burial of Antigone's brother, but Antigone resolves to
   bury him so his soul can rest. That is where the tragedy begins. Antigone disobeys her uncle's
   command and performs the funeral service; Creon orders her buried alive, and she hangs herself
   in the tomb.
3. Mendelssohn included three of Fanny's songs in each of two books of his songs. After the queen
   sang Fanny's song, Felix confessed that Fanny was the composer.
4. Ernst was Rebecka's two-year-old son.

# nine

For weeks after Lea's death, Felix avoided social gatherings as much as possible. At the beginning of January, he wrote to Paul, "The mere thought of letters, even to good friends, made me so frightfully sad that I didn't know how to get hold of myself." Whenever someone mentioned his mother, he sought comfort alone in his study. He was unable to write new compositions, yet to Klingemann he expressed gratitude:

> I'm thankful to my parents for my heavenly art, my calling. It leads me
> far away from city, country and earth itself; it's a blessing sent from God.
> Heaven preserve our family and give us strength to be better...My wife
> and children make me forget even music and cause me to think how
> grateful I should be to God for all the benefits He bestows on me.

As part of his reply to Lindblad's letter of condolence, Mendelssohn told him that talking and playing with the children were consolation and refreshment even on the first day, that he loved them more every year, and that he must thank God for His goodness as long as wife and children were well.

Cécile soon became her calm self again and in her quiet, intuitive way was balsam for her husband's soul. He was cognizant of this and mentioned it to both his and her family members. Thus he added a few lines at the end of one of Cécile's letters to her mother:

Leipzig, 22 January 1843
…Cécile is truly an angel in good, as well as in difficult days; she is always the same and yet always different, and always only following her own deepest feelings, and is always led aright; she is an angel, may God bless her for all the good she does for me and the children. And may He again bless you also.

Fanny sent Mme. Jeanrenaud kind words about Cécile as well:

You certainly know how boundlessly Mother loved Cécile; she truly adored her…she was constantly amazed at her, above all her total way of being and doing things. Thank God, she was still able to see Felix so happy and to have the great pleasure in his splendid children. On the other hand, it is a source of everlasting sorrow that my dear father never knew Cécile, as I know she would have been a person after his heart.

Three months after his mother's death, Felix still could not bear to remain at a social gathering for more than half an hour.

After Mendelssohn conducted his *Paulus* in Weimar, Richard Wagner wrote to Luettichau,[1]

The last Palm Sunday concert must be called one of the most brilliant, and left a deep impression in unusually numerous listeners…Mendelssohn Bartholdy showed us, in all perfection, a work which is a testimony to the highest flowering of art. The thought that it was composed in our time fills us with justified pride in the age in which we live.[2]

On the first of May—not in the first week of April 1843, as Cécile had feared—Felix and Cécile's fourth child, Felix August Eduard Mendelssohn Bartholdy, made his appearance. This time Mme. Jeanrenaud was unable to be present when the little one arrived.

In the spring and summer Mendelssohn made numerous trips to Berlin to again discuss his position at court. The first trip occurred less than four weeks after the birth of little Felix, and he told Cécile he would return in a few days. Cécile wrote to her husband almost every day during his absence. On the second day she penned words that soon became a constant refrain: that she was disappointed that he was remaining longer than he had said. However, except for other short trips to Berlin, Felix remained at home that summer; it was the first time in ten years that he did not conduct at a festival.

Before long he became more and more vexed about his relationship with the Berlin court. First, the king's ministers asked him to ratify suggestions that they and Felix had agreed upon but they had amended. He fumed to Paul, "The matter in Berlin cost me four most angry, disturbed and irksome days. If only I could have spoken to you for a single hour." After talking to the jurist Ludwig Muehlenfels in Naumburg, he politely wrote to the king's councilors that the changes in the agreement made the matter impracticable. But to Paul he wrote,

> I expected to hear some words spoken, but they have not been spoken, and they have been replaced by a thousand annoyances, and my head was finally so bewildered that I think I became almost as perverted and unnatural as the whole matter will probably finally turn out to be…I haven't been able to compose these days.

All the negotiations regarding Felix's duties in Berlin for the year 1843–44 were finalized to his satisfaction at the end of July. He would live in Berlin again, be in charge of the cathedral music, compose and direct the music for dramas, and once again conduct the symphony concerts.

Cécile let her mother know how she felt about the development: "I don't speak about our stay in Berlin, and I don't like to hear it spoken of before it's time to leave. I cried about it for several days, then I grumbled for a week, and now I have come to terms with it…Felix is very busy."

And Felix wrote to Mme. Jeanrenaud, "I *have* to go Berlin; I must keep my word."

At the end of July Felix went to Berlin alone to conduct the music for the 1,000th anniversary celebration of the German Reich. Cécile replied to his first letter by saying that she had heard that Mme. Viardot had sung at a court concert and thus knew that he was very busy "in [his] element as a little court flunky."

In another letter, from her *Tante* Schunck's country home in Priesnitz, Cécile made a telling observation to her husband: "Carl plagued me in such a comical way yesterday evening to remain in Priesnitz longer, and always reminded me of you…His wife will not be able to refuse him anything some day."

———————————

At age twenty-two, Jenny Lind did what was expected of a single young woman who was not under parental control; she chose a guardian, the forty-five-year-old judge, singer, and instrumentalist Henrik Munthe.

And in the same summer, Adolph Lindblad wrote about Jenny to his wife,

All I can tell you about our evil spirit [*bösen Geist*] is that I read her last love letter to Guenther, strange, most strange. What we have endured together. With every day the matter of boundless pain departs further, and in the end we have won in every way.

Lind went on her first foreign concert tour—to Finland—together with Julius Guenther[3] and Jakob Josephson, in July 1843. Her first concert in Abo was hailed by the local press as one of the most brilliant occasions in living memory. And when she arrived to sing in Helsinki, a newspaper reported, "Jenny Lind regarded the throng with a gaze so virginally pure, grateful and gentle that she was everyone's favorite before she had sung a note."

At her first concert in Helsinki Jenny wore a simple pale blue gown and flowers in her hair. The audience listened in a state of ecstasy. But when the conductor put a laurel wreath on her head at the end, there was near hysteria in the audience. Critics were lyrical about her modesty, her sincerity, her appeal to "heart, feeling and imagination." After a second concert in the Finnish capital, she left for Stockholm. On her return to Sweden she gave more concerts, several times together with Guenther.

During this time she confided in the Swedish writer and novelist Frederica Bremer[4] that she loved her singing partner. To the wife of the royal councilor, Lagerheim, she wrote about a "young man of whom [she was] fond":

I don't know what will happen in the future; every time I see him, I discover a new characteristic, and I would not be able to describe his conduct towards me; it is so indescribably tactful, prudent, gentle—*jo,* he is all that. I can't describe how amiable, how selfless he is, how the mere thought of him comforts me...We are very similar; he needs some one to love—I am convinced that the lot of the woman he marries must really become one of the purest bliss...Don't think that it is definite; everything will be deferred to the distant future.

Tired after the concert tours, Lind went to Copenhagen for what was intended as a private visit and rest. There she chanced to meet the ballet master August Bournonville, who invited her to stay with his family. Because *Robert of Normandie* was on the playbill at the Royal Theater, he arranged, without telling her, for her to sing the role of Alice in the Swedish language while the rest of the cast sang in Danish. Jenny panicked when he told her. She had sung in no opera house other than the one in Stockholm, and she was so fearful about singing in Copenhagen that she wrung her hands and cried so long that the director cancelled the performance.

Bournonville then sent for his countryman Hans Christian Andersen to determine if the fairy tale author could perform together with Jenny on some occasion. Andersen had felt rebuffed when he had met her three years earlier. Since then, however, she had read and enjoyed some of his fairy tales, and now she met him with a big smile and outstretched hands. She expressed her fears to Andersen: "I have never performed outside of Sweden; in my country everyone is so kind and good to me, and what if I should sing in Copenhagen and be hissed at? I don't dare attempt it."

Andersen replied that he could not judge her voice because he had never heard it and did not know her acting ability, but he was convinced that the mood in Copenhagen was such that she would be successful now with only a tolerable voice and limited acting ability. He advised her to take a chance. So Jenny decided to perform in the opera after all. At the first rehearsal of *Robert* she so charmed the other musicians by her person and art that her fears evaporated, and she sang the role twice in the Royal Theater. Her hostess described her performances as "unbeatable triumphs."

Among the many callers at the Bournonville home, Andersen came most frequently. Before Jenny's first concert in Copenhagen, he wrote in his diary, "In love." Later he repeatedly proposed marriage to her. On one such occasion she gave him a small mirror and told him that only Guenther could make her happy. A few days after her last concert, Andersen made another note in his diary: "I love her." He had spoken to Jenny in Danish when the two were alone together at the Bournonville home. When he wrote her an ardent letter in September, she replied, "Good brother, I believe you have completely misunderstood me. You read more into what I said than I meant. I can never be more than a sister to you. Don't ever doubt that I will be kindly disposed to you, but not more than that."

Three weeks after Jenny left Copenhagen, Andersen completed *The Ugly Duckling*. A few days later he wrote *The Emperor's Nightingale*, about a nightingale who drives death from the emperor. Then he wrote the story of Kai and Gerda, who "were not brother and sister, but were just as fond of each other as if they were." His fourth fairy tale was about the terrible snow queen, "cold and distant to her lover's protestation."

He sent her the first three stories and waited for acknowledgment that she had received them. Only after Bournonville told Jenny that Andersen had already waited six weeks did she write to her "dear brother": "I find the tales so divinely beautiful that they must be the purest and most glorious things that ever flowed from my brother's pen."

Meanwhile Guenther confided in Jakob Josephson:

10 October 1843
[My] matters of the heart are at the same point as when we parted, only with the difference that the fulfillment of my most ardent desires appear perhaps more distant than before. I can't cite the reason…The most important meeting about which we so often spoke, and the expected outcome that was so dear to my heart, did not take place, for on the same day that I came to the city, [she] developed a high fever, so that she could receive no callers. From this you can see that unrest, uncertainty, concern and fear are what occupy me at the moment.

Several weeks later, Jenny confided in Andersen,

27 October 1843
I have a difficult life! Many cares, much sorrow. Much happiness—and divine moments! I have parents, but oh! we don't have the least affection for one another, and I must seek other friends. After countless quarrels and bitter, bitter tears I left an unhappy parental home and found two friends for my entire life—the Lindblads! She is an angel, he a genius! Real greatness of spirit! A demon, a god, whatever you want. He developed the strongest passion for me; I was everything to him, his only delight. He pursued me with his entire being. I could desire whatever I wished

from him. His wife knew it. One day she sat down in order to make a writ for a divorce…Oh! my God! What a moment! I didn't consider it, my brother, I thought of their three children—I left them in God's care and withdrew, in order to see them again when *he* could calmly look at me! If you understand what I have suffered, and can imagine how much I love these people, then you would imagine the state in which I now find myself. All this happened just recently, and therefore the wound is still bleeding. It was precisely at the most difficult time, my good brother, a *Mensch* appeared who loves me deeply with all the purity of his heart, with the highest power of his soul – in one word: a man who could be said to be my fiancé. He is not. But no one but he can make me happy, I can rest on no one's breast but his. He will be faithful to me until death, and so don't wonder, when a girl—so *lonely*, so much the talk of the town, so highly regarded because of her fame, and as a result, not particularly happy—listened to the words of first love, and when I ask God every evening to give me the right love for him who has earned it to such a high degree! That is the way things stand, my brother!

Subsequently Jenny's confidante, Frederica Bremer, informed Andersen about Guenther's life and relationship to Jenny: "He led a loose life in the past, but it seems that this, his last and loveliest love, has made him steadfast and ennobled him. Jenny doesn't hide her feelings for him but is afraid of marriage and would prefer not to marry. Poor child, she is so alone."

And Josephson wrote in his diary, "Guenther believes that he no longer has enemies who hold his earlier imprudence against him. They would become an estimable artist-couple, although her genius is far greater than his."

At the end of 1843 Andersen composed another ardent love letter to Jenny, the last great love of his life. Much later he commented about her art, "Through Jenny Lind I first became aware of the holiness of art; I learned one must forget oneself in the service of the Supreme…Her appearance in Copenhagen created an epoch in the history of our opera; it showed me art in its sanctity—I had seen one of its vestal virgins."

---

In an attempt try to recover her health, Rebecka Dirichlet had been in Italy with her two children and a maid since the beginning of July. As soon as Felix returned to Leipzig, he began a letter to her with an amusing story about his children:

8 August 1843

…Recently Paul was screaming unbearably in the next room, and Karl kept saying, "Again, again." and then he screamed again, and the other one said, "Again, again." When Cécile came and asked for the reason, Carl said, "Mama, I wanted to see what kind of voice Paul had. We are having auditions." And Marie stood there and very seriously said, "Paul can sing very loud." They are all good and a blessing, and even the youngest already has goodness and intelligence shining out of his blue eyes.

On Monday I attended the performance of *Medea* by Euripides in Potsdam…How bad, *ja,* how wretched most of the scenes in this piece are…The basis on which they all rest is foul and spoiled.[5]

Shortly after Mendelssohn returned to Leipzig, Herr von Massow, councilor at the Berlin court, informed him that the king wished him to conduct his incidental music at a performance of Shakespeare's play *A Midsummer Night's Dream* and a few other plays in the "new" *palais.*

He delayed moving to Berlin with his family as long as possible. At the beginning of October he went alone to rehearse and direct the music for *A Midsummer Night's Dream* and told Cécile he would return in two weeks. The first performance of *A Midsummer Night's Dream* did not take place until the 14th however, and he remained in Berlin for three weeks. Niels Gade, a Danish composer and conductor, Joseph Joachim, a violin prodigy, Ferdinand David, and Ferdinand Hiller all came from Leipzig to attend the premiere. The French composer Hector Berlioz later complimented Mendelssohn:

Permit me to tell you that I heard your *Midsummer Night's Dream* in Dresden, and that I have never heard anything as profoundly Shakespearian as your music. As I left the theater I would have given three years of my life to be able to embrace [*embrasser*] you. Believe me when I tell you that I love you as much as I admire you, and that is a great deal.

At a moving farewell in Leipzig at the end of November, Mendelssohn assured the Gewandhaus board that he would return to participate in numerous concerts. Then he and his family moved by train to settle into his parents' newly decorated suite at Leipzigerstrasse 3. Only two days later he reported to Konrad Schleinitz:

Berlin, 27 November 1843

We are set up in a large, lovely, empty and somewhat sad house…it was more difficult for us to leave than words can say; I cannot describe all the love and goodness I have left there. Nowhere can I find it replaced, and only our return can bring it to me again, but you also know that I and all of us think of the much love and goodness every day with thankful hearts.

The children, as usual, express their thoughts most freely, and Marie cries all day and says, "I want to go back to Leipzig," and when I say, "Do you want to go there alone?" she replies, "If you don't want to go with me, I'll go alone." Carl is quieter already and only asks about his grandmother every minute, and if the whole house did not really belong to her. "I am certain she always sat there at the window," he says—and of course that doesn't make us more cheerful…I would rather immediately go back with him…But if God only keeps us all well, the concerns and unpleasantness and everything are welcome.

Members of his family feared that Felix's antipathy to Berlin would manifest itself in moodiness and anger. But two weeks after his arrival, Fanny reported to Rebecka that Felix was in a very good mood. And at the end of the year she thought that their brother's state of mind towards Berlin was still positive for the most part. In fact, at the beginning of 1844 Mendelssohn was actually considering the possibility of remaining in Berlin for a few years. Unfortunately, however, he experienced new vexations: the cathedral preachers and he were at odds about the liturgy, and he had difficulty making music an integral part of the liturgy. Even the Leipzig papers commented on the disagreements.

---

In his inimitable way, Mendelssohn's concertmaster, Ferdinand David, faithfully sent news from Leipzig and countered his friend's bad moods with humor and lightness. On one occasion he alluded to Cécile's musical taste:

Last week I thoroughly enjoyed Beethoven's last quartets…The fugue, of course, is difficult to swallow, but when one has chewed on it up to the

Andante, one can savor it; from that point on it becomes splendid, even though I would not wish to risk playing it for your wife on account of the *Knoddeln*. But the three notes in question aren't in it, and perhaps precisely this fugue would find favor in her sight.

---

Mendelssohn attended a performance of Wagner's opera *The Flying Dutchman* at the Berlin Royal Opera in January. Before Wagner departed for Dresden, he left him a note: "*Mein lieber, lieber* Mendelssohn, I am very happy that you are fond of me. The fact that I have become a little closer to you is the most important aspect of my entire Berlin expedition for me."

And he informed his wife that Mendelssohn had come to the stage, heartily embraced him, and congratulated him most cordially.[6]

---

Mendelssohn had been in Berlin for six months when he decided he would not remain. He informed the royal councilors about his decision, and in May he and his family left Berlin for Frankfurt. From there he went to London to conduct the London Philharmonic Society Orchestra. In the two months he was in London he either conducted or played the piano in thirty-eight compositions.

Because Cécile was exhausted and suffered from a respiratory ailment, her mother prevailed upon her to remain at the Fahrthor for five weeks before going to the spa at Soden. Again Cécile repeatedly expressed her longing for her husband. Two days after Felix left for London, she wrote,

> Today Marie very sadly said, "I feel so sorry for my papa." To the question "Why?" she replied, "Because he has to be so far away, and he loves me so much." I can say the same with even more right, but feel more sorry for myself all the time…The impossibility of seeing you for two months is very hard for me to bear…I wait patiently for everything when I'm not with you; I feel like a machine that has absolutely no will of its own. I don't care about anything.

In accordance with Felix's strict injunctions, Cécile reported regularly about her and the children's health, thus about the youngest,

Frankfurt, 22 May 1844

...Felixchen, poor boy, looks like a boiled lobster on his whole body today; in addition, he has the other rash on his head, arms and legs, sore ears and swollen glands. I feel so very sorry for him; when I bandage him in the mornings and evenings he is remarkably patient and often very happy throughout it all. You wouldn't be able to look at him in this condition...I only hold the child on my lap sometimes; you will allow me to do that, won't you?

In another letter she said she would write again in two days or grant the privilege to Mme. Jeanrenaud: "Mother greatly longs to pour out her heart; you already know what you must skim off from her letters."

Like a mother hen, Mme. Jeanrenaud kept careful watch over her brood and reported the slightest indisposition to Felix. After Cécile joined her in Soden, she noted that she was coughing, but she voiced another, to her more serious, concern:

The doctor here regards Cécile's illness only as exhaustion. He believes that the main condition for her recovery is a standstill of a number of years, so that her strength would not be taken into demand by more children. I'm convinced that you will make this sacrifice, as I know no man who is more loving than you, *mein lieber* Felix. And don't believe that it will be a sacrifice only on your part, for every day I am more convinced than ever that Cécile loves you tenderly and deeply, and nothing gives me more pleasure than hearing her speak of you. Every word expresses the purest love and adoration. But you know that better than I can say it.

---

1. Wolf August von Luettichau, 1798–1856, was director of the Weimar court theater.
2. After Mendelssohn's death, Wagner wrote only negatively about Mendelssohn and his music.
3. Julius Caesar Guenther, 1818–1904, was a baritone opera singer and later a teacher at the Swedish Royal Opera.
4. Frederica Bremer, 1801–1865, was an early advocate of equal rights for women.
5. *Medea* is the story of jealousy and revenge of a betrayed woman. Her husband, for whom she had left home and country and bore his children, left her for another woman, not for love, but for power and money.
6. After Mendelssohn's death, Wagner wrote that Mendelssohn had been ill-humored and implied that he was envious.

# t e n

LEA MENDELSSOHN DID NOT QUITE HIT THE MARK WHEN SHE TOLD HER SON "'Love is *histoire* for women, but nothing but an episode for men'…but for you, love is not merely an episode."

Felix had met the attractive, well-heeled Mary Alexander and carried on a brief dalliance with her in 1833. After he returned to Germany he had sent her a very long flattering letter, which gave Mary every right to believe that he wished to have more than a casual friendship with her. However, he did not write to her again for eight long months.

Now in 1844 Mary, who had been married for almost ten years to the parliamentarian Joshua Samuel Crompton, came to London from Norwich for the express purpose of meeting Mendelssohn for the first time since 1833.

When she first met him now, in the company of her two sisters, Joanna and Margaret, she felt constrained; the next day she wrote to Mendelssohn,

> Oh, let there be no cloud over our meeting; let us be friends once more, not merely outward seeming but in sincerity and mutual esteem. Two written lines or one kind spoken word or look from you when I see you

again will suffice to assure me of this, and I shall then feel quite light of heart, and truly happy in meeting with you again.

Mary assured Mendelssohn that her husband knew the purpose of her trip to London. Mendelssohn replied in what Mary termed a "charming true-hearted" note.

The next day Mendelssohn went to see her but was told by the valet that she was not at home.

In her second letter Mary informed him that she had waited for him until five o'clock but then left because she could not possibly tell her sisters that she expected him. At the end she told him that she would be at Benedict's concert the following day where Felix was to play the piano, that she had reserved a seat near the piano, and that because she would be "quite by [herself]" she expected him "to take a *little bit* of care of [her] when [he had] the time."

Joanna asked her sister to give Felix a number of messages at Benedict's concert. The following evening she sent Felix a note to express her indignation that their valet had not invited him to come in when he called and said she was sorry that Mary had not been able to speak to him at the concert. "She saw you looking sad and fatigued and not happy with your situation!"

Felix dined twice with the three sisters in the following weeks; they gave him Scottish keepsakes for him and Cécile and Marie.

A few days before he left London, Mary sent a short note with three bracelets, one of which Felix was to choose for Cécile, who was to wear it "for its *own* sake as well as *hers*."

The day before he departed for Frankfurt, Mary sent him a final letter:

Your earnest, sincere and friendly reply to the lines I wrote to you when I first came to town made me feel very happy, as did your assurance of your never failing friendship, and yet I could not but see that you were surprised at my having written to you—that you could not understand why I had thought it necessary to do what certainly (indeed by ordinary standards) might be considered inconsiderate, with the good sense and discretion becoming a woman. But I did not then pause to consider these things. I *felt* strongly and I wrote, for I knew I could trust you.

She said that if she were able to converse freely with him, she would tell him of the "many peculiarities of [her] mode of life and other circumstances that may have appeared to [him] wild and fanciful in [her] feelings."

She mentioned that she lived far from her family and former friends and led a very quiet and almost solitary life because her husband's occupation kept him away from home, and her children were too young for "mental companionship."

She admitted that she had acquired the bad habit of living so much in the *past* that sometimes she almost imagined it the reality and the *present* but a dream. She added that she had never experienced this illusion more strongly than when she met him again now, and she wrote under its influence.

> Your *truthful* and yet most feeling letter at once recalled me to the sense of this, and most sincerely do I thank you for it. *Thus* has yours been shown towards *me,* and believe me, I know how to value it. And should we never meet again, it will, whilst I live, give me happiness to know that I have in you a friend unchangeable and unchanging.
> Farewell, may God bless you and yours.

Mary and Mendelssohn did not meet again.

---

Cécile wrote to Felix at least every second day during his two-month stay in England. Sometimes she thanked him for the gentle way he dealt with her failings. Always she expressed her great delight about his detailed letters and her anticipation of his return.

Mme. Jeanrenaud also wrote regularly. In one letter she mentioned a slight indisposition that Cécile had not mentioned. Thereupon Felix reprimanded his wife, to which she replied,

> My mother has so completely exhausted the health item that all there is left for me to do is to defend myself to you, as I can see your angry face and your head-shaking from here because I didn't inform you of my slight illness. If I were with you I would make it up to you and torment you so long and kiss you until you completely forgave me.
> Now, however, I must be patient and wait for a severe reprimand. But you won't express your anger, but will carry it with you until we are together again, and you won't believe anything I write, will read something between every line I write. I have been wrong and will improve. Today I will once again ask for forgiveness. Don't be angry at me; it won't happen again.

In London, all the British critics made favorable comments about Mendelssohn's conducting. And the critic for the *Morning Post* expressed amazement at Mendelssohn's "indescribable power" as a pianist. But an otherwise astute critic, James William Davison, described the Bach concerto in which Felix performed as "somewhat of an oddity."

Mendelssohn remained in London three days longer than planned. On the last evening, at a soiree to which Klingemann had invited the composer's friends, he suddenly bolted from the room. Later he mentioned his sudden departure to Fanny Horsley Thompson: "At some moments I feel totally unable to be or to speak with many persons in society."

---

From Soden Cécile sent what she believed would be her final letter to Felix:

Monday [8 July 1844]
*Lieber* Felix,
I have never before been as happy about the prospect of seeing you again, and it seems impossible to me that I will be able to manage without you for such a long time again. It's always becoming worse, and last night, in the middle of my dreams, you stood before me all of a sudden, completely embodied, just the way you are, so that I awoke from the fright. I have absolutely no other thought than to see you again, and often I don't know what's going on around me.

Felix did not return to his family in Soden until the middle of July. From there he apprised his brother about his musical activities in London. This time he did not state that playing and conducting had no lasting value:

My stay in England was glorious! I have never been received with so much kindness anywhere or at any time, and I made more music in those two months than I usually make in two years…My main purpose, to be of service to the Philharmonic Society, was achieved beyond all expectations; according to all the judgments, they have never had a season like it for many years.

About Klingemann he wrote, "There is something glorious about such a friend, and one can find him only once in a lifetime."

Felix had been back in Germany for less than two weeks when he left to conduct a festival in Zweibrucken, near the border of France.

A few days later Mme. Jeanrenaud took out paper and pen again. She mentioned that a friend had declared that Cécile had never looked so well and so lovely. She spoke of how unreservedly cheerful the few days when Felix had been at home had been and how much they were all looking forward to his return. Finally she said that she always knew that he loved Cécile tenderly, but now she had really seen it and experienced it.

---

King Friedrich Wilhelm IV of Prussia had asked Meyerbeer, who was now the director of the Berlin Royal Opera, to produce a new opera for the gala opening of the newly reconstructed opera house in the fall of 1844.[1] Meyerbeer knew how Lind's reputation had grown in the Scandinavian countries. And in 1843, when Hans Christian Andersen had rhapsodized to Meyerbeer about her singing, and the composer asked, "But can she act?" Andersen had been equally rhapsodic.

Thus Meyerbeer invited Lind to sing the role of the heroine in the opera he was composing. Lind responded to the invitation by saying that although she feared singing in Berlin, she would trust him. So she tore up her unsigned contract with the Stockholm Royal Opera and prepared to go to Germany in the summer of 1844.

She arrived in Dresden at the end of July to begin German language lessons. Pleased to find Jacob Josephson there, she spoke much to him about her fears as well as about her love for Guenther. Consequently, Josephson made a diary entry:

August 23, 1844
Jenny Lind has an overpowering fear of singing in Germany. She loses all her courage when she thinks she could fail, and is having a great struggle...Sometimes she calms herself and sings the chorale "*Jesus, der ist all mein Gut*" [Jesus, he is my entire treasure]. The next moment she forgets the happiness she has provided for thousands of others and regards her ability as zero. Poor Jenny. I have never experienced such a violent struggle.

The Swedish consul in Dresden offered Lind a contract with the Royal Swedish Opera for much greater remuneration than she had received heretofore.

However, she did not sign; she was now in such turmoil that she even considered abandoning her operatic career completely.

She had been in Dresden only a few weeks when she received a summons from Stockholm to sing at the coronation ceremonies of the new Swedish king, Oskar I, in September and October. It was only after a pitched inner struggle that she made up her mind to heed the call.

Fearing that Lind might not have time to learn the part of the heroine in his opera, in large part because it was in an unfamiliar language, Meyerbeer asked Leopoldine Tuczec, the leading soprano at the Berlin Royal Opera, to learn it.

Lind sang ten times at the coronation festivities in Stockholm. While she was there, the new director of the Royal Swedish Opera, Count Hamilton, offered her 7,500 thaler per annum for eight years, and the same annual pension for life. The contract was ready for her to sign, but Lind was so enraged by a clause that stipulated that she would have to return 1,500 thaler if she accepted that she tore up the contract.

Despite her overwhelming fear, Lind prepared to return to Germany, saying that if she did not win over the fastidious Berlin audience, she would never step on the stage again and would never return to Stockholm.

After Lind returned to Germany, Frederica Bremer mused to Malla Silfverstolpe, "It's a blessing for [the Lindblads] that the enchantress and tormentress is gone."

---

In mid-September of 1844 Felix found an apartment on Bockenheimergasse in Frankfurt and helped his family to settle in. On the 27th he left for Berlin. His intention was, he said, to quickly extricate himself from his Berlin position in the most pleasant way possible and return to Frankfurt. He told Cécile that he would be home in two weeks.

The next day Cécile wrote to her husband,

The parting was very, very difficult for me, and I must ask your forgiveness for having made it more difficult for you. I am in a completely different mood now and look at everything with rose colored glasses. I believe your promise that you will soon be back, and I will make my life without you as pleasant as I can.

She reported that the children were all well, that she was fine, "not yet naughty [*vilaine*]," that she had only a slight cold, and that she was feeling more at home at Bockenheimergasse.

The next day Mme. Jeanrenaud informed Felix about Cécile's health and merely intimated that she was sad about Felix's absence. "She didn't tell me so, as you know how reticent she is about certain things; of course you will know from her letter."

Cécile wrote to her husband almost every day for two weeks, primarily about the children and their and her health. And she repeatedly expressed her longing for him.

Several days after he arrived in Berlin, Felix assured Mme. Jeanrenaud of his love for Cécile and said that he could hardly wait for the time he would be with her again.

> I cannot often enough hear that Cécile is well and cheerful, that her and the children's health is completely restored, that everything is transpiring according to their wishes. How I long for them daily and hourly. I was very happy to find my siblings so happy and healthy again…yet I long every hour to see who is my happiness and everything to me. I hope it won't be too long before our *Wiedersehen*. I have every hope that I'll be able to end my affairs soon and completely according to my desires, and you can imagine that I will stay no longer than is necessary. Cécile is writing as well and as punctually and faithfully as ever, but you will make me very happy if you write to me on her non-mail day.

One day Cécile sent an amusing account about their three-year-old son to her husband: "Paul has very many of your habits; when he is angry, he chews [*frißt*] his apron, and when he would like to have something, he snuggles up to me like a little earwig."

On her birthday, more than two weeks after Felix had left for Berlin, she responded immediately to a letter from him:[2]

> Frankfurt, 10 October 1844
>
> …I must give myself the special birthday pleasure of writing to you; my thoughts have been with you all day already, and everything that happened here today only intruded on my special wish to tell you how happy I am, and that the only thing lacking in my complete contentment

is your presence. But I shall have that soon, as you assure me in every letter, and also in today's inexpressibly dear, kind letter.

How can I give thanks for so much love? I cannot, and accept it as the blessed sunshine of my life. I feel the benefits of this love every day, but doubly so on a day like today. I cannot imagine my life without you; I also cannot imagine what would have become of me, but when you tell me that you are not worthy of me, I would like to weep, as all my efforts and endeavors are to always become more like you and form myself after you.

By this time, Felix had informed Cécile only that he would be coming soon; to her mother he wrote that he would not be gone "too long." However, at almost the same time he wrote to Cécile's sister that he would return to Frankfurt via Leipzig on the 29th of October. And to Klingemann he wrote that he hoped to leave Berlin in the middle of November and return to Frankfurt at the end of that month.

Shortly after her birthday, Cécile again wrote to her husband:

*Mein lieber* Felix,

…I must thank you for the dear, detailed letter I received yesterday. It made me very happy, and I hope all your expectations will be realized. You can write nothing that makes me happier than that you are coming soon, as my longing for you is worse now than ever. I have hardly any other thought than you, and you will see how much I am in love with you. I am well, thank God, the children also. I don't feel my twenty-seven years yet. Now I am eleven years younger than you again.[3]

Mme. Jeanrenaud also reported to Felix,

At this moment she's in church and is thinking of God and you, *mein lieber* Felix, who are everything to her, her joy and happiness, and with whom God in His love has so deeply joined you together. When I went to Bockenheimergasse at eight on Thursday morning I could not help thinking…of you and Soden, and to quietly say, "Oh, if only we were still there together, or if only he were here with us."…Cécile seemed as happy as she could be without you, for we couldn't give her what she loved the most.

On the morning of the 21st of October Felix informed his mother-in-law that he would leave Berlin in two weeks. And again he included assurances: "I long every day and every hour to hear from Cécile, whether she's well and unchanged, and whether the children are well, and if they are all thinking of me."

On the evening of the same day Felix met Jenny Lind at the home of the sculptor Ludwig Wichmann and his wife, Amalia.

In a letter to Cécile four days later he stated that he would remain in Berlin somewhat longer; to Schleinitz he wrote that he would remain in Berlin for three or four weeks.

After Cécile received the letter from her husband with the news that the king was assenting to all his wishes, she replied on the 28th, "[I must] congratulate you for—yes, for what? For your unheard of talent of getting everyone to act according to your wishes." In the same letter she assured him that she would be content to live anywhere, as long as she could be with him.

At almost the same time Mendelssohn informed Devrient about the contents of the king's letter:

> My position here has been modified during the last few days, and completely according to my wishes. I will continue to have the relationship as composer to the king, for which I shall receive a moderate salary, but fortunately I am free of all my obligations in connection with public performances and residence in Berlin. I hope to return to my family in Frankfurt soon, and to come to Berlin often for short visits, but never again to remain…
>
> P. S. I have another opera in my head which you must write for me.

In another letter to Cécile, without citing a definite date of his return to Frankfurt, Felix wrote, "Only the thought of seeing you again has helped me through this period of separation." But Cécile responded, "I wager that I cling more to you than you to me. We should put it to the test. I can assure you that if I didn't have the lead weights, the children, no power on earth would keep me here. I would have been with you again in Berlin long ago."

In another letter to her husband, after writing about an alphabet game her children played and noting that Marie could not play as well as her younger brother Paul, Cécile continued,

You will again say that I wrong Marie when I say that she has less intelligence than the boys. God forbid, I'm very satisfied with her. She is good, is easygoing, has a good measure of ambition, and that's all that's necessary for a girl…Actually, she's becoming prettier all the time and is particularly well built.

In the middle of November the king requested that Mendelssohn conduct a performance of *Paulus* "this year or next year." However, Felix reported to Mme. Jeanrenaud, "I had fully expected to leave on the 17th of November but have to remain in Berlin for two more weeks to conduct *Paulus* against my wishes."

When Cécile learned of the developments in Berlin she made the less-than-flattering observation, "When one has a little court flunky as a husband, matters don't proceed according to one's wishes."

In Felix's next letter to his mother-in-law, he wrote,

Each time I count the hours very impatiently until I see her, without whom I can no longer know any happiness or joy…The only thing that comforts me now…is the plan (another plan, you will say) that beginning three weeks from today, when with God's help I will be reunited with Cécile and the children, I will not leave them until the following autumn, not for a long nor for a short time, neither for short nor extensive travels.

Although Cécile said she didn't want to accuse him, she did so obliquely:

Is it not remarkable that it occurred to the king only on the day of your departure what he could have given you to do during all the time that you were there?…But I hope you are perhaps not remaining in Berlin on account of Hensel's picture. That could also have occurred to both of you before.

Several times that fall Felix was critical of Cécile's handwriting style.[4] She responded by saying she would try to improve.

Felix had planned to stop in Leipzig and Dresden before returning to Frankfurt, but when he received frantic letters from Cécile in Leipzig about Felixchen's serious illness he boarded the fast mail carriage in Leipzig and arrived in Frankfurt on the 6th of December.

1. The theater that was built in the reign of Frederick the Great was destroyed by fire in 1843.
2. Felix's letter, presumably a birthday letter, has not been found.
3. Cécile was born in October 1817, Felix in February 1809.
4. Cécile's writing style was such that she used four or five times as much paper as did members of the Mendelssohn family. Postage costs *were* very high.

# e l e v e n

ALTHOUGH MENDELSSOHN RECEIVED MANY INVITATIONS TO CONDUCT IN THE winter of 1845, he insisted that his life would be sans trip, sans music festival, sans everything until the following autumn. He admitted, however, that he was flattered to receive an invitation to conduct in New York for one thousand pounds, but he told Paul, "I regard that trip as unlikely as one to the moon."

In the same letter he included a humorous anecdote about his almost four-year-old son:

> Paul beat Marie's doll and yelled again and again, "I will marry you, I will marry you." Cécile asked him what it was all about, and he said, "I think that is marrying, when someone really beats a woman." The masses of wrong and wise concepts, all mixed up, are too cute.

Far from Berlin, Felix sorely missed his siblings, especially Paul, who often served as a sounding board for him. He now longed for the frequent walks and talks they had enjoyed since the completion of the railroad between Berlin and Leipzig in 1843. And Albertine confided to Cécile how much her husband also needed Felix. To rectify the matter somewhat, Felix proposed a "congress" of all four siblings and their families on the Rhine in spring, when Fanny and Rebecka were due to return from Italy with their families.

Without public duties in Frankfurt except those he chose, Mendelssohn composed diligently in the winter and spring of 1845. He completed six organ sonatas—Schumann described them as "perfection"—and in January he sent his newly completed violin concerto to Leipzig for publication. Ferdinand David premiered it in Leipzig and complimented the composer heartily.[1]

Mendelssohn was pleased that the Prussian king commissioned him to compose music for more ancient dramas. He completed the music for Jean Racine's *Athalie* and two Greek tragedies, Sophocles' *Oedipus Coloneus* and *Oedipus Rex,* at the beginning of March.

He spent much time with his children; often they went to watch the ice floes fly like lightning under the bridge in the Main River.

---

Two young Americans, poet and novelist Bayard Taylor and music critic Nathaniel Parker Willis, were in Frankfurt at the time of the great annual fair in March. As they slowly strolled along the northern bank of the Main River they encountered Mendelssohn. Taylor described the meeting:

> It was a deliciously warm, sunny day…and the long stone quay was thronged with thousands of strangers from all parts of Europe…As we pushed through the crowd, my eyes, which had been wandering idly over the picturesque faces and costumes around us, were suddenly arrested by the face of a man, a little distance in front, approaching us. His head was thrown back and his eyes, large, dark, and of wonderful brilliance, were fixed upon the western sky. Long thin locks of black hair, with here and there a silver streak, fell around his ears. His beard, of two or three days' growth, and his cravat, loosely and awkwardly tied, added to the air of absorption, of self forgetfulness, which marked his whole appearance. He made his way through the crowd mechanically, evidently only partly conscious of its presence.
>
> As he drew nearer I saw that his lips were moving and presently heard a deep, rich voice chanting what appeared to be a chorale, judging from the few bars that reached me in passing…My companion grasped my arm and whispered "Mendelssohn!" as he slowly brushed past me; and

for a single moment the voice of his inspiration sang at my very ear. I stopped instantly and turned; yet as long as I could follow him with my eyes, he still pressed slowly onward with the same fixed, uplifted gaze, lost to everything but his art.

The next day Taylor informed Mendelssohn in a note that he had attended a performance of *Walpurgisnacht* and asked if he could have a souvenir. Thereupon he received a few measures of the score of *Walpurgisnacht* with an invitation to Bockenheimergasse. Taylor was struck by the simply furnished apartment and again by Mendelssohn's appearance:

I remember, particularly, that the nostrils were as finely cut and flexible as an Arab's. The lips were thin and rather long, but with an expression of indescribable sweetness in their delicate curves...The composer Benedict once told me that when he was pursuing his musical studies under Carl Maria von Weber, the boy Mendelssohn was a picture of almost supernatural beauty.

At the end of April Mendelssohn informed Devrient about his life in Frankfurt: "For the first time in a long time I feel what it's like to live quietly and compose, and what happiness it is to have not only one leisure hour, and now and then a leisurely day, but a long series of leisurely days ahead for composing."

He read voraciously every day and attempted to contrive a plot for an opera, but nothing came of it. So he pleaded with Devrient to write a libretto for him:

Please, Devrient, do what you can for me...it should be German and noble and cheerful; let it be a Rhine legend or some other national event or tale, or let it be a powerful type of character such as in *Fidelio*. It is not to be *Bluebeard* or *Andreas Hofer* or *Loreley*, though there might be something of all of these! I want you to help me!

---

In a letter to Meyerbeer in November, Adolph Lindblad enumerated what he called Jenny Lind's "quite great faults": that she was irresolute and harbored "unnatural" doubts about her abilities; that she had said a thousand times that she didn't want to and couldn't, but at the same time she could and wanted to.

With that he advised the composer, "Disregard her doubts. She knows exactly how to overcome all difficulties."

When Meyerbeer talked to musicians, members of the court, and all his friends in Berlin, he described Lind as "un vrai diamond de genie."

Several days after Mendelssohn left Berlin, Lind was invited to sing at a court concert arranged by Princess Augusta. The person whom the elegantly dressed aristocratic guests saw sitting near the piano was extremely pale and clothed in a simple dress. She looked like a shy schoolgirl, not an operatic diva. Thus the celebrated soprano, Henriette Sontag, now Countess Rossi, and Lady Westmoreland, wife of the English ambassador at the Prussian court, speculated that perhaps Meyerbeer was playing a practical joke on them. When Lady Westmoreland asked Meyerbeer if he was really going to bring "that frightened child" out in his opera, Meyerbeer merely replied, "Attendez, [wait] miladi."

After she heard Lind sing a few songs at the concert, Lady Westmoreland described those few minutes as the most extraordinary experience she could remember. They heard wonderful sounds, she said, but what was most astounding was the transfiguration that came over Lind's entire face and figure, "lighting them up with the whole fire and dignity of her genius." Everyone in the gathering was transfixed; and as word about her spread, all of Berlin talked about her and waited anxiously for her to perform publicly.

Lind subsequently wrote to Judge Munthe:

…I have sung at court and been so fortunate as to please greatly. This may sound conceited, but I do not mean it that way. Countess Rossi was present, and my modesty prevents me from telling you what she is reported to have said. I am meeting with extraordinary success everywhere, and go into fashionable society much, because this provides the first entrance into the world of art. And I am already known in Berlin, and people talk of me with interest, so lively and so flattering, that I am beginning to think I must be in Stockholm. Forgive me, dear Mr. Munthe, for thus openly speaking of things as they occur. I promise not to become vain and conceited, only glad and happy when things go well…

When Lind invited Josephson to celebrate a Scandinavian Christmas with her at the Wichmann home, where she now lived, she wrote, "O! this Mendelssohn, how he has charmed me," and "That unusual Julius, I believe he is not happy. O! What a man he is."

Josephson came to Berlin and was pleased to note that Jenny's feelings had again become more tender towards Guenther and that she spoke endlessly of what he had done for her in the last three years "in making her life more even, and her humor better." Yet to his diary he confided:

> What storms still rage! She is uplifted by the enthusiasm of the people of Berlin, yet she is sick with longing for Stockholm and Guenther, poor girl … She received an infinitely noble letter from Guenther; it seems he has offered to break their relationship so that she could pursue her career.

In addition to her personal turmoil, Jenny was terrified about singing in Berlin; she realized that filling the royal opera house was quite another matter than singing a few songs at a soirée.

Furthermore, in her Berlin debut she had chosen to sing the title role in *Norma* in the German language for the first time. Although she continued her German lessons, she was sure that her German would be inadequate. Lind had other fears; she had heard that the Berlin audience and critics were known for their great fastidiousness. She admitted that her courage was "desperately low." What she wished most of all was to go home to Sweden.

Despite her emotional turmoil, Lind transported the audience to an ecstatic state in her Berlin debut in *Norma* on December 15. At the end of the aria, *Casta diva*, the tumult was so great that she had to repeat it immediately. Such a thing had never before occurred in Berlin, and the critic Rellstab* hoped that this "barbarism" would never again occur. At the end of the opera, the audience demanded that Lind appear again and again.

Jenny Lind created a furor again in January when she sang the lead role in Meyerbeer's *Das Feldlager in Schlesien*.[2] Her fame was now so great that Alfred Bunn, lessee of the Drury Lane Theater in London, went to Berlin with a contract needing only Lind's signature. During the intermission of the second performance of *Das Feldlager* on the 10th of January *1845*, Meyerbeer and Count Westmoreland persuaded her to sign for twenty performances in six months at £40 per night.[3] She almost immediately regretted signing the contract, even though she could not possibly imagine how much agony that signature would cause her.

Six weeks after signing the contract with the Drury Lane Theatre, Lind wrote to Bunn that she could not come to England because she did not know the

English language and because she needed a rest. Bunn replied that she could sing in German and threatened to demand compensation if she did not honor her contract.

Lind's performance in Weber's *Euryanthe* caused one Berlin critic to quibble for the first time. He opined that her features exhibited too much "morbid bodily fatigue" and that perhaps "a trifle rouge" might remedy this slight defect. Her performance of the title role in *Norma* continued to so electrify the audience that she had to repeat it four times in quick succession and sang the role a total of seven times in January. Yet before each appearance in Berlin, despite the overwhelming audience response, Lind feared that she would fail. Therefore she did not invite Jacob Josephson to come to her benefit performance in March. Afterwards she informed him about the evening:

> My benefit was the *loveliest day of my life!*...But then who could have guessed that in such a short time I could have grown so much into the hearts of the people of Berlin. It's impossible to express to you the emotion that was engendered in the audience each time I was called back at the end of the performance. I can only say that I can never experience, have never experienced a more wonderful moment. And do you know, I left Berlin with a heavy heart. The way they have appreciated the finest I can give can never happen again. And how I have grown at each performance!!!

On this emotional high she said she looked forward with mixed feelings to returning to Sweden:

> I think it will be so strange to be back in Stockholm. Those Lindblads, Jakob! who live in my heart as vividly as ever. That passionate man, to whom I am united to the tiniest roots of my soul...May God wave peace with his blessed hand over the restless minds of me and others.

When Lind returned to Stockholm on the 13th of May, she was greeted by thousands of people and fireworks. So she was shocked and angry by the unenthusiastic applause and a few hisses at her second performance of *Norma* at the Royal Swedish Opera. She complained that she was not used to an empty royal box and didn't want to sing for "rabble"; she even threatened to not sing again. The director cancelled the performance of the next opera, but three days later she appeared as Agathe in *Der Freischuetz*. This time she enchanted the audience. However, before she could celebrate that evening, she had to deal with her mother, who took her daughter to task for not sending her enough money and accused her of bribing Louise to not talk about Jenny's supposed lovers. In desperation, Jenny called for Munthe, who had *Fru* Lind thrown out of the theater.

Some time later, Lind introduced Donizetti's *La Figlia* (Daughter of the Regiment) to the Stockholm audience. She was fond of military music, and with its vivacity the opera was a perfect fit for her. She sang the lead role a total of eighteen times to great applause in the nine-week season.

During this time Jenny regularly appeared on the stage with Guenther again, but the baritone no longer pursued her. She described their relationship to Andersen on June 17:

> I won't get married. The one I love doesn't want me despite the fact that he loves me more than anything in the world. He doesn't want to rob me of my career. I am too much of an artist and would never be happy if I were not free…it would be a constrained attachment [*Zwangsbindung*]. Perhaps he's right.

Yet at the same time she expressed a strong desire, one that she would express again and again: "Listen, you! I need support! A man! A real, *strong, healthy* man! You need never be ashamed for me, for I shall never give my hand to anyone but one who is worthy. Oh, I could tell you strange things, but am silent!"

---

For months Felix and Cécile had considered where they should settle down for their sake and the sake of the children, and they narrowed their options to two cities. They shilly-shallied a long time, not able to decide whether to live in Frankfurt or Leipzig. Finally they chose Leipzig, because they had been very happy there. In Leipzig Felix could be outwardly much more effective and active than in Frankfurt, and he would still have spare time to compose. But if that did not turn out to be the case, Felix told Bernus,[4] they would go to Frankfurt after six months and always stay there, because that was where Cécile felt most at home.

At the end of May Felix informed the chairman of the Gewandhaus orchestra board that he would like to return as their conductor, and the board immediately sent him an invitation.

The "congress" of the Mendelssohn siblings that Felix had proposed did indeed take place at the beginning of July. Only Paul and his family were missing, because he and Albertine expected their second child soon. Rebecka with her two sons and the thriving five-month-old Florentine Fanny Auguste Dirichlet and the Hensel family arrived in Freiburg from Italy, and the following day Felix arrived there from Soden.

They spent some time with the law professor Franz von Woringen and his wife, where they made much music. Afterwards the Mendelssohn siblings and their children spent two happy weeks in Soden with Felix's family.

Mendelssohn expected to go to Berlin soon, but at the end of July a minister of the crown informed him that the king would not return to Berlin before September and that he should come to Berlin in a few weeks to rehearse *Oedipus*. So a week later Felix and his family and Mme. Jeanrenaud left their beloved Rhine region early and set out for Leipzig, because Cécile wished to give birth to their fifth child there.

---

Not much later—at the end of August—Lind arrived in Frankfurt. There she met and spent much time with an English couple, society woman Harriet Grote and her husband, George. Lind explained to Mrs. Grote how she felt about the stage:

> The theater and entourage are distasteful to me, curious people bother me, I'm exposed to many indescribable ennuis; the cold drafts in the wings, after singing on the heated stage, are bad for my chest; singing and acting simultaneously is exhausting, rehearsals are dreadfully tiresome, and I dislike appearing before ever new audiences.

Furthermore, she said, she disliked not having a stable home and was tired of learning ever new languages.

At the age of twenty-four, Lind had already joined the brightest stars in the operatic firmament and received ever more invitations to sing. One came in August via Lind's German coach, Charlotte Birch-Pfeiffer, from the spokesman for Franz Pokorny, lessee and director of Theater an der Wien in Vienna. Lind asked Mme. Birch-Pfeiffer to inform the director of her decision:

Frankfurt, 4 September 1845

...Although I know of the prestige of Vienna, and *Fürst* Metternich encouraged me to go there, turn it down, Mother Birch. This life doesn't suit me at all. If you could only see me and my despair each time I have to go to the theater to sing! It's altogether too much for me...I cannot understand why everything goes so well for me. People all receive me so well. But that doesn't help. Herr Pokorny would not be very pleased, for example, if I were to sing and fail once. For the money he offers me he can get singers who are not as difficult to please as I am, and who at least wish for something, whereas I wish for nothing at all!

In Frankfurt, Lind appeared in four operas and was well received each time. But afterwards she suffered from migraines and depression; her success, she said, left her feeling empty. Bernus du Fay heard Lind sing in all four operas and promptly sent his assessment of the star to Felix:

So, I have heard Jenny Lind—I heard her each time! You're right, *lieber* Felix, I, too, have seen more beautiful singers, have heard better voices, but I have not been as captivated! She is one of those rare phenomena in the arts who are artists not only by way of talent and training, but who are that in their souls, whose whole being breathes art. I've become acquainted with her, have even conversed with her about art and poetry...She reveres you and raves about the thought of singing in your concert. I think she will accomplish more than usual.

Mendelssohn did not mention Lind in his reply. Instead, he mused about where he might like to live, about his profession, and about what was occupying his mind more and more, the political and moral climate in Germany:

I have the same feelings I had before, that I shall remain in this place only as long as I feel pleasure and interest in those public occupations that seem the most agreeable to me. But as soon as I have won the right to live solely for my composing, conducting and playing in public only occasionally, then I shall certainly return to the Rhine...I have always followed all my public musical pursuits, such as conducting, etc., purely out of a sense of duty, never from inclination, so I hope to turn up as a house builder before long...Let's hope that by then either a solid, genuine nucleus will have been formed among the German Catholics in favor of enlightenment…or that the whole business will have vanished without leaving a trace and be completely forgotten. Should neither one nor the other occur, I fear we will run the risk of losing our finest national characteristics, thoroughness, constancy, honesty, perseverance and the like, without getting any substitutes for them. A collection of French phrases and facility would be too dearly bought at such a price. Let's hope for something better!

---

Alfred Bunn continued to send veiled threats to Lind, but she left his letters unanswered.

---

In 1845 Lindblad published the songs he had written to his own texts about the struggles he went through when he was so smitten with Jenny. The critics were not favorably impressed; they regarded the harmony as "too modern."[5]

---

Twice in August, and once in early September, Felix left his family. The first time he went to Berlin for a week of rehearsals, the next time to Dresden on command of the Saxon king. During each absence Cécile anxiously waited for her husband's return.

During Felix's third absence, she wrote that she hoped that he would return before the middle of September as she expected to "still be on her feet" until then. Cécile had calculated correctly this time; on the 19th of September, a few days after Felix returned to Leipzig, dainty little Elisabeth Fanny Henriette (Lilli) Mendelssohn Bartholdy arrived at the Mendelssohn apartment at Koenigstrasse 5.

The oldest of the five children in the Mendelssohn household was now seven-and-a-half years old. Lilli was christened on the 21st of October.

Two days after the christening, at a dinner after a subscription concert, Felix sat next to Charlotte Dolby, the beautiful English contralto who had been hired for the new subscription concert season. There he remarked to her, "The female roles in *Elijah* are a real woman's part, half angel, half devil."

The next day Mendelssohn left for Berlin. The performance of *Oedipus* was scheduled to take place four days later, and he expressed the hope that he would subsequently have a respite and be able to compose. He promised Cécile that he would return to Leipzig in two weeks and informed Schumann that he would definitely be back by the 10th of November.

A few days after arriving in Berlin he wrote to Cécile that he would soon return. And on the 30th of October he tried to pacify Mme. Jeanrenaud, who longed to see him before she had to leave:

> *Liebe Mama,*
> I am *very much* longing to come back, regardless of how dear my siblings are, and no matter how much I enjoy being with them. I would like to look into Cécile's eyes again, and would like to see the children again, and you, *meine liebe Mama*, who looks after us all so well and gladdens us with your love and your presence.

He said he hoped his absence would not be prolonged later than previously indicated and thought perhaps he could come even earlier. He promised to let her and Cécile know when it was decided.

Lind sang in three different operas in Copenhagen in October, with tickets at quadrupled prices. She also sang at a benefit concert for abused and neglected children at double prices. Hans Christian Andersen heard her each time; he noted that the only time he heard her express joy about her talent was after the benefit, when she said, "Isn't it beautiful that I can sing as I do?"

Even though Mme. Jeanrenaud stayed in Leipzig with her daughter Julie, now wife of Julius Schunck, she succeeded in enforcing her rule about not writing letters until Cécile's entire six-week childbed ended. But she herself wrote regularly to Felix.

Finally she relinquished this right:

31 October 1845
Today I'm writing the last bulletin, my dear Felix, and from now on will give the pen to the rightful owner, who is very happy, I believe, to be allowed to write to you herself. She looks very well and is fine today, although she told me that she had a little earache yesterday... I hope that when you return, I'll have your support in a matter that causes

me a great deal of concern, but Cécile doesn't want to listen…I hope she'll get over the bad mood she was in when I left her. Cécile kisses her dear husband, whose hope of his imminent return she doesn't really understand.

---

On the same day Jenny Lind arrived in Berlin. A day or two later Mendelssohn met her for the second time, again at the Wichmann home.

---

1. Joseph Joachim said of Mendelssohn's violin concerto that Beethoven's was the greatest, Brahms' the closest to Beethoven's in seriousness, Bruch's the most enchanting, but Mendelssohn's the "dearest, the heart's jewel."
2. Leopoldine Tuczec had sung in the premiere of the opera, but not to the satisfaction of the audience and critics.
3. The payment of £40 was somewhat less than she received in Berlin. Ten years earlier Bunn had paid Malibran £125 per evening.
4. Bernus, or Bernus-Du Fay, Franz, 1808–1884, was the husband of Cécile's childhood friend Marie Du Fay.
5. Thereafter Lindblad withdrew the songs and returned to writing in his older style.

# t w e l v e

NOW THAT HER MOTHER ALLOWED IT, CÉCILE WROTE TO FELIX ALMOST EVERY DAY.

Leipzig, 1 November [1845]

My very dear Felix, I found it easy to carry out everything you asked me to do, but the one arrangement, not to write to you, was too barbaric. I often wondered if you would be very angry if I wouldn't obey that command, because I so often wanted to say a few words to you, to thank you for your dear letters, to tell you how very happy I am, especially at this time because of your love, and for the evident blessing of God, for which I cannot be thankful enough.

Today the six fateful weeks are over and all is well, thank God, except for a little earache and toothache. But despite that I will freely endure my imprisonment until your return…

Little Lilli is really adorable, but my joy about her black hair and dark eyes was short-lived. Now she could not be more blonde and could not have more sparkling blue eyes…Carl practices the piano for ten minutes morning and evening. Paul is very well behaved…Felixchen is very lively and cute. You are to bring him bonbons. Farewell, *mein geliebter* Felix, until our happy *Wiedersehen.*

Sunday the 2nd [November 1845]
*Liebster* Felix,
You must forgive me that I'm writing again in order to recover lost ground, if only to tell you that I am fine today, praise God, that the earache is completely gone, and that I have nothing to complain about; on the contrary, I must give thanks daily and hourly for our well-being. You have no idea how much I'm looking forward to seeing you again. I can see that our life will be very beautiful, and I am in extremely good spirits. I'm enjoying the concerts and music, and am only sorry that I was unable to hear the lovely music for *Oedipus.*

Monday
....Last evening Herr Baseto gave me the pleasure of bringing me news about you...and I was very happy to hear that everything had gone well and I can hope to see you again, but I won't allow myself to look forward too soon to your coming.

The next day Felix asked his sisters if they wished to hear Vincenzo Bellini's opera *Norma* on the following Sunday, or perhaps all the operas in which Lind starred. Although he had little regard for Bellini's operas—they were Cécile's favorites—he was eager to finally hear and see Lind perform.

---

Shortly after meeting Mendelssohn, Jenny Lind wrote to Mathilde Arnemann, wife of the Swedish consul in Germany:

[Berlin] 5 November 1845
*Liebe* Mathilde,
...You know, I spoke to Felix Mendelssohn recently, and casually asked him if he enjoyed writing letters—you should have seen him then, we both laughed, he told me that there was nothing more terrible for him in the whole world, and if he wrote, it would only be "I am well and love you will all my heart." That's how I feel too.

---

On the same day, Mendelssohn informed Schleinitz that he had to remain in Berlin for fourteen more days but hoped to be in Leipzig to teach at the conservatory at the beginning of December.

Probably on the same day, in a letter dated Wednesday, Cécile wrote that she almost believed that in his last letter he had given her a gentle hint not to rejoice too soon, but that she was dealing with the situation by replying to the people who asked about his return "Unfortunately I'm used to it" or "My children help me pass the time" or "I know less than a newborn child."

Mme. Jeanrenaud expressed her regret that she would have to leave before Felix returned and voiced the matter of great concern that she mentioned in her previous letter:

6 November 1845

…I have something else on my mind that is very difficult for me to write about, but it has to come out, otherwise I will have no peace of mind. It concerns a matter which we have discussed before, your and Cécile's too great tenderness [*zu große Zärtlichkeit*] towards one another. I'm warning you about this with all the love of a mother, for whom your happiness is the dearest in all the world. Nature finally really exhausts itself also in the strongest! When you saw the picture of Herr [illegible], I deliberately did not tell you that he lost his wife with her sixth pregnancy. She was beautiful and well, surrounded by her children, and her death was the cause of her husband's death; he could not bear her loss.

In a letter to her husband on the same day, Cécile did not disguise her melancholy feelings:

The news of your prolonged stay has saddened me, having half-and-half believed that you would come this week already. But I can see all the reasons and am being reasonable. When you definitely know, write to Mother, who isn't always reasonable and wishes you back with all her might.

I'm not at all surprised that the king shook your hand…I'm surprised that I don't hear anything about the concert in Potsdam…

Herr David asked me to plead that you come here for the concert on the 24th. I gave him hope. Mother is leaving on Monday or Tuesday and is still hoping to see you.

The next day Cécile began a letter to Felix by asking him to forgive her for costing him unnecessary postage because she forgot to write *per Fahrpost* with the address. Then, after complaining about the uninteresting countryside around Leipzig, she wrote about the children:

> Marie is…very pleased with her lessons, goes and comes alone, and does her work much better. Paul writes a great deal too, but only for fun, not to learn…Felix is very good, goes out into the cold, and comes back with blue hands…Lilly is thriving. I hope you have a kiss for her; you write nothing about your siblings and nephews and nieces.

On the same day Felix fashioned a long conciliatory reply to Mme. Jeanrenaud's last letter:

> *Liebe Mama,*
> …Unfortunately I won't be able to meet you in Leipzig when I can finally return…I cannot get away in the next few weeks, and I fear I'll come too late to see you again after all. I don't need to tell you how sorry I am…
> We have experienced many serious and, thank God, many happy days together. I again owe you new thanks with all my heart, not only for the happiness you have given me in my beloved Cécile, as I thank you for that daily and hourly in my thoughts, but for the care and interest and love you have always shown her and the children and me…
> We are hoping for a happy and possibly a long *Wiedersehen* soon, and a *wieder*-living-together!…I will flee to that foreign, very dear land…and all your family, and we living happy, undisturbed lives with you, and the children happy, and Cécile happier and more tranquil than anywhere else, and I myself so really blissfully happy because of all the good I have received from you and the dear Lord all my life…
> *Auf Wiedersehen! liebe Mama*, I kiss you in my thoughts and thank you for all the goodness and kindness you have shown us during this time, and hope we'll meet again in good health, and happy and unchanged.

He did not mention the matter that was so important to Mme. Jeanrenaud. The next day, Cécile sent a short letter to her husband:

Your letter made me very happy except for the definite news that you're not coming. I only wish that I could surprise you and suddenly sit in the cab when you drive to the theater...Herr Schleinitz...seems very unhappy that you're staying away so long.

On the following day she wrote about their four-year-old son:

9 November 1845

...I must tell you a few nice stories about Paul. He had noticed that when I say "Goodnight" to the two oldest children, I remind them not to forget to say their prayers. Recently he said, "I also say prayers at night. I say, 'Be faithful unto death and I will give you the crown of life'[1] or 'God bless you,' and 'Amen.'" Isn't that sweet?...He's very good, although a little unmanageable.

---

Before she left for Frankfurt, Mme. Jeanrenaud sent a series of instructions to Felix. She conceded that Cécile needed diversions but opined that it was not good for her to stay out late and to "engage in many activities, etc., etc." Then she became maudlin:

Leipzig, 9 November [1845]

...And now, my dear Felix, my most grateful thanks for your dear, dear letter; it was a real source of encouragement, as I have not told you, and never will be able to, how sorry I am that I won't see you again.

You say that I am still so youthful in my feelings...yes, it even degenerates into childishness, and I torment myself and others with it, and am just as jealous and envious as children.

When I received definite word, and Cécile told me that you weren't coming, it occurred to me that I hadn't seen you since the christening, that you should not have promised to play for me, and that you had not given me the picture of Mme. Pleyel, etc. And Herr Mangnus [*sic*] became the object of my keen jealousy. Cécile said, half in jest, "But *maman*, you know that he loves you more than Herr Mangnus [*sic*], and why have you stayed here?" And I replied, half weeping, "That's why I am *fanati* [the rest is illegible]..."

The moral of the story, *mein lieber* Felix, is that one should be very careful about the promises one makes to one's mother-in-law. Oh no, you will make it up to me, and so I thank you for all future hopes of a reunion, even though my friends here deny it, and reason tells me that at my age my life will be highly uncertain and not long.[2]

In the evening of the same day, Mendelssohn heard Jenny Lind perform in Bellini's opera *Norma*.

---

In November the Berlin music journal *Allgemeine Musikalische Zeitung* published a review of Lind's performances of the previous September in Frankfurt-am-Main. The critic referred to her as a "fixed star among the planets" but continued by saying that he did not tremble like some reviewers when they took up their pens to write about her. Nor would he throw away his pen to avoid being accused of terrorism if he used "calm judgment." He praised her voice, her bravura and clear pronunciation, her technique and stage presence. And he noted that she felt the roles that suited her perfectly. But he declared that she was not able to sing the part of *Norma* as portrayed by the poet nor sing the part of a tragic heroine.[3]

---

On the 10th of November Cécile asked Felix to forgive her for having written too hastily and not having managed their financial affairs well. She feared, she said, that she would not have enough money until his return.

In another letter, Cécile asked Felix's forgiveness for not having asked if she should pay for a package at the post office and for having been so "stupid" as to pay two thaler for it. In the same letter she said she did not want to blame him for not returning to Leipzig for at least a brief visit. But she cannot have forgotten that when they lived in Berlin after the railroad from Berlin to Leipzig was completed, Felix had found time to travel to Leipzig on several occasions, and that his brother sometimes came to Leipzig to see Felix for just twenty-four hours. Surely she had also not forgotten that in the previous year she had congratulated him for his "unheard of talent of getting everyone to act according to [his] wishes."

On Fanny's birthday, November 14, Cécile sent best wishes to her sister-in-law:

I'm thinking of you a great deal today, *liebe* Fanny…Felix has written me so much about the happy times you spend together, and that he found both you and Beckchen so well; I'm glad to hear it, and I only hope it will continue…

Everything is fine here, praise God, and the little one gives me a great deal of pleasure…Without being vain, she is a very dainty, lovely child and behaves very well. And Felixchen, too, gives me just as much pleasure now as he gave me concern a year ago…

Send me back my Felix soon, *liebe* Fanny. I miss him very much.

Two days later Cécile sent Felix a description of a children's party in their home. All the children had been in a frantic state of excitement, and one of the maids had remarked to Cécile, "They're all like their papa." Cécile told Felix that she thought Christel's comment was "strange."

———————————

In Leipzig, Ferdinand David fretted about Felix's continued absence:

Leipzig, 17 December 1845
*Lieber* Mendelssohn!
I'm sorry to hear that you're staying in Berlin still longer and that we have to have the concert for the pension funds without you. If you were ten years younger I would very clearly inform you that there is a railroad between Berlin and Leipzig, that one piece played by you would net several hundred Thaler, that the program has not yet been completed, and other allusions of that kind. But we don't so easily do that at our age any more.

Felix equivocated several times in his reply:

18 November 1845
When I received your lines I again cursed the awful conditions here with all my heart, for I don't need to tell you that it isn't comfort that is keeping me from coming on the 24th to perform (and were it only for a day), to see wife and children. But the uncertainty which hangs over everything here hampers everything and everybody.

He mentioned that there was talk about a major court concert to be held on the 24th, and *Atrhalie* rehearsals after that. And he would be blamed if "things fell apart." Thereupon he asked if the performance could not be postponed, but not to the beginning of December, because he needed to recover from the strain in Berlin first.

More than three weeks after she had last seen Felix, Cécile made no attempt to disguise her anxiety:

Postmark, 17 November [1845]
*Lieber* Felix,
Although the news that I hear about you from the others upset me somewhat, I will trust your letter and hope to see you *here soon*. I don't know why I find this separation particularly difficult. I cannot come to terms with it.

When Felix assured her once more that he would come soon, Cécile responded that she did not really want to write to him again because it would cost him too much postage, but she wanted to thank him for his "dear" letter. She then explained how she had received the news of his protracted stay.

Mendelssohn heard Lind sing the role of Donna Anna in *Don Giovanni* on the 19th of November. On the same day Cécile informed him that she did not read a bulky letter from Dresden. It was unusual for Cécile to say that she didn't read a letter addressed to her husband. Before this time she had often read Felix's letters and, after informing him thereof, added one cliché or another, such as "Oh well, that is how one gets by."

None of the Mendelssohn siblings *ever* read each other's letters. In fact, in 1835 Fanny told Felix that she had unwittingly broken open the first of a number of packets of letters addressed to him because she had not looked at the label. "But I give you my word of honor that I did not look at the outside of a single letter, but pushed away the packet as if it were on fire." At another time Felix expressed his horror that by mistake he opened a letter addressed to Paul and assured his brother that he had not read one line.

---

In Frankfurt Mme. Jeanrenaud continued to fret about Felix's extended stay in Berlin:

Frankfurt, 20 November 1845

...Felix, yesterday was your queen's birthday. What more must still occur? When will my Cécile see her dear husband again? How are you, my good son?

It often seems so strange to me even now, that I cannot always, that is, as long as I know my children, speak to you of my great affection and love. I think you must have known it for a long time already, because I know it so well and feel it so vividly, that you, like Cécile and my other children, become more dear to me every year, so that sometimes it seems that the One whom one should love above all else demands too much. But He, Love itself, will have forbearance with our weaknesses...*Ihre madre* E J

In an undated letter, some time in November, Cécile wrote to her husband,

You'll laugh when I tell you that this is the fourth letter I've written to you since yesterday. I even laugh at myself, but I couldn't write to you yesterday because I was very sad that you weren't here...Today I'm reasonable again, and won't make accusations against you. What's the use of grieving...We're all fine. The children are well and happy, praise God. You'll find Lilli very changed—*ach nein*, you wouldn't understand that. I enjoy her very much and only pray to God every day that He'll keep her well. Herr David begs you to come back for the concert on the 2nd. I've given him hope...
When will the performance take place in Charlottenburg? I don't understand why one hears so little about all these things.

She also mentioned that she found his letters to be less informative than she desired.

After Felix had been in Berlin for four weeks, he still did not inform Cécile exactly when he would return to Leipzig. In her reply to one of his letters, Cécile wrote that she couldn't figure out from his letter when he was leaving Berlin but said he would "find [her] with curls and [expected him] to admire [her]." In the same letter she mentioned the household finances again:

Don't forget the shirts, but I can't pay for them, as I am already half bankrupt, but I fear you'll take the badly managed account books out of my hands again, and I'll probably never learn how to manage money. Forgive this fault and all the others.

By now "Forgive me" was becoming another refrain in Cécile's letters.

On the same evening, following several rehearsals, the big court concert at which Mendelssohn accompanied Jenny Lind at the piano took place in the beautiful Charlottenburg Palace.

---

In Leipzig the Gewandhaus board deliberated again, and David relayed the decisions to Felix:

Leipzig, 23 November

…The council of the gods and Grenser and David have decided for postponement…We hope that through your too long stay in Berlin *Athalia* won't become Fatalia for us, and all of us long very much, including all the students of the conservatory and many billiard players, for your sweet-tempered return…Your wife was here yesterday, is very well and cheerful.

---

From Berlin Jenny Lind sent a report about her blossoming career to her former vocal coach, Mme. Erichsen:

24 November 1845

It was with the wildest pleasure that I had the honor of receiving your kind letter, and I cannot thank you enough for it…I cannot forget that it was you who first guided my sensitive young mind towards high aims, or that it was you who saw beneath the surface and imagined you saw something behind those insignificant gray eyes of mine. How changed everything is now! All the musical talent of Europe is, so to speak, at my feet. What great things the Almighty has granted me in His grace!…

In only seven months I have succeeded in making my reputation here, while after seven years at home not a soul knew of me. At this moment I am offered all the most important engagements in the world!

The Berlin public is terribly critical, but I like this, for if I take pains, I am at least properly appreciated. They want to analyze my every gesture,

every shade of expression. Indeed, one has to be careful…I have to bear
no trifling comparisons, as at the moment I step forward I am measured
with the Sontag measure or that of the greatest artists that Germany has
produced. Perhaps you think I have grown vain? God forbid.

She still had not decided whether or not to go to Vienna but thought she
would return to Sweden and settle down quietly the following autumn. She
asked Mme. Erichsen to reflect on how difficult it was to be alone; she said that
the stage had no attraction for her and that she yearned for rest from all the
compliments and adulation.

---

In her next letter to Felix, Cécile offered her husband what she herself termed
a "tirade":

My dear, good and deeply loved husband, I have only good things to
report to you today, praise God, and we are all well and delighted with
the glorious weather. But we went for a walk and have red cheeks from
the fresh fall wind…I only wish you could see the little one when she
comes in. Even you would be pleased. You *Rabenpapa* [unnatural or bad
father] wouldn't even recognize her if you met her in the street.
*Ja*, if I had only known how I would fare with you, you *Musikantenblut*,
I would not have remained a church mouse, if I had reflected on the
matter more. Now it's certainly too late, now that you have left me with
a house full of children and have gone into the wide world and play the
part of a great man and court lovely singers.
I just received your dear letter which interrupted my tirade, and it acted
like a fist in the eye to my stupid joke. *Ja, mein lieber Mann*, we are truly
bound one to another; I feel here what you feel there, and that can never
change.

---

On the 27th of November Mendelssohn inscribed and presented one of his
favorite books, *Erbauliches und Beschauliches aus dem Morgenland* (*Uplifting and
Contemplative Writings from the Orient*) by Johann Rueckert, to Jenny Lind.

---

At the end of November Cécile still did not know when Felix would return. Did she know that Jenny Lind lived with the Wichmann family and that Felix often ate two meals a day at the Wichmann home, and that he was there again almost every evening until late at night, albeit together with Wilhelm Taubert, the court music director? And did he inform her that Lind and he would travel for seven-and-a-half hours on the same train to Leipzig?

---

1. "Be faithful unto death, and I will give you the crown of life" is a biblical text (Revelation 2:10) in Mendelssohn's *Paulus.*
2. Mme. Jeanrenaud was forty-nine years old at this time.
3. Lind did not interpret the role of *Norma*, a Druid priestess, as an inhuman demon of vengeance but as a pure and tender soul.

*Portrait of Felix Mendelssohn by Eduard Magnus, 1846.*

*Portrait of Jenny Lind, age 24.*

*End of song, "Ich Hör ein Vöglein", which Mendelssohn gave to Lind
in Leipzig in 1845.*

*Beginning of Mendelssohn's letter to Jenny Lind.*

# thirteen

LIND WAS EAGER TO SING IN LEIPZIG IN A GEWANDHAUS CONCERT, BUT THE opera director in Berlin was reluctant to let her leave Berlin. Nevertheless, eight days before the December 4th subscription concert, Mendelssohn presented his arguments to Schleinitz as to why Lind should sing in the Gewandhaus:

> You know that because of Dolby,[1] I wished that she wouldn't come until January, but I had convinced myself that despite the best will, she wouldn't be released here if there was no one who immediately removed the obstacles...Nothing would have come of it all winter if I had let this opportunity pass; the negotiations with Dolby will, of course, be difficult, but hopefully the board won't hold it against me that I didn't let the opportunity (which was offered) pass.

Mendelssohn went on to say that Lind "conducted herself very well in all the negotiations," and he expressed the hope that she would also sing in the benefit concert on the next evening. On the following day he informed Schleinitz that he hoped to "bring Lind with [him]" on Wednesday. On the 28th he wrote to

Schleinitz that he had received confirmation from Lind, and for Friday also, so it would be good if the concert for the musicians could take place on Friday. He asked Schleinitz not to announce the second concert yet.

In deference to the two female singers who had been hired for the season, Ferdinand David opposed Lind's participation in the subscription concert. But Mendelssohn asked if the two singers could not also sing together with Lind. He appealed to both David and Schleinitz, "Please reconsider, and we'll finalize the plans when I return to Leipzig." Would Mendelssohn get his way again?

When Cécile received word of Felix's imminent return, she penned a short note:

> *Lieber* Felix,
> You'll receive these lines on the day of the performance of *Athalie* if it hasn't been changed. You will have little time to read; they shall only say that we are all well and think of you with love.
> The children are very happy, and I much happier about your return of which you wrote. I will only believe it when I actually see you, and fear that the good people are making all the fuss about *you and Lind* in vain.
> I feel as if I haven't seen you for many years; I don't know why I feel like that this time. Farewell, I'll write on Tuesday unless you tell me not to. Ever your Cécile

Five days before the Gewandhaus concert, Mendelssohn pleaded with David once more to create a place for Lind on its program.

---

Prior to leaving for Leipzig, Lind described her relationship with Guenther to Josephson and gave reasons why she would never marry:

> I am no longer the person I was! So calm, wanting for so little. I have reached a turning point in my life. I will never change my position in life—will remain Mademoiselle Lind as long as I live. And this is what has caused the total change in me. I could give you the reason for this— but it isn't worthwhile. The one who is the reason for all this is probably wandering in the dark somewhere. He left Sweden months ago…I know

nothing about him since that time. May he be happy. He himself has chosen his lot…

But Jakob! Mendelssohn is here! I see him almost every day at Wichmanns. And he is an unusual man. My dear! We are going to Leipzig together tomorrow. Finally I shall sing under his direction at a Gewandhaus concert!…

The only kind of good life is home life. Apart from that, all is emptiness. But what is all that to me? I am suffering as much as ever from homesickness, and my only wish is to get repose away from the stage. And in a year I'll go home and remain at home, my friend. Oh, how I shall enjoy life! Ah! Peace is best of all. I have never had that as I have it now.

---

Meanwhile Cécile wrote to her husband that they were really on edge, not knowing if they would really see him in two days. On the same day Felix again expressed his wishes to Schleinitz regarding the subscription concert:

Berlin, 1 December 1845
*Lieber Freund,*
I've been able to speak to Lind only now, who immediately, and without any conditions, agreed to the duet from *Romeo* with Dolby, and only asked me which piece she should then omit, or if it would not be too much for the concert if she sang four times! I told her it would not be too much. It would not be possible to arrange it otherwise, as in my opinion she must begin with an Italian aria, and because I could not omit either the aria by Mozart nor the lieder.

---

Cécile was generally reticent in expressing her feelings to her mother. Now, however, she could not contain her anxiety, which was undoubtedly exacerbated by repeated questions from her mother.

*Ma chère maman,*
I would have answered your letter sooner if I had not wanted at the same time to write something definite about Felix's return. It's beginning to annoy me very much that his sojourn in Berlin is always prolonged. Not

that I have nothing to do, nor that I feel alone, which never happens to me, but this continual postponement from one week to the next, from one day to the next, has made me disagreeable and irritable... I'm expecting Felix *tomorrow evening*, barring all mishaps, as he is to conduct the concert. Mlle. Lind is going to sing, and tickets are in great demand.

*Toute à toi* [Entirely yours], Cécile

On the 3rd of December, almost seven weeks after Mendelssohn had left Leipzig, he and Jenny Lind boarded a train at seven o'clock in the morning and arrived in Leipzig in mid-afternoon.

Because Lind preferred to stay in a private home rather than in a hotel, she accepted the invitation of noted publisher and member of the Gewandhaus board Dr. Heinrich Brockhaus to stay with his family.

Three hundred extra tickets had been printed. At the subscription concert on December 4, Jenny Lind came onto the stage in a white satin gown, with white camellias in her hair, escorted by Mendelssohn. Heinrich Brockhaus's young son recorded his impressions of that concert:

The expectations of the Leipzigers—who pride themselves somewhat on their musical taste, and are sometimes a little hypercritical—were raised very high indeed; but the singer won them at once with the first air from *Norma*, and the enthusiasm rose higher and higher to quite an extraordinary pitch, first by means of a duet from *Romeo and Juliet* with Miss Dolby, and then a recitative and aria from *Don Juan*, and finally through some songs by Mendelssohn and some Swedish national airs. And with good reason. She is the most extraordinary singer, a most musical nature through and through; in full command of the most beautiful means, and besides that, so full of soul that a song sung by her goes straight to the heart.

Soul and expression so intimately associated with so beautiful a voice and so perfect a method will never be met with again; the appearance of *Fräulein* Lind, therefore, is truly unparalleled. And with all that, what noble and beautiful simplicity pervade her whole being, free of all coquetry, but nevertheless enjoying the effect she produces. One can only marvel and love her. And this appreciation of her is universal with young and old, and with men and women.

The audience demanded two encores after she sang Mendelssohn's little song "*Gruß*" ["Greeting"], a circumstance quite unprecedented at the subscription concerts. An English conservatory student, William S. Rockstro, opined later that never before or since that night had they heard it as superbly sung or as "deliciously" accompanied. Another student, Carl Reinecke, future conductor of the Gewandhaus Orchestra, was also particularly struck by the performance of that song:

> It is equally difficult to describe the transfigured face and luminous eyes of Mendelssohn, who sat at the piano, listening to the sounds of his own songs, as to describe the sounds that flowed from the throat of this God-favored artist.
> I think it's as impossible to sing with greater virtuosity and with more genuine feeling than Jenny Lind did…When she sang the [last] line, "*Sag ich laß sie grüßen*," it seemed as if the walls of the hall expanded.

The entire short song, on a text by Heinrich Heine, can be freely translated thus:

> Lovely sounds quietly encompass my being.
> Sound, little spring song, sound into the distance.
> Go to the house where the violets are blooming;
> When you see a rose, tell her that I send greetings.

On the morning of the concert, one young conservatory student had told another voice student, Elise Vogel, that she had seen *Fräulein* Lind on the street, that she was absolutely ugly, and that she would not attend her concert. But after the concert *Fräulein* Vogel wrote in her diary, "I didn't look at the features of the foreign singer at all—I received only the total impression of embodied poetry. I saw a genuinely feminine creature with blue eyes, deep as a well…And from the finely shaped mouth came the question '*Wie nahte mir der Schlummer bevor ich ihn geseh'n.*'"[2]

One critic described Mendelssohn's performance of his (G-minor) piano concerto at the benefit concert as unsurpassable. And he reported that the audience had been enthusiastic and uplifted by Jenny Lind in the first concert, but that in the second their enthusiasm had known no bounds, that this enthusiasm was "incessantly" expressed in the middle of a performance, even though Lind's performance had begun less well than on the previous evening. He reveled in the "unusual silvery tones" she produced in *Dove sono* from *The Marriage of Figaro* and opined that Lind surpassed even Sontag[3] in the finale of *Euryanthe,* which had not been thought possible. After much more praise of the many aspects of her singing, he declared that her performance of the aria from *Der Freischütz, Wie nahte mir der Schlummer,* was the high point of the evening; here there was "true drama, the genuine fervor of prayer, and a true depiction of fear."

Another critic reported that her performance of a Swedish song to her own piano accompaniment produced near frenzy in the audience. And like critics everywhere, he mentioned her diminuendo in that song, describing it as gradually becoming no more than "the most silent breath," and with a beautiful ornament during the pianissimo.

Yet another critic referred to the "magic of her tones" and her voice as one in many thousands. He exulted in her "noble, tasteful performance, and deep and intelligent understanding"; he praised her simplicity and modesty, charm and grace, and concluded that she lacked nothing as a singer.

Heinrich Brockhaus recorded a detail of the benefit concert that the critics did not mention: "Mendelssohn's delight in the artist and in her noble, feminine nature could only make him rejoice again. He was in a genuine state of enthusiasm. He took the viola away from Queisser in order to play in the finale of *Euryanthe.*"

Lind had promised to return to the Brockhaus home after the benefit concert but begged that no one other than the Mendelssohns be present. That, however, is not what occurred. She had just admired a painting in the Brockhaus home when all of a sudden Weber's *Jubilee Overture* sounded in the courtyard, where approximately 300 singers and instrumentalists had gathered. Lind repeatedly asked her host, "What shall I do?" and "How shall I thank the people?"

As she continued to look out of the window, the serenade ended, and most of the concert directors, with concertmaster David and Dr. Haertel in the lead, entered the room. David briefly and in a heartfelt way thanked Lind in the name of all the musicians as he presented a beautiful wreath of camellias and laurel on a silver salver to the speechless singer.

Lind was still tongue-tied when everyone went back into the courtyard. So Mendelssohn took her arm and said, "Gentlemen, you think this is Kapellmeister Mendelssohn who is speaking to you, but you are mistaken. It's *Fräulein* Jenny Lind who is speaking to you, and she thanks you heartily for the exquisite surprise you have given her. And now I turn myself back into the Leipzig music director again and ask you to wish long life to *Fräulein* Jenny Lind. Long life to her! And again, long life to her! And for the third time, long life!"

After everyone left, Lind embraced *Frau* Brockhaus and jumped up and down like a child.

When she and Mendelssohn parted at the railroad station the next day, he presented her with a song he had composed in 1841, "Ich hör ein Vöglein" ("I Hear a Little Bird"[4]):

> I hear a little bird so sweetly coaxing, wooing his beloved bride;
> He woos so loudly amid the perfume of the flowers.
> And from the blue lilacs the lovely bride continuously sings
> a million love songs to him.
> I hear quiet plaints, so anxious, so soulful,
> What may the voice, dying away in the wind, be asking?

---

In a note to his brother a few days after the concerts, Felix expressed no jaundiced views about Berlin or the burden of public performances; he merely thanked him for "six lovely weeks in Berlin."

Two days later he wrote his first letter to Lind:

Leipzig, 10 December 1845
*Mein liebes Fräulein,*
It was a week ago yesterday that you told me that I might write some time—perhaps in a year. Don't be angry, therefore, that it is already happening today; and don't believe that in addition to all your obtrusions I will annoy you too much with letters—but I have numerous reasons why I would really like to write to you today. Firstly, because I would so much like to know if you are well, if you arrived safely in Berlin, if the fatigue and exertions of those happy days were not harmful to you later. In posing this question, I am *not* concerned about the king of Prussia; I want to know only for my own sake, or rather much more for your sake! I knew that you had to sing in Berlin again on Sunday evening, also on Tuesday: and I thought to myself, if only this performing in rapid succession would not affect you adversely! Now I no longer know on which evenings you had to sing, and on which you are free; that also is not what I wanted to ask, but I really wanted to ask if you had arrived safely and remained well.

And then, it seems to me as if I had not even thanked you. You have simply done a good thing. I don't mean that you have provided for the widows of the musicians, also not that you have refreshed and uplifted us by means of your singing; rather, I mean everything from Wednesday morning at 7 o'clock to Saturday at 1 o'clock. I want to thank you very much for that. Moreover, I rejoice that what is right and good will never die, but will remain even though it doesn't appear so!

I just came out of the concert hall again; it looked just as it did a week ago, the gas flames made exactly the same noise as if it was raining outside; not one single beautiful tone of yours there, however, and you were also not at the rehearsal. It seemed like the past in that I again so vividly felt your presence in that I felt my joy and gratitude just as clearly, just as fresh, perhaps even more purely and undisturbed. Whilst I could tell myself that it would never be different, I also knew that the good remains and never leaves us. Thank you! These words say no more than that.

But there is another reason why I had to write today. I really wanted to remind you of *me*. I often continue (our) conversations in my thoughts, and sing the little song in F-major, or also the *rosen och de bladen* [roses and leaves], and leave out a note here and there to catch a breath, and when I do that, I would like it if you would remember me, for example, perhaps in the billiard room, or when the children above you play duets, or when you see Professor Tieck, or when a composer again comes with songs—or at other times. You probably do it *without* my asking you, for the fluctuating Berlin world will not wash away the memories of genuine affectionate joy, and no world and no waves will do that, as I know you; but I ask you nevertheless, so that you know that I am asking you...

Will you not forget the Swedish bread? I've told the children about it, and they won't forget, and are eagerly asking about it. What actually is in the letter? Not much, and yet many requests. But above all, this one request: remain unchanged and think now and then of your friend Felix Mendelssohn B.

On the following day Felix appealed to Eduard Devrient once more to help him with a libretto:

I again have a great desire to write an opera. Jenny Lind has persuaded me to write one for her...Please help me with this matter. You'll probably call me Cato,[5] and this kind of ending of the letter *denique censeo* [finally I understand]. It isn't much more than that, and after all, Carthage was destroyed, etc.

Six days after receiving Mendelssohn's letter, Lind mailed a reply. One can only speculate, if, à la Mendelssohn, she addressed the composer as "Mein lieber Herr."[6] Louise Johansson expressed her disapproval: "Jenny mailed a letter. Don't ask me if she considered what the consequences will be. Poor wife, poor children! *Jo, jo,* that's what happens when a person digs a ditch and falls into it herself."

Lind sent a second letter to Leipzig three days later—this one to Haertels: "I can honestly assure you that those two days in Leipzig belong to the loveliest memories of my life, and as soon as circumstances allow, I will be happy to greet the good people of Leipzig again."

In a letter to her friend Mathilde Arnemann on the same day, Lind revealed more about her deepest feelings than she had to Josephson several weeks earlier:

Berlin, 20 December 1845

Dearest soul!

Yes, I believe that you believe in platonic love, because you are such a pure being. Yes! of course he is married. I believe that you knew that already. And he is supposed to be very happily married, and you must not believe that I am so crazy as not to know that I am not worthy to be able to make such a man happy.

Yes, Mathilde! I admit it—deep in my heart I feel how much this man means to me, and it's true when I say to you: "No other man!" And even when I think about Guenther all day, it doesn't help. I feel drawn to no man the way I feel drawn to him. For God's sake, don't be angry at me. I can't help it. He has the purest, loveliest way of thinking of anyone I have ever met, and I can love him very much—for firstly, you have allowed me to; secondly, I am completely calm and happy. And I desire absolutely nothing, as I know that he is kindly disposed to me and likes me. And finally, I am glad that he is married, for this way I can continue to dedicate myself to my art.[7]

Again, don't be angry, Mathilde! My soul is open and pure! I feel no remorse. G. is in Kopenhagen now and presumably will stay there. He sent me a few lines—but Mathilde, these lines were not able to make any impression on me. What can I do about that? He is the best person in the world—but he doesn't want to marry me and I don't want to marry him; I cannot marry him. With my whole being I belong to that other man.

Oh, there is nothing I can do about that. Everything that I feel is so exalted, so noble, that the dear Lord can surely not be angry at me—and He will also forgive me when in the future I will practice my art with thoughts about him. You must know that everything has become easier since I have achieved this virginal outlook and—listen, I am perfectly content, I am not at all troubled. I desire nothing.

Did Lind really believe that she was expressing her deepest feelings when she said that she was glad that "the only man" was married?

---

Three days before Christmas Mendelssohn composed two songs, one beginning with the thought "There is no greater suffering than when two soul mates (or sweethearts—*Herzen*) must part."[8] In the second, "Tröstung" (Consolation), the poet Hoffman von Fallersleben tells the reader to take heart and be of good cheer, because God is merciful and good.

The next day Mendelssohn created a lovely album as a Christmas gift for Lind. He copied five of his songs, including "Tröstung," in the album. And he wrote a much longer letter than his first to Lind—in his most beautiful handwriting:

23 December 1845
*Mein liebes Fräulein,*
I wish to thank you so much for your dear, good, friendly letter, to tell you what pleasure you have given me thereby, and by means of the letter that you have remembered me! But you know how much pleasure you give me thereby, and thanks can never be expressed in words; precisely when one wants to say it best, it succeeds least well. Your letter often reminds me of Lindblad; he also had not studied German grammar, and wrote better, and in a more heartfelt way than most Germans are able to do…and the same holds true for yours…
Tomorrow is Christmas Eve, and ever since you left Leipzig I wished to be one of the people who brings you a gift that evening. There will

be many of them, but no one can do so more sincerely and in a more heartfelt way than I. So I beg you to accept the songs. Now it actually seems to me that I should say something about the fact that I am adding myself to the numerous composers who press in upon you, but I have stopped doing so, and recall that you already called it *malplacé* once. But what I should apologize for, in any case, are the drawings, but the fault lies only with the court concert and the compliments that were given me for my drawings. When you said that you could also dance, I immediately decided to draw something for you, as well (badly) as I could.

However, because of the many interruptions, they have turned out less satisfactorily than I had hoped—you will have to be satisfied; at least the *rosen och de bladen* and the little golden stars and the Swedish bread aren't missing.

I would again like to thank you especially for the Swedish bread. Please, *liebes Fräulein*, send us a loaf now and then, and please do not forget, as long as you are in Berlin, we all enjoy it so much; and the children are so happy when we receive a loaf from *Fräulein* Lind, and I believe that you sent it to us *yesterday*. When it came last time, the children had seen your picture hanging in the street and had all suddenly run to look at it and cried that it was you. I asked whether they had been able to read the name; they said no, they had recognized it, but it didn't resemble you. I wanted to make an instructive comment, that it must resemble you, but it occurred to me that I felt the same as they. And the bread arrived when we got home, and in the evening your letter came. That was a very happy day, *mein liebes Fräulein*, and I will never forget it.

And now I must end the letter, because the mail, which will bring you this letter tomorrow, is leaving now. If we were in Sweden, I would throw the package in through the door, would I not? If I were in Berlin, I would bring it to you, and that is what I would like best. So the postman will bring it to you, and tomorrow evening, please think once also of me. As for me, you know that on every happy holiday and on every serious day of my entire life I will think of you, and that you must share them, whether you like it or not, but you wish it, and you know that it's the same with me, and that that will never change.

Ever your friend, Felix Mendelssohn Bartholdy

And I wish you a happy holiday.[9]

1. Charlotte Helen Dolby, later Sainton, 1821–1885, alto, was hired for the Gewandhaus concerts in 1845–46.
2. "How sleepy I felt before I saw him," from C. M. von Weber's opera *Der Freischütz.*
3. Henriette Sontag, later Countess Rossi, was the most celebrated and beautiful operatic singer of the 19th century.
4. This song first appeared in print in a book of Adolph Boettger's poems in 1846.
5. Cato was an upright third century B.C. Roman statesman and moralist who despised the corruption and ostentation of Carthage and commanded that it be destroyed.
6. Unlike *Fräulein,* which always meant "unmarried female," *Herr* had multiple meanings: "lord," "master," and when used with a man's surname, "Mister." In accordance with Victorian mores, the young Mendelssohn wrote to the parents of young English women he admired, not to the young women.
7. At another time Lind said that her love for Mendelssohn was so great that she would gladly give up her career in order to become "his."
8. Mendelssohn did not publish the song "Wenn sich zwei Herzen scheiden," and there is no evidence that he gave it to anyone.
9. Lind's daughter, Jenny Maude, published a facsimile of this letter in her book *The Life of Jenny Lind,* n.d.

# fourteen

WHEN THE MANAGER OF THE BIRMINGHAM FESTIVAL, JOSEPH MOORE, ASKED Mendelssohn if he and Lind, "the reportedly great lion," might participate in a festival in Birmingham in the fall of 1846, the composer replied,

> If you can have Jenny Lind for the festival, by all means have her, for we now have no singer on the continent who is to be compared to her. But although she has no fixed engagement…I fear it will be difficult to make her come, as they are all mad about her and force her into more engagements than she can accept.

Lind's erstwhile suitor Julius Guenther had sent no more warm, affectionate letters to Jenny after she went to Germany. But from Paris he wrote to Jacob Josephson about his feelings:

> Jenny Lind, yes! That is a chapter with which I could still fill a page or two, as my soul and heart are filled with it to eternity, but that is better

left until we meet. If you write to her, tell her from me that she is, in my opinion, the greatest singer alive, for now I have also heard those who in some cases possess so-called advantages over her.

Another former suitor, Hans Christian Andersen, came to Berlin from Denmark in December with the hope of spending Christmas Eve with Lind. Although he had been forced to accept the fact that she did not wish to have a romantic relationship with him, they were now his Kai and Gerda, "not brother and sister, but…just as fond of each other as if they were."

Andersen had many admirers in Berlin, including the Prussian royal family. So he received numerous invitations to Christmas celebrations, but he declined them all because he was waiting for an invitation from Lind. When the invitation failed to arrive, he spent Christmas Eve alone in a hotel in Berlin. After he informed her of his disappointment, she invited her "dear brother" to celebrate a Scandinavian Christmas Eve with her and Louise Johansson at the Wichmann home on New Year's Eve.

———————

After Christmas, Fanny accepted her brother's invitation to come to Leipzig to see a new grand piano at the firm of Breitkopf and Haertel. Because Felix was scheduled to conduct the music for *Athalie* in Berlin again on the 8th of January 1846, the siblings returned together on the train to Berlin. Nothing could have given Fanny greater pleasure than having Felix to herself for seven-and-a-half hours.

While he was in Berlin, Felix called on Lind. Consequently she wrote to her guardian, Judge Henrik Munthe, that Mendelssohn sometimes came to Berlin and that she had often been in his company.

After he returned to Leipzig, Mendelssohn received another request from Joseph Moore—that he "endeavor to prevail upon Lind" to attend the Birmingham festival. "We think" he wrote, "your application will be most likely to induce her to come."

Mendelssohn replied that Jenny Lind's participation was very important to the success of the festival, as he considered her "without hesitation, to be the premiere singer of the day, and perhaps of many days to come." But he was unwilling to undertake the negotiations that Moore requested. She had been adamant when she told him that she would not go to England and had already refused two invitations. Alfred Bunn, lessee of Drury Lane Theater in London, was now threatening her with prison if she refused to honor her contract.

---

In part of a six-page especially affectionate letter to Felix, Mme. Jeanrenaud quoted a Frankfurt friend on the 22nd of January:

Mme. Pleyel, who radiates the purest innocence, said about you, "Although I may be deceived, nothing can rob me of the comforting belief that this soul will be saved and will return to its purity, which it has lost because of nefarious people."

Felix responded immediately, without commenting on Mme. Pleyel's statement. Knowing how unhappy his mother-in-law was about his frequent absences from home, and having declared—at least to others, if not to her—that he would remain in Leipzig until the summer, he wrote another flattering account of Cécile:

26 January 1846
For several days already I have wanted to write to you, and do you know why? Actually only in order to tell you that Cécile looks so very well! And that is certainly reason and substance enough for a letter, is it not? When I came home and found her with her very shiny brown curls and her good, healthy color and with such a cheerful expression, I thanked God first, and then thought I wanted to write that to you and say no more in the letter than that. I told Cécile that, and she laughed, and then I let myself be deterred from doing so. And now your dear letter has arrived…It has been a long, long time since I have seen her look so well and sprightly, and so cheerful.

Only then did he inform her that he planned to conduct at the Aachen festival in the middle of May and be gone from home for two weeks. He ended that part of the letter, "Another trip, you will say. Can I help it? The people force them on me, and of course, once I have been forced, I don't find the coercion as bitter as some others."[1]

---

When Hans Christian Andersen heard, at the end of January, that Lind had received an invitation to the court at Weimar, he quickly accepted his invitation from the grand duke of Weimar to be his guest as well. Lind sang five times at the little court theater and spent much time with Andersen on excursions in the duke's carriage.

After he learned that Lind would be in Weimar, Mendelssohn invited her to spend some time on the 30th of January with him and his family. She came, and they discussed the roles she might sing in Birmingham and Aachen if she chose to go there.

On the third of February Felix enjoyed an all-day celebration of his birthday: an orchestral fanfare in the morning, receipt of fifty-three flowerpots—eighteen camellias—three big cakes, a speech by Ferdinand David, and a big party at the home of Schleinitz in the evening. Ostensibly as a birthday present for her husband, Cécile painted roses and the third verse of a poem by Lenau on the cover of a tiny datebook:

> *Nie mag weiter sich ins Land Lieb von Liebe wagen,*
> *Als sich blühend in der Hand, Läßt die Rose tragen.*
> [A lover should never leave his beloved for a period longer than the time it takes for a rose to wilt in the hand.]

---

In their great desire to recruit Lind for their festivals, members of the committees of both the Birmingham Festival and the Lower Rhine Festival in Aachen bombarded Mendelssohn with letters throughout the winter and early spring. Each offered further inducements: Joseph Moore offered to increase Lind's honorarium to £450; and the Aachen Pentecost Festival committee said that if Lind hesitated to decide to come to Aachen, they would try to arrange a number of guest appearances for her in Cologne, with suitable remuneration.

The members of the Rhine festival committee wished to feature Mendelssohn's *Athalie* on the next program. But the composer disagreed with their choice because he believed none of the parts in *Athalie* were suitable for her. He argued that it was important that she sing on the first day of the festival, and that she herself had suggested Haydn's *The Creation*. He reminded the committee that the oratorio had not been sung since 1818, at the very first Rhine festival. The committee agreed to include *The Creation* in the program.

---

A newly married English couple—both singers—Adelaide Kemble Sartoris and her husband, Edward, had become good friends of Mendelssohn's. They were now in Rome for the winter, and from there Adelaide replied to a letter the composer had written on the 14th of February:

> Dear Mendelssohn…I saw the old *Abbate* today—he spoke with great affection of you, and desired me to remember him to you—he heard from Berlin that you are *quite in love with Jenny Lind,* or as he delicately added, with her talent—tell me about her—if she will not let us hear her in England.

Mendelssohn did not mention Lind in his reply.

At the beginning of March Felix and Cécile went to Berlin for the baptism of Paul's second child, another daughter, Cécile Katherine (Kaetchen). Because Cécile had not yet heard Lind on stage, they planned to attend a performance of Meyerbeer's *Les Huguenots* after the baptism. Unfortunately, four days prior to that day Lind sprained her ankle.

The next morning Mendelssohn went to see her at the Wichmann home and stayed for three hours. Lind did not invite Louise to be present during the visit, and Louise did not record in her diary whether any members of the Wichmann family were present during all or part of the three hours. Her notes suggest that they were alone at least some of the time, and she expressed her opinion about the visit: "3 March 1846. Mendelssohn was at the Wichmanns till noon. But he knew how to take advantage of his rights, that is, if he has such rights as a married man."

Louise also noted in her diary that Mendelssohn went to see Lind at least three additional times:

> 6 March 1846. Three hours before lunch and three after lunch! Of course, it's true that he's an artist and music aficionado. But did they not speak about other things than music?
>
> 7 March. The same person was there, with the difference that his wife was with him in the evening. It seems to me to be most calamitous to love the husband of another woman, and in such an undisguised way.

The next day Felix and Cécile and their daughter Marie returned to Leipzig. Two days later the Aachen committee received confirmation from Lind that she would assist in their festival and in all the roles that Mendelssohn would determine.

A few days later, in a letter to Wilhelm Taubert, Mendelssohn added a postscript: "*Glömm intet din goda vän.*"[2]

After Taubert came to Leipzig the following week to perform in a subscription concert, Mendelssohn wrote another long letter to Lind:

Leipzig, 18 March 1846

The news that Taubert brought regarding your condition did not satisfy me as I had hoped it would; and just as in such circumstances I would like to sit at the piano and play for you, I come now (as I cannot, unfortunately, be there) with written words, and imagine myself asking on the ground floor if I can speak with you, and hear the reply, "Yes," and *Fräulein* Louise opens the door for me, and you have one of the ten thousand pictures and copper engravings you have been given, in your hands, and I seat myself beside you and begin this way: O *mein liebes Fräulein*, what a great joy you have given me with your dear, good letter! First of all, just the address, for I would not have thought that you would have found the time, and I was quite surprised when I really saw your letter.

Then also, that you do not scold me a great deal because of the old stupid distrust and all the wearisome doubts that went through my head and then through the pen when I last wrote to you.[3] I should actually be very ashamed of that, but do you also know that I am not? Forgive me, but I told you ahead of time that at times I would have to bore you with these things. Now it shall not happen again for a long time; and how I thank you that you have talked me out of it in such a kind and good way. (I also do it myself, but I like so much to hear it from you.)

Shall I remember you to Marie? She speaks to me about *Fräulein* Lind all day, and that she once was so good to her. And yesterday when I came into the children's room, chubby Paul had a piece of paper to practice his penmanship, and when I looked at the paper, I saw that he had written "Liebes Fräulein Lind" at least ten times. Thereupon he composed a whole letter to you today, and I had to promise him that I would send it along, and one has to keep one's promises. At first Marie wanted to send her own letter—I presumed, however, that one was enough, and thus she only signed her name. Carl said he couldn't sign his name because he hadn't written the letter. The children think of you every day and every hour, as do their parents!

We long very much to hear that you are feeling better, and that you will soon be free of the boredom that comes with such a long "imprisonment." Please send us word soon, and, God willing, may you soon be perfectly well again!

After describing the morning rehearsal with Taubert and musing about the public, Mendelssohn became more personal:

This evening something strange happened at our house. Cécile said, "It's too bad that we haven't received Swedish bread for such a long time." I replied, "I'll write yet today and request it for you." Marie said, "Paul has already written to *Fräulein* Lind." I asked him to show me the letter, and when Paul came with the letter, the servant came in the other door with the package with today's Swedish bread. That reminded me of the time that you were going to give me theater tickets but had no more left, when suddenly the nicest tickets lay on my writing desk, and you said, "That often happens to me." This time it happened to us, but you were certainly involved.

Tomorrow Taubert will be envious that I have Swedish bread. Today we both sang "Komm Kuh, komm Kalb" à due; it was a glorious artistic achievement. Taubert sings better, but I pronounce the Swedish words better.

You wish to know how I felt these days when I was completely quiet in my room and wrote notes without end, and only now and then went for a walk in the fresh air. I felt quite well again and believed I was well. But since the day before yesterday, when I was halfheartedly occupied with concert matters and all sorts of correspondence…since then I have been greatly agitated and in such an unpleasant mood that all the people say to me, "How well you look," whereas you would say, "What's the matter with you?"…

I don't see why I shouldn't also fill this page; when I begin to chat with you, *mein liebes Fräulein*, it becomes difficult for me to stop; I am looking forward so much to the Rhine and before that, to your coming here, which you promised us, and to a real spring…and spring will end, like my old song in your book. And I also look forward to the day, as you also do, when I no longer conduct and concern myself with the public and am involved in a so-called sphere of action, and have no sphere of action other than simply staff paper, and conduct no more than I wish, and when I can again be quite independent and free! It won't be for another few years yet, *but no longer*. I hope that with all my heart and that is something we have in common. I believe this is so because we both truly love our art with all our souls.

Now I must think, however, that I have sat with you long enough and should leave, or perhaps it may be *Norma* tonight, and the clock has already struck half past 2, or you have suddenly received visitors and I would have to take my hat, even though much against my will...I soon hope to hear that you walk, tread, stand, jump, dance, play billiards, sing in a Ries lieder concert[4]...and are rid of all demands.

You have promised to think of me now and then, and you must keep your promise! As concerns me, you know that I experience with you what you experience, the good and the sad, and that no day passes in which I do not thank God that I have met you; and even though you have many friends, and will have many more, there is no one, and there will be no one who is as much yours with all his heart, unchangingly yours, as your friend Felix Mendelssohn Bartholdy.[5]

---

At the conservatory, in accordance with his custom, Mendelssohn meted out praise and blame frankly and impartially. But at times his irascibility took the upper hand. In records that William S. Rockstro kept of the 1845–46 school year, he quoted Mendelssohn as "almost shrieking, 'It isn't there'" after a pupil added a note to a certain chord. The same student noted that on another occasion, after a student scrambled through a difficult passage, he cried with "withering contempt, 'That is hopeless.'"[6] Rockstro also commented, however, "Wherever Mendelssohn saw an earnest desire to do justice to the work in hand he would give direction after direction with a lucidity which we have never heard equaled."

---

From Berlin, Lind informed the Frankfurt businessman Herr Buettner that she was very happy, "in fact, happy, in good spirits, cheerful and delighted, in a much better state" than when she had last seen him in Frankfurt. She also stated that because she had not yet accumulated enough money, she would not retire from the stage until 1847.

----

On or before the 27th of March, Mendelssohn sent another letter to *Frl.* Jenny Lind.[7]

----

Lind made her last appearances in Berlin on the 2nd of April. Having finally decided to sing in the imperial city, she prepared to embark on her trip to Vienna. After she left, Mme. Birch-Pfeiffer wrote a letter of introduction of the singer to a friend in Vienna:

> On Sunday our angel fled from us, and only today have I brought myself to introduce her to you by this letter. Jenny Lind, of course, needs no introduction to a lady as truly artistic as you, and I will only venture to give you a few slight indications of her northern temperament, which your own fine tact would easily have discovered without them.
>
> She is reserved and self-contained, pure through and through, and sensitive to the highest degree; so strangely tender that she is easily wounded, and as a result, becomes silent and serious for no apparent reason…A word will often quickly shut her up in herself; and I tell you this in order that you may see how you fare with her. When she suddenly becomes dumb to you, you may be certain that something has wounded her delicate sensitivity. She is a true mimosa, which closes itself at the slightest touch.
>
> Don't conclude from this that she is *sans esprit*. She speaks little and thinks deeply. She is very perceptive and has the finest tact—a mixture of devotion and energy such as you have probably never met before. Being free of the slightest trace of coquetry herself, she regards all coquetry with horror. I adjure you, tell all your coterie that Jenny must be received brilliantly; otherwise she will never forgive me for having persuaded her to perform in so large a theater, for she fears that her voice will not fill it. She stands alone in her great modesty as she does in everything else. If you invite her to your home and she won't sing when first you ask her, let it pass. Don't allow any one to pressure her, otherwise it's possible that she may not come again…

She is passionately fond of dancing, but not of dinner parties. Nothing is more hateful to her than sitting at a table for a long time…Since she has left I have felt as if I were in my grave. I can listen to no singing now.

---

1. No response from Mme. Jeanrenaud has been found.
2. Swedish for "Don't forget your good friend."
3. The letter has not been found.
4. Lieder recitals were new at this time.
5. Holland and Rockstro omitted the last sentence of this letter in their two volumes about Jenny Lind's career. This letter is one of only three of Mendelssohn's letters to Lind that is housed in public libraries. None of Lind's letters to Mendelssohn are in the composer's correspondence albums.
6. Rockstro quoted Mendelssohn as saying "So spielen die Katzen" (literally translated, "That is how cats play").
7. Only the envelope of that letter has been found.

# fifteen

LIND COULD HAVE ENJOYED A FEW WEEKS OF NEEDED RESPITE BETWEEN HER
Berlin guest appearances and her debut in Vienna. But Mendelssohn had prevailed
upon her, albeit with some difficulty, to sing in Leipzig on Easter Sunday. She
arrived four days before Easter, bearing a letter from Fanny to Felix, and another
for Cécile from Felix's *Tante* Hinny Mendelssohn. The latter referred to Lind as
"everyone's darling."

Lind's host for the second time, Dr. Heinrich Brockhaus, noted her arrival
in his diary:

April 08, 1846.
I found everyone well and in a good mood at home because of a lovely
visitor—*Fräulein* Lind, who came to stay with us this morning, as she
had previously promised. I, too, was heartily glad to see the amiable,
simple girl and great artist. She was talkative and warm all evening, and
this was further enlivened by Mendelssohn's presence.
April 09, 1846…One has to love the girl from the bottom of one's heart,
she has such a noble, lovely nature. And yet she is not happy. I am

convinced that she would gladly exchange all her triumphs for simple domestic happiness. She observes that at the Mendelssohns, where wife and children make for Mendelssohn's happiness.

The next day Lind and the young poet Dr. Emmanuel Geibel came to the Mendelssohn home for a long drawn-out noon meal. Geibel brought his fourth revision of the plan for a libretto of *Loreley*. The protagonist in this story is a young woman of humble birth who is courted by and falls in love with a nobleman who comes to her disguised as a hunter. At the same time, however, he is courting a noblewoman. Ultimately, Loreley discovers that he is planning to marry the noblewoman, and in her feelings of betrayal and despair, and desiring revenge, Loreley goes to the Rhine. There the water sprites promise revenge for a very heavy price: she must consecrate herself to them forever.

On Saturday before Easter, Lind made an entry in Cécile's album in the Swedish language: "11 April 1846. *Saknad. Jag hade en van.*[1] Jenny Lind."

The concert on Easter Sunday was scheduled for early evening. But at some time during the day Mendelssohn found time to write letters—not mere notes—of introduction of Lind to four friends in Vienna: to amateur composer and journalist Dr. A. J. Becher, to the professor of piano Joseph Fischhof, to his friend Franz Hauser, and to the widowed Baroness Dorothea von Ertmann. Lind was to deliver the letters personally. To Dr. Becher he wrote,

> 12 April 1846
> …[Jenny Lind] is the best [female] artist with whom I have become acquainted in my entire life, the most genuine and noble, and at the same time the most fine and quiet and upright person. Thus I believe I will have done my duty toward her when I request that you go to her as soon as you receive these lines, and be kind and helpful to her…She is very shy and retiring, but when you will have heard her sing a little song or a great aria you will know more than I am able to tell you about her. So I commend her to you. But tell me also that she will not become too deeply rooted in Vienna, as we will not be able to make a go of the Aachen Music Festival this year if she isn't there.

With his request to the pianist Joseph Fischhof to help Lind in any way he could, he described her somewhat differently:

Never in my life have I met a [female] artist as noble, as genuine as Jenny Lind. Nowhere have I found natural gifts, training and deep sincerity in this combination, and probably never will; and whereas *one* of these qualities may have appeared much more prominently here or there, I believe that the combination of all three has never occurred before.

To his old friend Franz Hauser he wrote less formally, and even more enthusiastically:

You will receive these lines through *Fräulein* Jenny Lind; as soon as you have received them, go to her and be kind to her; you will surely do me that favor, won't you? I will regard all the good you do for her as if done to me. Not a day passes in which I do not feel happy anew that we are living at the same time, that I have learned to know her, and that she is kindly disposed to me, this glorious, genuine, good artist.

I imagine that you will feel as I do, to whom she has actually never been a stranger, but has rather appeared as "one of us," the invisible church about which you sometimes write to me. She draws from the same well with all of us who take our art seriously; thinks the same, strives for the same, so that all the good she experiences in the world is as flattering to me as if it happened to me, and helps me and all of us…When she sings the first time, write to me on the same day and tell me how it all went… because I want to hear it especially from you.

Always and forever your friend, Felix Mendelssohn Bartholdy

He began his letter to Dorothea von Ertmann by thanking her for the "never-to-be-forgotten" days he had spent with her and General Ertmann in Milan in 1831 and assuring her that few days had passed without thinking "long and often of her kindness and friendship." He introduced Lind to her in approximately the same way as to his other correspondents in Vienna.

Only three artists were scheduled to take part in the Easter Sunday concert: Jenny Lind, Felix Mendelssohn, and Ferdinand David. No orchestra was available, because an opera was scheduled for that evening. Thus Felix had saddled himself with the onerous task of playing alone and accompanying every other number but one on the program. However, as soon as Clara Schumann came to his home in the afternoon, he was able to persuade her to play once in his stead.

*Frau* Schumann had not heard Lind sing before the Easter Sunday concert; immediately afterwards she wrote in her diary,

> Lind is a genius in singing, the likes of which one seldom hears. One is captivated the first time one sees her, and although her face is not beautiful, it appears so because of her wonderful eyes, which enliven her whole face. Her singing comes from the depths of her heart. It is not striving after effects and not passion which moves one, but it goes directly to the heart; a wistfulness and melancholy transport one into the realm of feelings, whether one wills it or not.
>
> Lind may appear cold to some on first meeting, but that is not the case. She seems so only because of the simplicity of her singing; one hears no howling, no sobbing or trembling tones, absolutely nothing in bad taste. Everything is lovely the way she does it. Her coloratura is the most perfect I have ever heard; her voice is not big, but penetrates the whole room because she sings with all her soul...
>
> After the concert...I learned to love Jenny Lind twice as much because of her unassuming—I could almost say retiring manner; one hardly noticed that she was there, she was so quiet—to state it briefly, she is as original a creature as she is a great singing genius.

The concert review in the *Allgemeine Musikalische Zeitung* was equally laudatory:

> *Fräulein* Lind reproduced the longing of youthful love in *Euryanthe* and the childlike devotion and complete faith in God of Agathe with such truth and sincerity that it did not fail to make a deep and lasting impression...At this evening concert she also delighted the public with Mendelssohn's charming song "Suleika"...Herr General Musikdirektor Mendelssohn Bartholdy played Beethoven's *Sonata quasi una fantasia* with his usual consummate artistry.

In her diary entry, Louise Johansson noted that Mendelssohn was truly pleasant and charming and had gone to a great deal of trouble for Jenny's concert.

On her way from Altona to the spa at Carlsbad,[2] Mme. Arnemann stopped in Leipzig to attend the Easter Sunday concert. After the concert and dinner,

Mendelssohn went to the hotel where the two women lodged and found an extremely agitated Jenny Lind. Later that evening he penned a letter to Mme. Arnemann. Mme. Arnemann replied on the 15th of April,

> I now know that there is one person in Leipzig who knows what it means to *have* to leave when one would so gladly have stayed, but it wasn't possible. Jenny didn't want to remain under any circumstances. O, it was a bad evening yet after you left...
>
> The surprise of seeing her here already on Monday was entirely too much, and I, together with you, thank God that He has led matters so that I have had the opportunity of getting to know her; even though I am unable to understand the *complete fullness* of her art, I believe that I understand her heart...and as long as she wishes mine, it is hers. The thought that she might no longer desire it still makes me literally shiver...Tomorrow it will be dreadfully empty here, as she is leaving at ten o'clock to go to Prague and Vienna.

After the concert Lind wrote to Mme. Birch-Pfeiffer, "Mendelssohn's praise is the greatest artistic pleasure that can be granted on earth."

Felix sent a succinct report about the concert to Fanny:

> Jenny Lind again provided us with unbelievable pleasure, and half by force, and half against her will, she gave the most brilliant concert I have ever heard in the hall of the Gewandhaus; she sings "Suleika," my E-minor song, *zum Hinwerden*,[3] as Baermann from Munich expresses it.

The text of "Suleika," written by Goethe's erstwhile beloved Marianne von Willemer, reads,

> How I envy you, west wind, that you can give him the news that I suffer because we are apart.
> You awake quiet longing; your breeze causes eyes, woods and hills to be in tears,
> Yet your mild, gentle wafting cools sore eyelids.
> O, I would die of sorrow if I had no hope of seeing him again.
> So rush to my love, speak gently to him, but do not make him sad, and

do not let him know of my pain.

Tell him, but tell him simply, that his love is my life, that his nearness will make me happy.

Cécile ended a four-page letter to her mother with only one line about Lind's concert: "Mlle. Lind was here for a week and gave a concert that was full as an egg."

A few weeks before Felix went to the Pentecost Festival in Aachen, Fanny sent a short letter to Cécile: "The string of music festivals on the Rhine must be very nice; I would like to go if I were not as poor as a church mouse this year... Will you totally remain a wallflower while he raves?"

In reply, Cécile lamented to Fanny, "Felix is so dreadfully busy that I see very little of him. Soon I will be alone again, without him."

---

1. *Saknad* can be translated in various ways: "missed, missing, regret, loss, lack"; it is followed by "I had a friend."
2. Carlsbad, now Karlovy Vary in the Czech Republic, was part of the Austrian Empire at the time.
3. Rietz dated the composition of "Suleika" as 1837. *Zum hinwerden* may be translated as "to drive you crazy."

# s i x t e e n

MME. ARNEMANN WAS NOT THE ONLY PERSON WHO WAS TOTALLY ENAMORED with Jenny Lind. Clara Schumann wondered, "What would my Robert say about my passionate outbursts about what Lind and her artistry mean to me?" The singer cast a spell on grown, dignified, rational persons, on university students and professors, and equally on men and women. Professor Geijer's daughter Agnes described the phenomenon in her diary: "She is a witch and always will be, for it is quite impossible to see and hear and be together with her without being bewitched, enchanted, falling completely in love with her, over and over again!"

When Lind arrived in Vienna on the 18th of April, however, she did not feel as if she enchanted anyone; here she felt like an insecure and tired stranger. Whereas in Berlin, Meyerbeer had paved the way for her in musical circles and Mme. Wichmann had provided a warm home, in Vienna she felt terribly alone. And because of her inordinate fear that her voice would not fill the Theater an der Wien, she refused for days to even try to sing. As she had in every other new city, however, she overcame her fears, and she made her debut in the imperial city on the 22nd of April in Bellini's tragic opera *Norma*.

The Viennese were so eager to hear her that all the seats were already filled in the early afternoon. And she created the same kind of furor as in almost every other city where she sang the role of the Druid priestess.

The next day Lind posted letters to Mendelssohn and Mme. Birch-Pfeiffer; to Birch-Pfeiffer thus,

*Liebe Freundin,*

It's over at last, thank God, and I hasten to describe it to you, although I know that the kind-hearted director Pokorny[1] has written all about it to you today.

Well then! Yesterday was the all important day on which I appeared in *Norma,* and the good God did not desert me, though I deserved it for my unreasonable nervousness.

Don't be angry with me, I beg you! I can do nothing with regard to that, and suffer enough for it myself. The three previous days were dreadful. The idea of turning back was always in my mind, but I should have given offence to so many if I had done so.

But now we shall be merry here for a little while and sing nine times; and then we can go still further. But this public! At the end I was called back sixteen times and twelve or fourteen times before that. Just add that up! And the reception! I was quite astounded!…

I have never met kinder people than the Viennese, I don't have words to describe my time here! I thank God that He helps me so much.

Hauser attended a performance two days after her debut and complied with Mendelssohn's request that he send a report immediately; in fact, the singer wrote after midnight,

*Mein lieber* Felix,

How can I ever repay you for all the love you have shown me, and today you will receive only a few confused lines from me, as I am so overcome— having heard Lind for the first time last night…Last Wednesday, the 22nd, she appeared for the first time in *Norma*…and in fact under the most unfavorable circumstances in the world—in the worst conditions, at quadrupled prices, with the rivalry of the two theaters, each of which had its nettled faction in the audience. I sent both children and remained at home with apprehensive agitation and fear…yesterday I acquired a seat and listened with a kind of delight that I wouldn't have believed possible, to the very last note—really, whoever did not give his heart to this dear being immediately after the first scene of this dear child must have something other than a heart where a heart should be.

I must say that of all the many female singers I have heard in my lifetime, none can be compared to Lind. This chasteness, this purity, in short, the whole phenomenon has never before existed—and then there is but One Voice here.

Now it doesn't matter how she sings—she has conquered—and it would be sad if it were not so. But I will rather say no more about her, as I cannot express what is inexpressible. Today Lind said, "When you will hear *Athalie* und *Oedipus,* you will be just delighted."

After Lind attended the performance of *Antigone,* she mentioned the play in her second letter to Mendelssohn from Vienna:

How nice if a subject just like *Antigone* could be found for an opera; no doubt you are laughing and asking: Where can we find material such as this in our time? But I have always thought of *Antigone* as the nicest problem to solve, for example, at her last struggle, when she almost dies—O, how simply beautiful—and then the old men who murmur, etc., etc.[2]

The following week Hauser prated on about Lind to his friend Moritz Hauptmann, a violinist, composer, and professor at the Leipzig conservatory:

Jenny Lind is singing here, and I will say no more than that I have caught the Lind fever, and in its most violent form. I tell you that she is a dear one, irresistible [*zum auffressen*], and a dear, amiable, honest, intelligent, lovely etc., etc., etc., etc., [*sic*] child. I have never heard such a voice in my life, nor have I ever met such a genial, womanly, musical person… On the stage she is the loveliest, purest, most charming creature one can possibly see or hear…Lind soars above everyone.

Hauser knew that Mendelssohn was pressed for time because he had not nearly completed *Elijah,* which was scheduled to be performed in Birmingham in fewer than five months. Nevertheless he wrote a second long letter to the composer:

Vienna, 7 May 1846

*Lieber Alter,*

Not a word about Jenny Lind, everything the people say about her sounds stupid to me. All of Vienna is lying at her feet and I more than anyone…

Laugh at me, scold me, do what you want with me, but I don't know what comes over me when I just see that lovely face. I feel as if I have never seen anything lovelier, and when she opens her mouth to sing, and the sweet voice sounds, I think of the dear little angels who would sing something like that if they had flesh and blood.

Tell me, *lieber Alter,* how can one do something kind for the dear child? I could have my hand cut off if she wished it—it seems to me that everything must be a bother to her and I bother her a great deal; for I have even succeeded in giving her praise, for which most receive abuse. Recently she said to me, "I'm glad that you like it—that is much" [*das ist viel*]…and "When I don't have to sing, I begin to be a Mensch again, and to live"…But do you know why I'm actually writing to you today?…She asked me several days in a row, "No reply yet from Mendelssohn?" When I told her that we were very irregular people in our correspondence, she said, "Oh, he will definitely reply." Now *Lieber,* don't make a liar out of her, for you cannot imagine that friendly dear face when I come to her with your letters…I have the knack of getting her into the best of moods when she's in somewhat of a bad mood. I talk about you, and you should see how her dear face is transfigured to the beauty of an angel, and so two hours pass and we never run out of material and I don't know where the time has gone. I don't want to think about the time when I will no longer see her.

On the same day Mendelssohn interrupted his work on *Elijah* to take the time to answer Lind's two letters:

Leipzig, 7 May 1846

*Mein liebes Fräulein,*

You are certainly a good and excellent and very kind *Frl.* Lind, that's what I wanted to tell you (and I have said it often enough in my thoughts) after receiving your first letter from Vienna, which you wrote so soon after your first performance.

That you wrote to me on the very next day, that you knew that there was no one to whom it would give greater pleasure than to me, and that you found time for it and let nothing hinder you or hold you back—all this was too good and kind of you!

Your description of the first evening and of the twenty-five curtain calls etc., etc., reminded me of an old letter written to me by my sister when I was in London a long time ago, and I looked for the old letter until I found it. It was the first time that I had left the shelter of my parental home or had produced anything in public, and it had gone well and a great load was off my mind, and I had written an account of it all to her, and thereupon she replied. She said there was nothing new to her in all that, for she had known it all with certainty before; she could not, therefore, very clearly explain to herself why, in spite of this, it had been so very pleasant for her to hear it all confirmed—but it was very pleasant nevertheless. It was precisely the same with me when I received your letter...

Hauser also sent me a very nice description. I have never received a more jovial letter from him, and in this way you give me so much and such great pleasure even in secondhand...But I am really more pleased by the enthusiasm of the Viennese and the twenty-five curtain calls than these few lines will perhaps express to you. I enjoy it also—not because of what people call triumph or success...but because of the succession of pleasant days and evenings they express...You must tell me all about this in detail, or rather, I must worm it out of you...

And now let me express a thousand thanks for what you wrote to me about *Antigone*. Yes, I would like to do that over again. But I must weave that into material for a new letter, and consult with Mme. Birch-Pfeiffer...But my paper has come to an end. We're all well here, and think of you every day.

Soon I shall write to Vienna once more, and then, please God, we shall see each other again on the Rhine and will make a little music together and converse a little, and I think I will enjoy myself a little because of that.

*Au revoir.*

Your friend Felix Mendelssohn Bartholdy

One evening Lind was so dissatisfied with her performance in the first act of *La Sonnambula* that she declared she would not sing again. That night at 11:30

one of the directors came to ask Hauser to talk to her. Early the next morning, he called at Dr. Vivanot's home and found Lind in a dreadful state. He had to talk to her—about Berlin, about Leipzig, and Mendelssohn—and joke and cajole for three hours before she became cheerful and followed Hauser's suggestion that they go to the home of Dr. Jaeger. There she played games in the garden and danced in the evening. Three days later, Hauser said, she was more extraordinary in *Norma* than ever.

Soon there was another problem. All the seats for the next performance of *Sonnambula* had been sold long in advance, when all of a sudden Lind said she did not want to sing before Joseph Tichatschek[3] replaced the inadequate tenor. That storm was weathered also.

While she was in Vienna, the opera director in Pesth[4] invited her to be guest artist there for 1,000 C.[5] for each role. She told Hauser that the offer surprised and pleased her very much. He countered, "You may not sing for less than that." When she told him what she had received in Berlin, Hauser scoffed, "You sang for that pittance in Berlin?"[6]

Hauser was opposed to her going to Aachen to sing at the Lower Rhine Festival because she would be able to make a fortune in Vienna. Pokorny had told him that he wanted to draw up a contract for one hundred performances, pay her in advance, and let her choose when she wanted to perform, in one or two or three years or immediately. When Hauser told Lind, she responded, "Then I'll jump into the water." Yet she admitted that she wanted to amass a fortune.

Fischhof informed Mendelssohn that Lind had aroused the most fervent enthusiasm, and that it was so much more notable because her appearance occurred at the end of a season of an overabundance of performances for a music-weary public and in which a rival Italian opera society, as well as Eskeles[7] and Franz Liszt, tried to divert attention from her. In fact, he termed Liszt's farewell concert as "almost a fiasco."

Four days after writing to Lind, Mendelssohn replied to Hauser's two letters:

> I knew very well that Jenny Lind would provide you with so much pleasure—I never doubted it for a moment. And yet I was very pleased to discover from your letter that I hadn't been mistaken, and that you also had been truly refreshed by this splendid, pure, good artist. Tell her that no day passes in which I do not rejoice anew that we are both living in the same era, that I have learned to know her…that her voice sounds

so lovely, and leaving all music out of the equation, that she is exactly who she is, and then give her my heartiest greetings…

But really, I must come to Vienna some day, I hear everyone speak of it, and you all say such kind things about my music and give me such extraordinary accounts of their performances that you make my mouth water. Perhaps I can bring *Elijah* when it is completely new, some time before the winter—or I'll wait until I have found an operatic subject and composed the music—and until Jenny Lind will be there again—and the latter would make me happiest of all …[*das wäre das Beste*].

When you greet her from me, tell her also that I'll write to her this week, but she must forgive me if my letter is stupid, for I cannot do better just now.

On the same day, the 11th of May, fewer than four months before the Birmingham festival, Mendelssohn asked William Bartholomew to translate *Elijah* into the English language. Bartholomew in turn reminded the composer that all the orchestral parts were to be completed by mid-August.

Meanwhile, members of the Pentecost Festival committee in Aachen were concerned that Mendelssohn informed them that he would arrive on the 27th of May. The first rehearsal of the combined forces of orchestra, choirs, and soloists was scheduled for that day, and the festival was to begin four days later. They strongly urged him to come before the 27th.

While he composed *Elijah*, Mendelssohn's mind was also occupied with the thought of an opera for Lind. He harbored serious doubts about *Loreley* but was unsuccessful in his quest for another operatic subject. In the middle of May he again appealed to Devrient for help; he told him that any libretto that was truly dramatic would do. He wrote to Lind on the same theme in another rather long letter:

Leipzig, 15 May 1846

…Sometimes it seems to me as if it were my solemn duty to compose an opera for you, and to see how much I could accomplish in it—and it is, in fact, my duty.

However, it doesn't depend only on me, and it will certainly not be my fault. If only it were possible! If I am not mistaken, my last letter to you must have seemed very stupid—with absolutely nothing in it. Moreover, I fear the present one will be no different, and that the two of them will be no more than a hearty greeting.

You must have suffered a great deal from homesickness!…But I hope this has passed long ago, and that you're cheerful again, and are making music, and gladdening the hearts of the people by means of the many great gifts with which God has endowed you…

How happy you made my dear Hauser again! He wrote me such a delightful letter after you had been to his house the second time. And I always think about this: what if, of all the true joy that you shed around you, the brightest rays could fall back upon you, and could as thoroughly warm and refresh you as you refresh others! But that cannot be, and when we meet again I will show you a passage in Goethe in which it's written why it should not be so. Yet how I wish it could be so!

He informed her that *Elijah* had given him immense pleasure throughout the last few weeks. But then he returned to the first subject of the letter: "If only the opera were already as advanced as this! I would then play some of it for you. But what if it wouldn't please you at all?"

The following week, Mendelssohn received a letter from Dorothea von Ertmann. It had been impossible for her to get tickets for the first seven or eight performances, and when Lind found out about it, she had brought two tickets to the baroness. She described Lind's singing as being that of an angel, "most pleasant and soulful."

On the same day Hauser composed his third long letter to Mendelssohn in less than a month; Lind was to deliver it to him personally in Frankfurt. Hauser's enthusiasm had not waned:

21 May 1846

*Lieber* Felix,

…Lind is leaving tomorrow, and I don't know how I will continue; it will be the beginning of another era. I'll have to return to the old ordinary bourgeois life and will live with the memory of the hours I spent with her; they were the most beautiful!…Now, least of all, should she have left us, but she is making the sacrifice, and is doing so with all her heart, and one must give her credit for that…

Yesterday she sang *Sonnambula* in a benefit for herself, and the widowed mother of the emperor herself threw her a wreath—such a practical demonstration from a woman who actually lives only to support the

poor, the hospitals and similar institutions has never happened before…
But the other members of the imperial family also give evidence in all
kinds of ways how much they admire Lind…

*Lieber alter, guter* Felix, I couldn't tell our good Lind everything you
wrote in your last letter, but long ago I already said that everyone who
lives in the same era with her must consider himself fortunate and must
thank God every day that he has met such an artist. But *Lieber*, I would
really like to see you and speak with you. It's been three long years, and
we've changed so much, and I have become gray—who knows how long
it will be—I'm melancholy about you today.

Lind had been in the imperial city for only five weeks when she prepared to
go to Aachen. By choosing to leave Vienna, she not only made a great financial
sacrifice; she also made a personal sacrifice, as the journey by carriage to the
Rhine region was long and arduous.

When she left the theater on the eve of her departure for Aachen, she found
such a huge crowd that she went back inside and did not venture out again
until two o'clock. When she stepped into her carriage, a band of young men
unharnessed the horses and would have dragged her carriage themselves if a
cavalry detachment had not prevented it. In the scuffle, Lind's manservant was so
seriously hurt that he needed medical assistance. Because of her concern for him,
Lind delayed her departure for Aachen by twelve hours. How then could she
possibly meet Mendelssohn in Frankfurt four days later, as they had planned?

---

1. Franz Pokorny was director at the opera house Theater an der Wien. Lind lived not far from
   the theatre, on the same street, Am Graben, a main thoroughfare in Vienna, with Dr. Vivanot
   and his family.
2. This excerpt is what Mendelssohn quoted to Mme. Birch Pfeiffer from Lind's letter to him.
3. The Bohemian born Joseph Aloys Tichatschek, 1807–1886, was the most famous tenor in
   Dresden from 1838 to 1872.
4. Pesth is now part of Budapest, Hungary.
5. The currency denoted by *C.* could not be determined.
6. Lind received as much for five weeks in Vienna as she had received for five months in Berlin.
7. Presumably Eskeles was a son of the wealthy Viennese financier Bernhard von Eskeles, husband
   of Lea Mendelssohn's aunt Caecilie Itizig.

# s e v e n t e e n

MENDELSSOHN HAD PLANNED TO TRAVEL, WITH FRIENDS, DOWN THE RHINE by steamboat from Mainz to Aachen, a distance of almost two hundred miles and lasting almost two days and one night. Because Lind did not know the Rhine region, he looked forward to showing her all his favorite spots during the cruise.[1]

He arrived at the Souchay home in Frankfurt on schedule at dawn on the 25th of May and hoped to meet Lind at the Weisser Schwan (White Swan) Inn in Taunus later that day. He sent word to a former young student, Emil Naumann, that he should meet him at the railroad station the following morning. Mendelssohn waited for Lind at the inn, but when she still had not arrived at midnight, he returned to the Souchay mansion.

Emil Naumann went to the Taunus railroad station punctually at eight o'clock the next morning. While he waited for Mendelssohn, he overheard a woman ask every person at the station, "Is Mendelssohn actually coming?" Emil informed her that Mendelssohn had told him to meet him at the station at this time. It was only then that he learned that he was speaking to Jenny Lind.

Minutes later, Mendelssohn arrived somewhat out of breath, expressed his profound relief that Lind was safe and sound, and greeted all the friends who were joining him on the Rhine cruise.

Naumann carefully recorded many details of the Rhine journey:

> I have never seen Mendelssohn happier and more high-spirited than during the steamboat voyage in the Rhine region, beginning in Mainz in the loveliest weather. Besides Jenny Lind there was a group of Mendelssohn's closer friends on the deck, some of whom accompanied him to Aachen; others went only as far as Bingen. Jenny Lind had never before seen the German paradise, the Rhine with its mighty current, the islands which suddenly appear like bouquets out of it, and its banks which gently ascend to the mountains. She was radiant with pleasure.
>
> Mendelssohn increased the same by his most charming exuberance when he named the most famous vineyards on the hills and plains for her and compared each, according to its quality, with the great classical and mediocre composers. Thus he said that the Johannisberger on the gently rolling hills was the Mozart among the wines; those from the craggy rocks, the Rüdesheimer, on the other hand, was Beethoven... When the ship passed a vineyard that was less well known, the modest artist called out, "That is a vintage of doubtful medium quality, like us, who are fellow travelers among the great ones."

In Biberach, in the midst of much revelry, the boat was met by a choir singing Mendelssohn's choruses from *Antigone*. This prompted one of his friends to say, "Felix, how fortunate you are; your journey resembles a triumphal entry everywhere." As if a shadow passed over Mendelssohn, he replied with a sudden melancholy expression, devoid of all mirth, "Don't begrudge it to me—sometimes it seems to me as if only the spring of life will be my portion!"

That somber mood did not last, however; in St. Goar Mendelssohn was again so out of hand that he suggested to Lind with deceptive seriousness, "Let's get out and spend the whole day enjoying ourselves in this beautiful region. What can they do in Aachen without us? They have to wait for us. We have the right as the main persons in the whole show to keep them somewhat in suspense."

On the afternoon of the 27th of May, in lovely weather, Mendelssohn and his party arrived at the old city of Aachen, some fifty miles southwest of Cologne, near the Belgian border. Lind went to stay with the family of the Marquis von Sassenay; Mendelssohn lodged at the Hotel Grand Monarque.

Although he was to take part in the rehearsal that evening, Mendelssohn sent word that he was too tired to make an appearance. As a result, there was chaos at the rehearsal. Although everyone was familiar with his prowess as conductor, some people still wondered if in only two days he could really consolidate all the forces—the orchestra and the choirs from Aachen, Cologne and Duesseldorf—for the three-day festival.

That evening Mendelssohn wrote to Julius Rietz, who was now the music director in Duesseldorf. When he had promised to play in Rietz's concert after the Pentecost festival, he had suggested to Rietz that Lind also sing a few songs. Now, however, Mendelssohn informed his friend that he had second thoughts about Lind's participation because she had been very agitated and was scheduled to sing in Hannover shortly after the festival. He explained why he did not want to speak to her about the concert: "As she had decided to come to the music festival here only because I asked her to, I find it impossible to present her with another travel itinerary, and I doubt that she would be able to do it. I leave it to you; you know her."

One day prior to the festival, Mendelssohn rehearsed for seven-and-a-half hours. Yet when he heard that Lind's friends Professor Erik Geijer from Uppsala, Sweden, and his wife and daughter, Agnes, happened to be in Aachen, he had a piano sent to their rooms. Mme. Geijer informed her son-in-law, Count Hamilton, now director of the Royal Theater in Stockholm, about the evening:

> Jenny also promised that she would arrange for Mendelssohn to play for us, and since the world now turns around according to her wishes and commands, one may feel quite certain when she has pronounced her fiat in one's favor.
> In the evening we were present at the rehearsal of *The Creation,* and then heard the good news that Mendelssohn had declared his willingness to play for us...So in the evening Jenny and Mendelssohn came to us. Jenny sang some lieder, and I need neither to describe nor praise them. Geijer was quite beside himself with delight and pleasure.

The next day everyone's fears vanished. Mendelssohn worked his magic at the festival again, and Jenny Lind dazzled the audience in two oratorios: Haydn's *Creation* and Handel's *Alexander's Feast.* But the critics were most taken with her singing of Mendelssohn's songs—to the composer's accompaniment—"Auf Flügeln des Gesanges" and "Frühlingslied."[2] They described the effect as wholly unparalleled. "Auf Flügeln des Gesanges" may be translated thus:

> I bear you away on wings of song, my little love,
> Away to the meadows by the Ganges, I know the loveliest place there.
> A garden full of red flowers lies there in the still moonlight;
> The lotus flowers await their dear little sister.
> The violets giggle and caress and look up at the stars;
> The roses clandestinely whisper sweet fairy tales into each other's ears.
> The good, wise gazelles leap towards them and listen,
> And the waves of the sacred stream murmur in the distance.
> There under the palm tree we will sink down
> And imbibe love and peace, and dream a blissful dream.

---

Critics in the Scandinavian countries and Germany had all been effusive in their praise of Lind's vocal artistry in operas and lieder, of her acting and her personality and purity. But no audience had yet heard her sing in an oratorio. A sophisticated French music critic, Georges Onslow, who had never been at a Lower Rhine Festival, published some of his impressions.

He began by declaring his great respect for the energy, tenderness, precision, and the most delicate nuances with which the more than 600 performers played and sang under Dr. Mendelssohn's leadership. He was amazed that after only four rehearsals they produced the most stunning effects: precision in the fugal sections and absolute unison in the most delicate nuances, at times so energetic, at others so tender. He praised the calm and precision and the unusual talent of Mendelssohn as conductor. He declared that such power, such force, in choral singing could be found only in Germany.

He stated that he found it difficult to describe the enthusiasm that *Frl.* Lind aroused. He regarded her talent to be extraordinary in every respect and said that no one could perform sacred music more perfectly.

The festival became known as the "Jenny Lind Festival."

At some time during the weekend Mendelssohn gave Lind another of his songs on a text by Klingemann. He added the superscription *Ein noch viel älteres Lied* (A still much older song), and she placed it after his "Ein Altes Lied" (An Old Song) in the album Mendelssohn had given her.

On the third day of the festival, Lind wrote to Taubert in Berlin,

*Herr Capellmeister und Freund!*
I would like to write about many things, but I write such a bad German that I hardly dare to do it, but I have to tell you that it was nice that you came to Vienna and that you can count on me if I can be any kind of help to *you*…I hope that your amiable wife and children are all well! *Ach!* Give my greetings to all your darlings, and I hope that your wife has nothing against it that I love you with all my heart!

And she informed Mme. Wichmann's son, Rudolf, whom she addressed as "brother," that Mendelssohn would accompany her on another Rhine journey after the festival.

The festivities in Aachen ended with a ball on the 2nd of June, to the delight of both singer and music director, as both were passionately fond of dancing.

Before Lind went to Hannover, Mendelssohn showed her his favorite haunts. They sailed up the Rhine and spent a pleasant day together in Cologne and Bonn. Near Koenigswinter they ascended the jagged rocks of the approximately 3,500 feet high Drachenfels.[3] From there they had stunning views in every direction: the Drachenberg castle and Drachenberg ruins on the mountain itself, and the Rhine valley, running mostly south to north. To the north, not far from the mountain, they could see Koenigswinter and Petersburg; further north, Bad Godesberg and Bonn. Even the Cologne cathedral, still incomplete in 1845, was visible in the clear weather. A few miles to the northeast they could see the *Siebengebirge* (Seven mountains); five miles to the south and slightly west, Ramagen with the remains of Roman walls and the railway bridge over the Rhine, then Sinzig with its 13th century Romanesque style church. The Ahr valley and a fortress at Reineck were visible between Ramagen and Sinzig. In the southeast, they could see Koblenz.

The composer and singer returned to Cologne at nine in the evening. There Mendelssohn found a letter from the inquisitive Hauser; after inquiring about the Bach catalog, he asked his friend, "Tell me, Felix, how was it in Aachen and at the Rhine and on it and in Frankfurt? Tell me a great deal, and don't be taciturn, and if you see a rose, tell her I send greetings."

Hauser will surely have exulted in what Mendelssohn wrote a few days later:

Duesseldorf, 8 June 1846

…You asked me, as if in passing, to tell you about the music festival in Aachen. You rascal, you are just as anxious to hear about that as about the Bach catalog! Well, it was very good, very splendid, towering above all the others, and chiefly owing to Jenny Lind, because, as for the orchestra, I have heard it better on some other occasion perhaps, and the choir, though splendid, has been equally as good at previous festivals. But they were all so uplifted, so animated, so artistically moved by Lind's singing and manner that the whole thing became a delight, a general success, and they worked together as they never had before. I had the clearest evidence of this at the last rehearsal when I begged her, for once, not to be the first and the most punctual in attendance, but to get some rest and come towards the end of the rehearsal. She agreed to this, and it was quite miserable to see how feebly things went—so devoid of life that even I became listless like all the others, until, thank God, Jenny Lind appeared, when the needed interest and good humor returned to us, and things moved again. Of course there were wreaths and poems and trumpet blasts again and again, and the people were as excited as they are wherever she goes…

*Frl.* L. brought me only your first melancholy letter in which everything went sour for you. When we spoke of many things she suddenly asked me to do her a favor and write to you soon. I asked her if she had a message, to which she replied in her manner: "I guess you can greet him and tell him that he must not forget me, as I will never forget him." So there you have it…

One day after I accompanied her down the Rhine she traveled to Hannover, and I, here, where I participated in a concert which would have been nicer if Jenny Lind had been there.

Lind sang at the Hannoverian king's birthday celebrations, then performed twelve times in Hamburg's *Stadttheater* and gave two benefit concerts. Some journals published satires about Lind in reaction to the extreme adulation she received everywhere.

---

In Frankfurt Mme. Jeanrenaud was anxious again. Fifteen days after Felix had called on her, she could not resist sending him a note:

I don't know where you are, or which route you will take. I know you are very busy, but do me one favor—not to disappear from our area without a trace. Write but two words before you leave, and I will be deeply grateful. What a glorious Rhine journey you must have had with the glorious weather and the amiable company.

In his reply Mendelssohn said he might return to Leipzig via Hannover but wrote not a word about the Rhine journey.

From Duesseldorf, Mendelssohn went to Liège, Belgium, to hear his new commissioned composition, *Lauda Sion*. He then returned to Cologne to conduct a male choir of 2,000 voices in another commissioned composition, a setting of Friedrich Schiller's *An die Künstler* (To the Artists). He was surprised and delighted when all two thousand men, as if spontaneously, sang his song "Es ist bestimmt in Gottes Rat"[4] from memory.

Bernus du Fay, now a Frankfurt senator, was sorry to miss both the Aachen festival and the male choir festival in Cologne. However, he heard a great deal about both from his friends, and from Darmstadt he wrote to the composer,

Jenny Lind is supposed to have outdone herself, and I gladly believe that; she was singing under your direction, and, it seems to me, was singing more for you than for the audience. I don't hold that against her; true art finds true satisfaction only in itself and in the approval of the directors.

---

From Bremen Lind wrote to Hauser,

16 June 1846
*Bester* Herr Hauser,
I have often thought of you since I left Vienna, and have often written to you in my thoughts, but suddenly I am forcefully struck by the thought that I must speak to you with a bad pen, bad paper and in the German language, but what does all that matter when I write to a *Mensch*?
There is something in my heart that I want to tell you, but first of all to thank you for the time in Vienna. I thank you for your friendship with all my heart. I thank you that you immediately recognized that the dear

Lord gave me a heart also! And now my tale: I have learned to love you
very, very much, and I know that I shall *never* forget you all my life and
that you are one of those people for whom I could make a great sacrifice
if it were necessary…

It was lovely on the Rhine. But the time went *very, very* quickly, but it
lives on in glowing colors in my grateful heart, for the greatest happiness
is to be found in *pure, noble* human hearts. You certainly will not doubt
that this applied to my traveling companion. O, life is beautiful, life is
rich. The other will be calmer and longer, or I would rather remain here!
But on the other hand, may we soon see one another there where there is
no parting! but also—no *Wiedersehen*, and that would be too bad. May
God keep you.

Forever your faithfully devoted Jenny Lind

---

Felix did not stop at the Fahrthor before he returned to Leipzig. Cécile
reported most succinctly to her mother on the 17th of June, "Felix seems to have
been pleased with his trip."

Two days later he arrived in Leipzig—two weeks later than he had assured
Mme. Jeanrenaud. Again Cécile wrote only briefly to her mother about his
return: "Felix has returned *très glorieux* from his trip, looking much better than
when he left."

On the same day Mendelssohn sent thanks to Mr. and Mrs. Seydlitz, daughter
and son-in-law of Herr Verkenius, for their hospitality in Cologne: "I have again
arrived here safely, and found my family well and happy…My Cécile thinks it's
clear that you must have spoiled me and looked after me, because I look so well,
and she thanks you, along with me."

---

Following her guest appearances in northern Germany, Lind stayed with
Arnemanns in Nienstaedten, near Hamburg. One day while she was at a rehearsal
in Hamburg, Mme. Arnemann composed a long letter to Mendelssohn:

Nienstaedten, 22 June 1846
*Lieber Doktor*,
If I weren't convinced that you enjoy hearing about Jenny, you must
believe me that I would not dare to burden you with a few lines. She

has been here since the 19th, when I met her in Hamburg well and happy, which makes me very glad, as her condition in Carlsbad caused me some concern. She recalls the lovely time on the Rhine with pleasure, Bremen with less, and Hannover with more because of the arrival of the Wiechmanns [*sic*]…yesterday at breakfast they surprised Jenny with your portrait by Mangnus[5] [*sic*], and so you are truly among us, not only by means of your picture; you know that, do you not? Not only by means of your divine songs which Jenny continually sings with all her lovely soul. Do you also know that?…The public is really wild this time; there are no more seats left for the first four performances, and the tenor Cornet is doing all he can so that Jenny's six performances become twelve…

We are hoping and thinking very much about your going to London via here…But Jenny must not know about your coming…She doesn't know that I'm writing to you, but as she was away I felt the urge to talk to a friendly soul about her.

Because Lind planned to leave the stage in a year and hoped to sing in an opera by Mendelssohn before then, she appealed to Mme. Birch-Pfeiffer:

Nienstaedten, 26 June 1846
…But the most important point of all is, how is the opera coming? Are you still thinking about it? You can depend on me until next autumn, but not longer than that. Please do it, I beg you. Mendelssohn is deeply interested in it, and is in agreement with the idea, as I also am. I beg you to complete the work for the sake of the three of us, for it will certainly bring us honor.

---

Fanny demanded to know the details of her brother's experiences at the Aachen festival. But what he wrote to her about the festival is remarkable primarily for what he did not relate:

Leipzig, 27 June 1846
*Mein liebes* Fenchelein,
Whoever is able to resist the kinds of incantations you employed must be Satan himself…Thus I am taking a great folio of paper and am

writing to you, even though a huge part of *Elijah* still has to be notated, and although they are already rehearsing the first part in England; and Spohr, whom we had to entertain every noon and every evening…and for whom we gave a concert of his compositions at the Gewandhaus… and who is always a kind, welcome and refreshing guest, but this time he helped to make my head dizzy…

I should really have taken a week to relax after the Rhine journey instead of taking part in new festivities, and now, in addition, I must write a long letter. So if it's stupid and confused, place the blame on yourself, Fenchel, because I am stupid and confused; but I will fill these four pages, that I swear by my beard; and when that is finished—from early tomorrow morning—I'll lock myself in and not move an inch until *Elijah* is finished; that I also swear by my beard.

So you want to know something about the Rhine, now there is the *malheur* that Cécile's letter, in which, at my request, she communicated my very detailed report of the trip to Paul, has crossed with yours, and now it's impossible for me to know what you know and what you don't know. It will be best if I write only those things which Cécile could not have written, and that you cannot know…

I have never experienced such a packed, full three weeks such as these; always up until midnight or one o'clock, and up again at six o'clock, and then the bustle began again at 6:30 and lasted until midnight or until one. The major thing in Aachen was that the Marquis von Sassenay and the mayor, Nellesen, tried their best to provide me with milk rice (because Lind said I like it), but that they didn't succeed because their French chefs always made something different, more elegant, but which was not milk rice.

Then once I took a bath, and as I sat in it, I noticed it was warm Aachen water, and I became so barmy that I was close to falling asleep all day… But the choirs went really well, and if Paul would have heard Lind sing the first two arias in *Alexanderfest* he would again have clapped the way he did at the concert.

He included a detailed account of the hectic Saturday schedule with its seven-and-a-half hours of rehearsals and mentioned the evening with the Geijers: "At nine in the evening I went to Professor Geijer…we made a little music, I played the C sharp minor sonata, *Songs Without Words,* etc., etc."

He did not mention that Lind was present at Geijers, nor that she traveled with him on the Rhine after the festival, nor about his return route from Duesseldorf. Fanny responded,

Berlin, 9 July 1846
*Mein lieber* Felice,
Thank you for your letter with the loveliest news, among which you placed the one about the milk rice at the top, of course. I would have been able to stand more news, for if you think that Cécile has written much, you are gravely mistaken. Cécile is too easygoing to write details, but I'm grateful that you have given me half an hour…
Actually we should sign a contract that after every music festival, every important event, you write a long letter…When we meet after a long period of time, many of the details have been forgotten…Now an entire oratorio by you is going out into the world, and I don't know one note of it.

---

As Lind was now totally exhausted, a doctor ordered her to go to a spa. Although invitations continued to pour in, she accepted no engagements until after the middle of September but gave one benefit concert in Nienstaedten. At the same time Hauser declared to Mendelssohn that it was "absolutely clear that he must write an opera" and enquired what the composer and Lind were up to: "Tell me in greater detail what you are doing, where you are going, and at the same time faithfully tell me what Jenny is doing, etc., etc."

Mendelssohn should have rested after the festival but had no time for such luxury. Although the Birmingham Festival was scheduled for the end of August—in less than six weeks—he still corresponded with Bartholomew about the translation of parts of *Elijah* and told the translator to omit the aria "O rest in the Lord," because he thought it sounded too "sweet." Bartholomew forcefully and successfully argued that it should remain. The choirs were already rehearsing the chorus parts they had received.

At the end of the month, Felix wrote to his brother that he longed to speak to him—that he had a thousand things he wanted to say to him. When Paul came two days later, his brother was, as he said, "as happy as a marmot."

Felix did not meet his deadline; he wrote the last notes of his oratorio fifteen days before the festival. Yet despite all the pressures, he still found time to write

to Lind to ask her to let him know her travel plans. He also informed her that
Geijers had invited him to come to Sweden to feast on roasted reindeer and that
he looked forward to eating milk rice at her house.

After *Frau* Wichmann returned to Berlin from Hannover, she deemed it
important enough to write about some ivy, a symbol of affection to the German
mind, that Lind had brought with her from the Rhine and carefully nurtured.
Among other things, Amalia Wichmann informed Mendelssohn what had
happened to that ivy:

Berlin, 31 July 1846
Honored *Herr Doktor*,
…My two sons and I were with Lind in Hannover for four days. I could
tell you about very many merry antics there, but I fear the letter would
become too long, and so I will only convey the many, many greetings
which she asked me to send to you and your wife. The ivy from the
Drachenfels has, unfortunately, already died; the great deal of water that
she wasted on it could not bring it back to life, which made her very
sad.
Respectfully yours, Amalia Wichmann

1. Apparently Louise Johansson did not accompany Lind to Frankfurt and Aachen.
2. It has not been possible to identify which of Mendelssohn's three Frühlingslieder Lind sang.
3. *Drachen* is "dragon" in the German language. *Fels* is either "mountain" or "rock." *Berg* is "hill"
   or "mountain."
4. The song begins "In the counsel of God it is ordained that we must part from those we love."
5. Eduard Magnus, 1799–1872, was one of the foremost portrait painters in Berlin.

# eighteen

On his way to England in the middle of August 1846, Mendelssohn again did not stop at the Fahrthor. Instead, he wrote a letter to Mme. Jeanrenaud en route and spent a night with the Seydlitz family in Cologne. He arrived in England on the 17th. Three days later, Mme. Jeanrenaud wrote to him,

> When I think of the past and the time when we first became acquainted… that I felt so clearly that Cécile would be happy with you, and that my love for you grows every year, then I recognize and am grateful that a Higher Hand brought us together…Adieu, *mein lieber, bester* Felix…No one *trusts* you more than Your tenderly loving E J

In London, Felix was delighted to stay with Klingemann and his new bride, the young former Sophie Rosen. As always, Felix basked in Klingemann's, and now also in Sophie's, friendship. Cécile immediately expressed her gratitude to her husband's friend:

*Lieber* Herr Klingemann,

Felix cannot praise your kindness enough, on which, however, I counted with special confidence when I saw him leave here unwell. Your care seems to have agreed splendidly with him…If he happens to still be there, tell him the children and I are well, *Gottlob*, and that we are very much looking forward to his coming.

Mendelssohn rehearsed with the soloists and orchestra in London and left for Birmingham by train with the musicians. Josef Staudigl[1] sang his role as the prophet at sight at the final rehearsal. And at 11:30 on the morning of August 26, 1846, the composer conducted almost four hundred musicians at the premiere of *Elijah*. Despite strict injunctions against all clapping at performances of sacred music in England, the audience encored four numbers in each part. *The Times* declared the performance to have been "an absolute triumph."

The next day Felix wrote to his brother about the festival: "No work of mine ever went so admirably the first time it was performed, or was received with such enthusiasm by both the musicians and the audience, as this oratorio."

Three days later Cécile informed Fanny about the "tiny bit" of information she had received from Felix from London and the "two lines" from Birmingham:

But of course [Felix wrote] absolutely no *details* because he has so terribly much to do. He seemed to be pleased with the rehearsals, which I really had not expected. He wrote, "My *Elijah* sounds glorious and is so powerful in the great hall that I wish you were here; the musicians and singers compete in demonstrating their goodwill to me."[2]

Mendelssohn only conducted at the festival; he had stipulated that he did not want to play the organ, and definitely not the piano, in Birmingham, because conducting had become more of a strain than previously.

Although it was possible to travel from London to Leipzig in four days, Felix did not hurry home from England; he spent eleven days en route and arrived in Leipzig on the 15th of September. He had planned to delay his return even longer in order to meet Lind again in Frankfurt but had received a letter in which she said she would not arrive in Frankfurt until the end of September.

A letter from Mme. Jeanrenaud was waiting for Felix when he arrived in Leipzig; it began thus:

9 September 1846
Welcome to German soil!...I have received a letter from Adelheid [Benecke] from which, if you don't know it yet, you can discover what kind of man you are...In my poverty I would actually offer nothing to such a celebrated man as you if you were not my beloved son, and today it is exactly ten years that I can call you that. Do you sometimes think of the country outing to Kronenthal [*sic*]. *Ach,* how the years fly.

After that friendly beginning, the tone in her letter changed:

I haven't succeeded very well in the task of weight gaining, for which a certain Herr M., I believe, must take the blame. I won't say more today. If you should not know the man, *lieber* Felix, he will come to see *you,* as well as Mme. Mendelssohn, after your return, and unfortunately I say this to make you a little jealous; unfortunately the ladies cannot resist him, and then one feels sorry for the mothers...With all my heart, your E J

Felix did not respond to his mother-in-law's comment about Cécile's weight loss, nor the "certain Herr M."

Fanny also mentioned Cécile's weight when she wrote to her sister-in-law:

I'm so sorry that you have had to spend this most heavenly of all summers in the city; we have enjoyed the garden more this summer than in any that I remember in my lifetime...I would really have wished that you could have shared this existence with us; I'm not pleased with what you say about your being so thin, and your lack of appetite.

Two weeks after he returned to Leipzig, Felix reported to Fanny about the Birmingham festival:

I have never heard a better, more spirited first performance than *Elijah,* and will probably not hear another again. Now I would like most of all to take the score under my arm and play it for you from A to Z this morning.

But so far I cannot make up my mind to go on a trip or do anything else, but after the exertion of the summer and the much traveling back and forth, I will vegetate like a shrub. Because after one look on my return, I saw that everyone here was well and happy, I do nothing the whole good, long day but eat, go for walks and sleep, and I still haven't had enough of all three. I should prepare *Elijah* for publication now…and have the German text added so that a performance would be possible in this country very soon, but, as I said, first I have to do things in moderation.

---

Chorley had been instructed by Mendelssohn to meet him and Lind in Frankfurt. When the journalist discovered that neither he nor Lind were to be found, the annoyed critic wrote to Mendelssohn,

Frankfurt, Friday, 18 September 1846
…Here I arrived last night, *no Lind, no you*—nothing for *me.* But I hear she is now coming next week, so I [shall] return here on Saturday, the 27th, *expressly to hear the lady.* Now won't you give me a line to her, that is, if you think we should suit, which may excuse presenting myself to her, still less to force myself on any one, because I am, unhappily, a journalist. So if I don't find a note from you that will justify me in waiting on her here…on the 27th…Aff'ly yours, Henry Fothergill Chorley

Mendelssohn replied that he could not wait for him in Frankfurt because of homesickness and commented that he liked Lind better at the piano than on the stage and concert room and hoped that Chorley would like her as much as he did "which [was] a great deal."

---

In September Lind mused in a letter to Josephson,

I would like to live a simple life…and help poor people as much as I can…I will never change my present life, you are to know that, in case you hear about my many suitors now and then. Nothing but lies! I am too happy to desire to exchange my present status with another. Up to this point my career has been the loveliest one could imagine, and I praise Germany greatly for this.

She was still agonizing: should she or should she not go to England? And once again she asked Mendelssohn for advice. This time he replied more briefly. First he said that if she wished to do him a great favor, she would sing one of his songs for Chorley. "I believe he is going to Frankfurt solely for this reason, so that I really have no choice but to come to you with this new request." Then he responded to her request for advice:

> I have so much to say about England and your trip there that I really don't know what I should write. In any case, everything depends on the way you establish yourself; for you have the whole thing entirely in your own hands, and English music lovers are looking forward to your coming and are speaking about you in terms that please me greatly, and that happens very seldom. So you can manage it exactly as you want to...Till we meet again, merry, happy and unchanged, Felix Mendelssohn Bartholdy

In the same month, the journalist Dr. Alfred Becher asked Mendelssohn whether he could and wished to conduct *Elijah,* with a cast of about a thousand performers, at the riding school in Vienna in November. He mentioned possible sopranos they might pursue: "Then we would have to think about the solo parts. I wonder if Meyer would be inclined to accept if we invited her, or very confidentially, would the incomparably glorious Lind take part in it, in case the contract with Pokorny allows it?"

Mendelssohn replied that he would have greatly enjoyed conducting the German premiere of *Elijah* in Vienna if they had invited him three weeks earlier but that it was impossible to print the scores with German texts in time. He did not mention Lind.

---

In September of 1846 Lind instructed Judge Munthe to invalidate the will in which she left everything to her parents. According to the new will, her parents would receive no more than they absolutely needed.

In the same month Louise Johansson commented in her diary, "The thought that she will die before she returns to her fatherland is firmly entrenched in Jenny's mind." Louise also noted that Jenny now brought her food and was kind to her in other ways, and she mused about her mixed feelings toward her mistress:

Jenny hugged me and brought me presents. She is so tenderly concerned about me and she does not become silent for many days…I will recover if this continues, for my illness in summer was a result of Jenny's hardness towards me. Oh, how lovely life is when one is treated so heartily by someone whom one loves with all one's heart as I have loved Jenny since her earliest childhood. Jenny always has the right to do what she wants; she can, for example, eat without criticism. I have to hear that I eat too much. Jenny can work as much or as little as she wishes, but when I sometimes sit and sew, Jenny becomes angry. *Jo*…she can do what she wants and feel totally free, whereas I feel imprisoned within four walls in a foreign land. *Ach*, she has never felt what it means when one is dependent for everything.

---

In a letter to Klingemann at the beginning of October, Mendelssohn deplored the fact that he probably would not be able to see or hear Lind before the next spring or fall. He then described his pleasant home life. And he told how his oldest sons, aged eight-and-a-half and almost six, had delighted him and Cécile:

My two boys, Carl and Paul, sat together at the table today and spoke with pathos, and Carl suddenly got the idea to improvise a poem in the most sublime tone, "The moon, it shone in the nightly night," to which Paul added, "And brought everyone his love aright." The rest of the poem was never finished because we almost burst with laughter. And yesterday I got out my paints for the first time in one-and-one-half years and painted a speckled blue sky.

---

After Chorley heard Lind sing in Frankfurt, he sent a report to Mrs. Grote:

(Frankfurt) 4 October 1846
…And now let me tell you how thoroughly, with my whole heart, I like her as a singer; more by twenty times than I had expected. The only fault I can find…is that she is too fond of using all her powers, the end of which is a feeling of heaviness, the one tinge of Germanism that remains about her style…I was really delighted to find that I am not past the old

thrill or the old beating of the heart, and that I could not go to bed till I had written a note (in horrible French) to say "Thank you."

On the same day Chorley wrote to Mendelssohn,

After a fear of disappointment, I hardly know how to describe, I laughed and cried like a child again, with a sort of pleasure which reconciles to long dreary intermediate places of existence, when I begin sometimes to fancy I can hardly be human, so hard…so unkind to the world!
I heard the lady in *La Fille du Regiment,* shall stay for her *La Sonnambula* and *La Vestale*…I have seen her too, twice, but having here no matrons to vouch for my "pristine purity," we are obliged to be ceremonious, that I sit on the edge of my chair and make speeches and visits ten minutes long, when I should like to stay as many hours…She says *she will not* come to London.

———————————

In London Benjamin Lumley, lessee of Her Majesty's Theater since 1841, was near bankruptcy. He had lost the director, Michael da Costa,[3] and most of his best singers to the rival opera house, Covent Garden, of which Alfred Bunn was the lessee. Only Luigi Lablache, who was generally described as the "finest, most beautiful, powerful" basso of the century, remained with Lumley.

Lumley had invited Lind to sing in Her Majesty's Theater, but she had adamantly refused his offer, even after he promised to take responsibility for any legal damages arising from the Bunn affair. She told him to go to Italy for singers; she would not go to London. However, Lumley knew where to go for help. He went to Leipzig, told Mendelssohn about his plight and plans, and hand delivered a letter from Lind.

The next day, October 6, on her twenty-sixth birthday, Lind wrote to Mme. Birch-Pfeiffer that she would be ready to leave the stage in six months, but that Lumley still hoped to "get her," and if she should hear that she had *really* gone mad, she would probably be on her way to London.

———————————

Moscheles went to Germany in October, stopped in Frankfurt to hear Lind for the first time, and offered his impressions of her art to Mendelssohn:

October 12

I heard Lind here in *Sonnambula*, *La Vestale* and *La Fille du Regiment*
and am completely enchanted by her. Many here want to put a damper
on their enthusiasm by saying that her voice is veiled and too weak for
some roles, but I see her greatness as lying in her emotional, sensitive
performance. I can well imagine how the impression of her glorious
talent influenced yours when you accompanied her at the Aachen music
festival. Many people have told me about this.

From Naples, on the same day, Lablache wrote to Lumley—and later also
to Lind—about her dilemma. He asked him to convince Lind that she would
be with "brothers and friends" in London, and not with intriguing artists, and
offered to help in any way that he could.

On the same day, a week after Lumley delivered the letter from Lind,
Mendelssohn replied with a letter of almost 1,200 words:

Leipzig, 12 October 1846
*Mein liebes Fräulein,*
I had intended to write to you on the day your first letter arrived, but
a few hours afterwards your second letter came, and Mr. Lumley, who
brought it. All that he said to me, and all that passed through my mind
in connection with it, and the different thoughts that went through my
mind made it impossible to write to you until today; and I told Mr.
Lumley that if he would come here again after his journey to Berlin, I
would carefully think it all over in the meantime, and would then tell
him whether I could advise you to go to London or not. He seems to
set great store upon that, that is, on my advice, and I already told you
in my former letter that the whole success of his undertaking depends
on your coming…I can only repeat what I wrote before—I would like
you to arrange, as far as is humanly possible, *as completely as you can*, for
your own comfort, and when that has all been settled, I would like you
to go there.

He continued by saying that he would have "strongly urged" Lumley to
"speak clearly and precisely" about money matters, because she "could, and ought
to make the kinds of terms" that no one else could, but that he did not have the
courage to do that, "not even for [her]." He then did his best to encourage her:

You will certainly meet with such a reception there that you will be able to think of it with pleasure for the rest of your life. I believe that once the English take a liking to someone, there are no people more friendly, more cordial and more constant; and you will experience that feeling there. For as I told you before, I have noticed that they entertain this genuine feeling there, not only about your singing, but also about your personality and your whole being, and they set even more store on the latter than upon the singing itself; and that is how it should be. In my opinion, therefore, I do not for a moment doubt that you will be received there as you deserve, more warmly, enthusiastically and heartily, perhaps, than in all your previous experiences…Therefore you will make your friends very happy if you go there; and I, for my part, should be very glad if you would go.

He urged her to insist upon "all possible conditions that could make matters agreeable for [her]" and again assured her that going to London and singing there would be "nothing but pleasant." Then he became more personal:

I'm selfish, too, in my counsel; for I hope that we shall meet there in this world again. When I was still in England I had half promised to return there next April; had I only known that you would be there at that time, or would be going there, you can imagine how much more willingly I would have settled it…

Lumley is hoping to procure a libretto soon…God grant that the results will be good…But apart from all this, I hope to visit London again next spring, and what a pleasure it will be for me to witness the most brilliant and hearty reception that can possibly happen to an artist!

He asked Lind to immediately reply in detail to his letter.

Would Lablache's encouragement and Mendelssohn's powers of persuasion be great enough to dispel Lind's fears of prison?

---

1. Josef Staudigl, 1807–61, studied philosophy, then noviced in the monastery in Melk, played oboe and guitar and sang bass and studied medicine in Vienna. When Count Gallenberg took over the court opera, Staudigl received a place in the chorus, then minor roles, and soon all major bass roles. He had no equal as oratorio singer. His voice failed in 1855; he died in a psychiatric hospital.

2. Cécile's letters to Felix in August and September of 1846 are missing from the "green books."
3. Sir Michael da Costa, born in Naples in 1804, went to London in 1835.

LIND VACILLATES

# nineteen

LUMLEY PERSONALLY DELIVERED MENDELSSOHN'S LETTER TO LIND IN DARMSTADT. A few hours after she read it, on the evening of the 17th of October 1846, in the presence of Lumley and Herr Buettner, Lind signed a contract for triple the remuneration Bunn had offered her. She was to sing eight times that summer for £4,800. Lumley was ecstatic:

17 October 1846
Dear Mr. Mendelssohn,
I am delighted to tell you that your letter has had its effect, and that the lady signed an engagement. Your letter charmed her so much. It was a most pleasing picture—her countenance, when reading it. No sun could have infused more joy into a beautiful landscape than your letter did on her...
I have prepared the engagement wholly in her favor; but I proposed to her to add anything else that you might think advisable, and I added a clause to that effect. She would not enter into the question of money; but I am quite sure you will be satisfied that I have done everything right in that way...

I need not tell you how truly grateful I am to you…I look upon the Engagement of Lind as a new era in the progress of Art in England. Her success will be transcendent. Independently of her great genius, she has that purity and chastity of manner which none but a really good person can possess. And which, in England, will gain her partisans on all sides…

My joy on the completion of the affair is not unsullied. I am fearful that she may, for a time at least, tease herself with fears…that may torment her…I entreat you to assure her of the absolute certainty of her great success, to give her encouragement.

Ten days later, Lind informed Amalia Wichmann that she was going to London and that "Mendelssohn alone" had been able to persuade her to do so. She also mentioned her hosts in Munich:

I'm living with the Kaulbachs, and am getting on well here. He is a dear, dear man, and his wife is very kind. I have lighted upon the best house in Munich, just as I did in Berlin. Besides this, things are fine with me here, as everywhere. I'm beginning to get used to it, although I cannot conceive what it is that pleases the people. But that's God's doing.

---

Louise noted that in September and October of 1846, Jenny had been calm and collected, but that in November she had become restless again and often imagined that she would die before she went home to Sweden again. Louise confided to her diary about Lind's moods:

Once when I said something inappropriate about a person, Jenny's mood immediately changed. She said a number of unkind things; for instance, she told me I was like her mother. *Jo*, it is my opinion that Jenny is to be pitied in many aspects, despite all her fame and brilliance. She is independent and takes advantage of that with the help of God, but she is lacking the most noble characteristics, regarding a calm spirit and devout religiosity, to spread calm and peace among her associates. I must learn to accept being suppressed; Jenny is and remains hard towards me. God, give me strength to bear this hardness.

In Berlin, Fanny expressed her melancholy in a letter to her famous brother:

26 October 1846

...It seems that your coming here is quite uncertain, and I am very sad about this. *Ja,* if only our lives wouldn't end this way, one year following another, without enjoying one another. It's now almost nine months since we have seen one another. It's sad...

You'll find Beckchen changed very much to her advantage; don't stay away too long, so that the winter won't have taken hold of her in the meantime. When I think of the wretched sad time we had to suffer last year, I cannot thank God enough that she has improved beyond all expectations.[1]

Farewell, *mein lieber, lieber* Felix, that's the only thing that sometimes makes me feel sad that we live so far apart, and hear so little from or about you.

The greater part of Felix's immediate response reflects his negative feelings as well:

Leipzig, 28 October 1846
*Meine liebe Schwester,*

A thousand thanks for the songs, the grapes, and all the goodness in today's letter! But I'm so torn by all kinds of people (dear and not dear) who want something from me or to do something with me, that only the positive question in today's letter immediately causes me to write. I should have expressed my thanks for so much kindness much earlier, but why do the dear neighbors take up so incredibly much time and state of mind!

*Ja,* and why are we not living together, as you say. But I am not without the hope that perhaps in several years we will again live together...

Isn't this a miserable letter?...But that is the way it looks in my head, and in addition I have had a toothache for several days, and Mme. Jeanrenaud is melancholy because she must soon leave, and still has no good opportunity, and because the weather is becoming so bad, and poor Johann has been ill below for four weeks...and who knows how long it will last, and visitors don't have to concern themselves about all this, but only want to sing or play in a subscription concert, or want their compositions looked at, or want only a few opinions or Thaler or letters of recommendation or to remain here a few hours, "cannot do otherwise."

Two days later Mendelssohn requested that the Gewandhaus board relieve him of solo performances because, he explained, he was so exhausted after every performance that he was unable to compose. However, he promised to take part in quartet evenings.

On the last day of October, after Mendelssohn had pored over Lind's signed contract, he replied in a letter of almost 1,700 words. First he stated that he regarded himself as the "most stupid person possible" when it came to contracts and legal matters, and that at first he had wanted to show it to someone conversant with legal matters but had decided against that. He assured her once more that both as a musician and a person, she would be received in England with the "kind of love and jubilation and delight" that even *she* had perhaps never experienced before and that she would have "warmer friends, greater triumphs, and a more heartfelt reception."

He then commented on the contract point by point. He did not agree with the length of her engagement and the number of times she would sing each month, or the financial terms; but because she had signed, he argued, that could not be changed. However, he opined that singing in England would be much more pleasant and less difficult than in Germany.

He also voiced his objection to her plans to go to Italy to study the Italian language, and disagreed with a clause that stipulated that she could not sing in "particular concerts," because "particular" could be made to extend to the queen. Striking the two words would create difficulties because she had "sanctioned them with her signature," he continued. But since he strongly disapproved of their intent and was allowed to *add* conditions, he wrote a new paragraph that, he hoped, would become a part of the contract. According to the new addition, she would be allowed to sing for non-paying guests in "particular apartments."

He sent the same paragraph to Lumley and urged him to make it a part of the contract. At the same time he entreated him once more to obtain a libretto.

At the end of his letter to Lind, he wrote more personally,

I would certainly be glad if…I could soon write something dramatic—and especially for you. I assure you that I will neglect nothing whatever in that regard. For I have always wanted to write dramatic music, but now, more than ever. And then I have a secret foreboding that tells me that if I don't succeed in composing some kind of decent opera *now* and *for you,* I probably never shall. But on that point again, I entertain a real Turkish fatalism—that if it doesn't happen, it never was meant to happen…and so I shall be content if we meet again in this life, be it with or without the opera. But in the final analysis it is you I think of first, and only much, much later of the singer you are; and I believe you do the same in regard to me.

He ended the letter with the sentence *"Bleiben Sie mir gut,* and I will remain your friend for the rest of my life."[2]

On the same day Felix wrote a birthday letter to his brother. Paul had managed Felix's business affairs for years, and in the last several years he had also more and more become his confidant. At times their roles were almost like those of father and son, with the younger man taking on the role of the father. Except for good wishes, Felix's letter to Paul is largely an expression of bitterness and sadness, particularly about his beloved fatherland, where, he wrote, "mediocrity, even worse, such tasteless superficiality is so rampant and where honest, able, true words are so seldom heard." And he complained again about callers:

I have never yet encountered so many strangers, inquiries, unreasonable demands—and almost all so fruitless, and many so modest, and many so immodest, ever so many singers, instrumentalists, composers, and almost none even mediocre, and yet full of the greatest words, full of national consciousness certainly not striving for the highest—but demands of the highest kind. And in contrast, the impossibility of fulfilling even one demand with a good conscience, or to recommend.

He continued by saying that he no longer wished to have public duties; what he desired was to live with his brother and to compose. When he wrote to Paul again a few days later, he said that a passage in Jean Paul's *Flegeljahre*[3] had now become clear to him, that he could have only one twin brother, and that Paul was that twin brother.

Mme. Arnemann informed Mendelssohn at the beginning of November about Lind's whereabouts and activities and expressed the hope that he would go to London via Nienstaedten in spring, that such a little detour would provide "lovely moments with Jenny."

Felix and Cécile spent several days in Dresden in November. Devrient, now a theater director there, saw Felix frequently, and he, as well as Felix's other friends, were struck by the composer's great irritability. Mendelssohn remained in Dresden long enough to hear Wagner's new opera, *Tannhäuser*. Hans von Buelow, a virtual Wagner worshiper and not an admirer of Mendelssohn at the time, described his impression of how the latter responded to the opera:

> By means of his heartfelt words that he directed to Wagner with evident emotion after the performance of *Tannhäuser* in Dresden, Mendelssohn has completely cleansed himself of the sad blemish[4] which was boundlessly unedifying, and during which the conductor had an ill-humored expression.

Mendelssohn's valet, Johann Krebs, who was almost like a member of the Mendelssohn family,[5] had been bedridden for almost two months and died one day after the composer returned from Dresden. On the morning after Johann's death, Felix wrote to Paul,

> It has hit us very hard; such a good, faithful and upright soul is something wonderful, the body being housed in whichever class it may be…He spoke absolutely cheerfully and optimistically and courageously to everyone *the whole two months,* and spoke the same way and acted the same way five minutes before his death.

Near the end Mendelssohn fashioned a sentence in his trademark prose: "And now thank you for your thanks in your letter in which you thanked me for giving thanks that you were born!" He asked Paul to send two thaler per month from his account, beginning January 1, 1847, to Johann's widowed mother.

At the beginning of December, Mendelssohn thanked Klingemann for his wonderful letter and paid him the ultimate compliment by quoting from Jean

Paul's book: "'Men can have only one friend, says Montaigne, said Vult,' thus it is written in *Flegeljahre*. And I said it with all my heart when I received your letter, my only friend."

That ended the positive part of the letter; he continued with one of his strongest complaints about the public life of a musician:

> Conducting, and even playing (actually everything and every official public appearance), has become downright odious to me, so that each time I can make up my mind to do it only with aversion and reluctance. I believe the time is coming, or is perhaps already here, when I will give up this kind of public regular music making in order to make music at home, to compose, and allow things to go their own way out there.

He said that he thought he would definitely go to London for a few weeks in April, this time not without Cécile.

Because, after several weeks, Felix still had not been able to shake off his sadness about Johann's death, Cécile suggested that because there was nothing in Leipzig to distract him, he should go to Berlin. He took her advice, stayed with Fanny for almost a week, and looked for a new valet.

How different his time in Berlin was, how tranquil in comparison to the time in the fall of 1845 and the early spring of 1846. Now he stayed at home all morning and played and sang with his sister.

And he rejoiced with Paul and Albertine when, during that time, they became parents of their third child, their first son.

---

Despite Cécile's fears, Felix returned to Leipzig in time for Christmas. On the 27th she wrote to her mother about the gifts she and Felix had exchanged, among them a "wonderful" velour coat "too beautiful to wear in Leipzig," and a "bagatelle" she had painted.

Felix heartily thanked his mother-in-law for the copper etching of a "favorite Rafael painting" she had sent him for Christmas. And he complimented her just as heartily:

> There is something special about mothers and grandmothers...no one else is able to give pleasure and to make life so nice—quite apart from the fact that they have given it to us—and when Cécile says "*der Mutter*"

I have such a strange feeling, as if I can feel more at home in the world because she can speak to "*der Mutter.*"

He then composed a paragraph calculated to make her happy:

I wish we would see one another often, and I am making arrangements so that it can occur, God willing. First of all I hope to travel through Frankfurt with man and mouse (Cécile is the man, and the mouse is the five mice) and have a nice time of rest there…Cécile and I are very fond of our travel plans and we speak about them every day. But still dearer to our hearts is the wish to have a very, very little house on the Rhine, to move there every spring…to have done with all directing, public performances and whatever the stuff [*Kram*] is called. I am heartily tired of the good and bad aspects, and think of the winter in Frankfurt, which despite little Felix's illness, was so lovely and happy and unforgettable.

---

Hauser had by now assumed his new position as conservatory director in Munich and could send news about Lind to Mendelssohn:

Munich, 29 December 1846
…I didn't receive *Antigone* from the Augsburg choral society, [so] the Munich choral society members wanted to buy the score themselves, and they can do that now. By means of Lind's boundless kindness, they took in more than 3,000 Fl. from the three concerts in which she sang. The dear soul left us yesterday morning, to everyone's regret…
I've tried to talk her out of the trip to Italy—I regard this trip not only as useless, but also highly dangerous. How triumphant the stupid, coarse Italians would feel! If she doesn't go, everyone will presume that she has no need to go and possesses all the qualities and dexterity that she needs for Italian opera.

He asked his friend to persuade Lind not to go to Italy, because "once she gets something into her head, it's hard to get it out unless one simply absolutely insists." Finally he described the effect that her singing had in Munich:

The girl…sang the role of Susanna for the first time, and one couldn't imagine anything lovelier and more charming. I wish you had heard her sing the passage, *Komm du mein Trauter, daß ich Dich kränze mit Rosen* [Come, my beloved, so I can bedeck you with roses]. She looked like an angel and nothing could possibly have been lovelier; for me, it was the most beautiful thing I have ever known.

Moreover, the people of Munich didn't conduct themselves badly either; the orchestra was maddest of all. For instance, she never came to the theater for rehearsals without being received with shouts and fanfare and applause.

He wrote nothing about the Kaulbachs or about the reception that *Frau* Kaulbach hosted for the singer after a performance of *Der Freischütz*. The artist Wilhelm Kaulbach had formed a negative impression of Lind even before he met her, because when she arrived at their home, the horses that pulled her big custom-built carriage had trampled on the carefully tended flowers and neat paths in front of the house.

Kaulbach's daughter described the two artists and the reception:

Jenny Lind was amiable to the highest degree, but was also a moody and spoiled artist, and was affected by her moods even more than my father. Mother must have gone through many a disagreeable hour because both artists were always in opposite moods: if one was out of sorts, the other was in a good mood; if one wished to be alone, the other wished to be sociable.

The high point of these extremes occurred on the lovely evening when Jenny Lind sang Annchen [*sic*] in *Freischütz*. During the performance she had the misfortune to lose her shoe; as a result, she lost her stage presence, and that affected the audience. The rapport between stage and listeners was gone, and the expected success did not materialize.

But Mother had invited a great many guests, and everyone was anxiously waiting with bated breath to see the famous singer face to face. But this did not occur. She locked herself in her room and answered to no knocking or calling. Father, who was angry at this lack of consideration, locked the door and left the surprised guests with Mother, who took pleasure in telling him the next morning how extraordinarily well things had gone, and how lively the evening had become.

---

Because Lumley fervently hoped that Mendelssohn would write an opera especially for Lind to perform in his theater, he had traveled to Milan to commission Scribe to write an outline of a libretto. The impresario believed Shakespeare's *The Tempest* was the perfect vehicle for Lind, as she could, he wrote, "so beautifully describe the gentleness, sentiment, naïveté, surprise, affection, and anxiety." He envisioned the stellar cast—Lind as Miranda, Lablache as Caliban, and Staudigl as Fernando. Mendelssohn replied that he would put all others matters aside in order to complete the opera for the following spring.

---

1. Rebecka had been severely depressed for most of the previous winter.
2. *Bleiben Sie mir gut* can be translated as "Remain kindly disposed to me" or something more affectionate, such as "Continue to love me." In their two volumes about Lind's career, Holland and Rockstro did not include that sentence, nor the previous one.
3. Jean Paul Richter's *Flegeljahre* (*Adolescent Years*) was a best seller at the beginning of the nineteenth century.
4. By the "sad blemish" Buelow referred to what he perceived to be Mendelssohn's negative expression and manner of conducting when he conducted the prelude to *Tannhäuser* in Leipzig earlier. Wagner later wrote, "All that Mendelssohn could find to praise in *Tannhäuser* was the canonic imitation at the end of the opera."
5. Doctors did not normally make house calls to see servants but came at Mendelssohn's insistence. And throughout the months of Johann's illness, Mendelssohn went downstairs whenever he rang, either to read to him or to patiently answer his countless questions about household matters.

# t w e n t y

NOT CONTENT WITH HIS TEACHING POSITION AT THE MILITARY ACADEMY IN
Berlin, and unhappy with the political situation in Prussia, Rebecka's husband,
Peter Gustav Dirichlet, considered accepting an invitation from Heidelberg
University. Neither his wife nor her siblings wished the strong family ties to
be broken, and at the beginning of 1847 Felix implored Dirichlet to remain in
Berlin:

> I'm asking for my sake also; for I now have decided to go to Berlin
> for the winter…I preferred a residence in a smaller town…and yet I
> now feel compelled to leave it, to rejoin those with whom I enjoyed
> my childhood and youth, and whose memories and friendships and
> experiences are the same as my own. My plan is that we should form one
> pleasant united household all together…and live happily together…for
> I consider it the greatest possible good fortune that could ever befall me,
> so don't frustrate all this with one blow, but remain in Berlin, and let us
> be together there.

Rebecka immediately expressed her misgivings:

Berlin, 8 January 1847

…Hensels are thinking of Italy…You want to buy a house on the Rhine in a few years and will probably stay there for most of the year; you will often have work on the estate, making alterations, supervising; so it could often happen that you would have to remain nearby, and that it will become troublesome for Cécile to travel every year, as it has been for *Tante* Hinny for a long time already, who travels with eight carriages— without children. Mme. Jeanrenaud will also do her part to keep you there during the winter every now and then; it has become known that you don't wish to have a permanent position, and you will receive offers of guest appearances from all the big cities, which you will not always be able to refuse. In short, it appears to me that having two places of residence would not be at all feasible for you…and since your estate would be the principal residence, the second would come out second best. Paul, who is also not enchanted with Berlin, says that if you come, he would stay…That also is only an "if." So it could happen that we would be the only ones remaining in Berlin, when it's becoming more expensive every day, when Dirichlet's difficult job robs him of time and energy. Those are the charms of Berlin without siblings.

The tension regarding Dirichlet's future dissipated in February. His salary at the military academy was increased, but what made him particularly happy was the respect and affection his friends and colleagues showed him.

———

Jenny Lind returned to Vienna on New Year's Eve to prepare for her second set of guest appearances at the Theater an der Wien. That evening she went to Jaegers and danced until two o'clock in the morning. A few days later she wrote to Josephson, "A new year, thank God. Now I can only wait with dreadful impatience for my liberation from this difficult, wearisome way of life. I will leave the stage in August and return to Sweden in September; perhaps we can go together."

On the 7th of January she opened her second season in Vienna with Donizetti's *La Figlia del Reggimento.*

———

Clara Schumann was giving concerts in Vienna at the time, and she and Robert called on Lind. As soon as Clara spoke of her concerts, Lind offered to sing in the next one; it was her "obligation and an honor" to do so, she said. Clara was delighted, as attendance and proceeds of her earlier three concerts had been very poor. In fact, at the third concert the proceeds had not covered the costs.

A few days later Lind sang a few songs at Clara's last concert. It changed the pianist's fortune, but it was not without a troubling aspect, as the pianist noted:

> I gave my fourth and last concert, which was packed to the rafters, so that many people could not get seats at all. Jenny Lind sang wonderfully. The concert was the best and most brilliant that I have given and paid for our whole trip, and we could even bring 300 Thaler to Dresden. And yet it belongs to one of my saddest memories...I could not rid myself of the most bitter feeling that with one song, Lind accomplished what I could not have accomplished with all my playing. Nevertheless, I was enchanted by Jenny Lind's performance of the songs, especially "Auf Flügeln" by Mendelssohn. I have never heard the song sung so well; here there was a twofold influence, for as I have seen from all her utterances about Mendelssohn, she loves him not less as a man than as a composer.

After the Schumann couple paid a long visit to Lind the following day, Clara made another diary entry:

> I am so fond of her. To me she is the warmest, noblest being I have yet found among *artistes*—and how can I ever forget her? One must know her and know her thoroughly to love her as I do...She made me promise that I would stay with her when I came to Stockholm and that I wouldn't go unless she was there herself, so that she might take part in my concerts.

Robert Schumann also made some comments about Lind in their common diary:

> I will never forget the rehearsal preceding the concert...this simple, clear, natural and deepest understanding of music and text at the first reading of a composition that I have never met before in such perfection. She

shared with Clara—with whom she was very pleased, just as Clara raves and glows about her—a number of things about herself and her inmost being. We also spoke a great deal about Mendelssohn, "the purest and finest of all the artists" she calls him and said that she thanked God that He brought this artist into her life; she mentioned that this might be the last time she would sing in Germany before she went back to Sweden permanently, but no sea was so wide as to prevent her from hearing Mendelssohn again. She showered us with apples and sweets for the children when she left; we parted from her as if we had encountered a divine visitation, she was so lovely and gentle.

Schumann also expressed his delight at the way she sang his songs in Clara's concert. And he opined that Cécile curbed Mendelssohn's imagination, whereas Lind "rejuvenated and inspired" him.

Lind, meanwhile, created problems for Pokorny, causing Mme. Birch-Pfeiffer to write a frantic letter to Mendelssohn. The Viennese opera director had informed her that after singing only once, Jenny had declared she would not sing until Tichatschek came, and that after he came, she offered other pretexts for not singing. Birch-Pfeiffer also stated that people were saying that Jenny wasn't content with her honorarium and had spoken about going to Pesth to sing. She believed that Jenny was hurting both the director and herself and was ruining her reputation. She begged Mendelssohn to rectify the situation; she was sure, she said, that a few lines from him would suffice. But by the time Mendelssohn received Mme. Birch-Pfeiffer's letter, Lind had already sung several more times.

———————————————

As soon as Mendelssohn heard that a dear friend in England, Mrs. Fanny Thompson, the former Fanny Horsley, was seriously ill, he took the time, as he frequently did when friends were ill or dejected, to write her a long, cheerful letter:

Leipzig, 19 January 1847
My dear, dear friend,
...I have two special subjects about which I want to write to you...I can, in fact, announce to you one of the most glorious works of art ever achieved by the brush (I am the brush!), a landscape that I have painted for you, and which is so beautiful that one might take the

earth for heaven, and the reverse. My own composition—an imaginary convent in cheerful early dawn; a cloudless heaven, some bushes, some distant mountains (wretchedly colored); an impenetrable wood (too green), a ruin (too brown), a cross beside a pathway…But don't lose this description, otherwise you might be unable to guess what it represents. I wanted first to announce this picture, and then something even better— namely Jenny Lind. You showed so much interest in her before, and wished so much to make her acquaintance, that I decided to write to you as soon as it was decided that she would come to London…Now, however, I am too late, as I hear it is generally known, but this you do not yet know, that I have made it a condition that she should not be in London long before going to Seymour Street and singing all her songs for you…I don't in the least doubt that she…will call as soon as she arrives…It isn't certain yet that I will come to London this spring, but I wish it very much…Cécile would certainly come too, and then you must invite us and the Klingemanns and Jenny Lind.

To this letter, Fanny replied,

I thank you about Jenny Lind and for the landscape which I long for and look for eagerly. The state of musical excitement just now in London baffles all description, and as Benedict is friendly with both sides, I have, while there of an evening, been much amused by listening to contrary statements. However, so as you and dearest Cécile do not disappoint us, I care for…comparatively nothing, for in that sweeping assertion, I cannot include Jenny Lind. I trust she will not be frightened away by the continued wickedness of Lumley and Bunn, but until she arrives I shall not confidently reckon on her…Ever your most sincere, affectionate friend, Fanny

At the end of January Felix composed a canon for his brother to the words "Gott fürchten ist Weisheit" (To fear God is wisdom).

As a birthday present for Felix, Mme. Jeanrenaud sent him a little album that she had filled with pictures and mementos of Cécile. He thanked her the next day:

*Liebe Mama,*

You must know what an extraordinarily great pleasure your present, which I received yesterday, gave me. How often, since yesterday, I have opened the little book and have been uplifted again and again by Cécile's face as a child, which is just the same as it is today, and yet quite different; and I like the landscape of Lyons so much, as well as Cécile's amusing drawing attempts and her sister's wedding poem, and the whole book speaks to me so clearly of your love and goodness. 1,000 thanks, *meine liebe, gute Mama.* I hope that you thought kindly about me once yesterday, as I did of you all day with the deepest and most sincere gratitude, you who have given me so much happiness!

Before Robert and Clara Schumann left Vienna in January, Lind asked them if they had friends in Berlin. When it appeared that they did not, she sent a letter of introduction of the couple to Mme. Wichmann and asked her to be hospitable to them. In the same letter she expressed her almost boundless longing for a calm life. No mortal, she sighed, could be happier than she when she would be free.

On the same day she wrote another letter to Mendelssohn, which the Schumanns were to deliver personally. However, eleven days before he received her letter, Mendelssohn assured Klingemann that he would not come to England without Cécile this time. And without any details, he mentioned the distress Schumann had recently caused him in Berlin, and perhaps also in Dresden:

I won't be able to send along a letter for you with *Frau* Schumann. Her husband has behaved in an ambiguous way, or worse, toward me, and has stirred up a real hornet's nest for me, which has caused my previous zeal to help him and do him favors to become damned cool. More verbally if it's worth the effort to you.

Almost a week later Mendelssohn heard from Schumann:

Dresden, 5 February 1847
*Lieber* Mendelssohn,
I'm coming to Leipzig on a flying trip on Monday and would very much like to talk to you. We also have a letter for you from someone whom we have seen quite often, and who raves about you, and of whom you also are very fond. Can you guess? If you're free on Monday evening, don't

write anything, then we'll come at eight o'clock in the evening. If you aren't free then, send us a line at the Hotel de Bavière on Monday. (We will also talk about the Babylonian state of affairs in Vienna.)

Schumann went to Leipzig three days later and delivered Lind's letter to Mendelssohn.

On the same day Paul and Albertine celebrated the baptism of their first son, Moses Ernst Felix, without Felix, despite the fact that Paul had written "Come" eleven times in his invitation.

-----

Even though Lind knew that she might meet Mendelssohn in England in spring, her inordinate fear about going to that country was again gaining the upper hand because of Bunn's threats. During the week when she did not perform, because *Vielka*—formerly called *Das Feldlager in Schlesien*—had to be postponed, she wrote to Mme. Wichmann,

13 February 1847
Dearly beloved,
…What can you be thinking! I going to Paris! Never as long as I live. Who could have told you that? And how could I have entertained such an idea without telling you? No, dearest Amalia, not only am I not going to Paris, but it seems as if I shall not even go to London. Bunn won't give up the contract, and I cannot go there…for he actually threatens to put me in prison!!! I tell you, Amalia, I should be wild with joy if I didn't have to go there. *Mein Gott!* Just suppose this happened! They have made me all kinds of offers from Paris;[1] but I didn't have to give it a moment's thought. *I am going to leave the stage* and then I shall want for nothing else in the world…Today is one of those days, my beloved Amalia, when I feel so lonely in this world without a protector to whom I can turn and see my own love returned in loving glances. O, the pure love between husband and wife is, after all—it must be—the most sublime feeling and a real necessity for us human beings. I have a loving soul. I should like very much to make someone happy. For I feel within myself the power to do so. But where does one find the right man?

By this time Jenny's expression of her desire for marriage and home life had become a constant refrain. In the same week Louise commented in her diary,

> But these eight days were not good. Jenny had time to think stupid thoughts that prevented her from sleeping and took away her appetite. She wants to get married. But where will she find a suitable man? There is no one. Perhaps she'll accept some devil-may-care tippler. Poor Jenny, who thinks about exchanging freedom for bondage, and in addition, an unfaithful man who will squander her money; she'll never find one with a character like Guenther's.

During the eight-day period when the Theater an der Wien staged no operas, Jenny and Louise went to the von Jaeger home almost every day. Another frequent guest there was Julius Pechwill; Louise disliked him intensely and let both parties know of her feelings. One day Jenny horrified Louise when she said she rather liked Herr Pechwill and thought he would be a good husband.

---

Mendelssohn completed his revision of *Elijah* in the middle of February. A few days later he replied to the letter from Lind that Schumann had delivered. This time he did not, as had become his custom, begin by expressing effusive thanks for the letter. And he merely alluded to what Schumann had done to anger him so much:

> Leipzig, 19 February 1847
> It's a long time since we have spoken to each other, *mein liebes Fräulein.* Some day I'll tell you in detail, by word of mouth, why I must begin my letter thus, and why my heart felt so heavy when Dr. Schumann brought me your letter—delayed since the 20th of last month. Before all else today, I have a favor to ask of you. You will think it a great bore; it is for that reason that I come down on it like a sledge hammer.

He asked to see the letter in which she said that Lumley was taking Bunn's contract wholly upon himself, because only then could he give her his opinion. If this vexed her, he continued, "I tell you that you yourself are to blame, since by telling me so much, you gave me the right to enquire further, in fact, made it my duty to do so."

Near the end he wrote less personally,

This letter is like a room in which there has been mayhem…It's very boring to pick things up and put them in their proper places. But it must be done, and only then can one again be comfortable there. Don't bore yourself too much with putting things in their places…I was at the Wichmann home again a few months ago and was very pleased with your portrait by Magnus, which is there now instead of you.

The ending of the letter is quite unlike those in all known earlier letters: "With a thousand greetings from Cécile and the children,[2] your friend, Felix Mendelssohn Bartholdy."

---

Edwin Hale Lewin responded to Mendelssohn's question about Lind's situation with Bunn, "The affair is a mere trifle, magnified to suit the purpose of the Covent Garden party." And he asked Mendelssohn to "throw [his] valuable influence into the scale to induce Miss L. to come to London without delay." He assured him that Mr. Lumley had undertaken every liability on behalf of her in the Bunn affair and she need have no fears.

---

Lind sang in the first performance of Meyerbeer's revised opera *Vielka* for the first time in Vienna on the 18th of January. Louise noted that she was so tired afterwards that she couldn't speak, more tired than she had ever seen her. Lind wrote to Hauser about the performance,

*Vielka* was finally produced two days ago. It was very well received and Meyerbeer received a stormy ovation…I was so afraid that I became very hoarse, and don't understand why I wasn't booed…At 10:30 the theater was almost completely full!!!! And so the people sat there for 13½ hours, O *Dieu!* I long so much for spring, and to leave the theater; this wish becomes stronger after every performance…
They're making such a fuss in London that I would rather do anything than go there. I want no part of the intrigues there; my talent cannot deal with that.

At the end of the month, without consulting anyone, Lind impulsively offered Bunn two thousand pounds if he would return the contract before she went to London. Bunn replied that he would return the contract for nothing if Lind would agree to sing in another season. So she asked Mendelssohn for advice again.

If he again advised her to go to London, would she heed his advice, only to renege again?

---

1. At another time she said, "What, me, with my potato nose, sing in Paris?" And when both Parisian opera houses offered her attractive contracts she replied, "I do not sing for immoral audiences."

2. This appears to be the first letter in which Mendelssohn conveyed greetings to Lind from Cécile.

# t w e n t y - o n e

In March 1847, Mendelssohn wrote to Dr. Heinrich Doerrien, chairman of the Gewandhaus board, about a decision he had made about the Gewandhaus concerts:

> *Hochgehrter Herr Regierungrath,*
> Although it's very difficult for me to write these lines, I cannot do otherwise than inform you…that I wish to resign from my position in [the Gewandhaus] concerts…and that I will henceforth do everything I can, without a binding relationship, to further its goals, and contribute to their realization with all my strength, whether here or far away.

In ten years he had elevated the ensemble to the finest of its kind on the continent.

———————————

In the winter Felix had made plans to conduct *Elijah* in London, Birmingham, and Manchester in the spring. The proceeds from the trip were to pay for an extended holiday in Switzerland with his and Paul's families. In one letter about the trip Felix wrote to Paul, "Above all, if only our wives will get along.[1] And we two also! Perhaps preventive measures can be put in place in advance. I long to see you soon. Keep your word, *Du guter Bruder.*"

The following week he wrote to Paul again:

Leipzig, 13 March 1847
I've never looked forward to the trip as much as I do now. I've been miserable the last fourteen days, I've had a cold and shoulder and back pains and all kinds of other pains, and in addition, I'm in a melancholy state as I always am immediately after the completion of a large composition...
But I'm thinking of the blue sea, of us there, and of the three crowns, one for Albertine, one for Cécile, and the third for the two of us, if we can wear them, if we can really manage things with bag and baggage, and in Vevay I will compose again, but above all, go for walks and breathe fresh air and live with you, *lieber Bruder.*
*Auf Wiedersehen, lieber Bruder, Dein* Felix

Mendelssohn hoped that Lind would sing in his *Elijah* in England and enquired of both his translator, William Bartholomew, and Klingemann if the performance could be postponed. To Klingemann he wrote,

Leipzig, March 10, 1847
But ask Buxton if the whole *Elijah* performance...could not be postponed until fall, when we would be sure of Staudigl, that I would be sure of having a vacation...and above all, that it would be certain that Jenny Lind was coming, and if Costa or Lumley will break their necks. I don't like a cock fight and will neither make bets nor wait to see how matters develop.

Bartholomew was indignant in his reply:

My dear sir...In reply I can give you 20 good reasons *why you should come* and *not one* why *you should not come*...Jenny Lind's and Staudigl's affairs are nothing to your *Elijah's*. If they manage them badly, is it a reason why you and your friends should manage yours badly too? Why does Staudigl not answer letters written to him weeks, nay months ago? Why did Jenny Lind sign a contract she cannot or will not fulfill? By the bye, if I see that matter rightly—she signed for the season 1845—that season is past—and Bunn cannot demand her services for another—this of 1847. He could only claim damages for non-performance in 1845, but never mind, return we to our mutton chops, if you please.

God bless you, dear sir,

W. Bartholomew

---

Meanwhile, Edwin Lewin arrived in Vienna as Lumley's envoy on the 8th of March. As soon as she saw him Lind was in a dreadful emotional state. She knew why he had come and could not rid herself of specters of prison. So Lewin did not even mention London.

Meanwhile, Mendelssohn replied to another letter from Lind:

Leipzig, 14 March 1847

*Mein liebes Fräulein,*

I'm sure you know how glad I am when I receive a letter from you. But your last one contained some things that make me feel very uncomfortable, or rather, the whole letter does. In one place you say that you are feeling sad and anxious and that you cannot sleep, and in addition to this, the letter seems agitated throughout. And this is what troubles me. That's why I'm writing you these few lines today…If you're still anxious and out of tune when this arrives, and if the English business is to blame for this, I beg you, *mein liebes Fräulein*, don't let your powers of reason, otherwise so clear and natural, be troubled by the dreadful outcry…and all the tumult and all the wretchedness. For after all, the great advantage of a good conscience…is that it's the one thing of which no one can rob us, and that under its guidance one is led through all the quarreling and fighting on the way, and unexpectedly attains one's goal.

He said he regretted that she had offered to pay Bunn two thousand pounds and wished she had not promised Lumley that she would go to England. But after all, he reminded her, he believed that she had wanted to "act correctly and honorably."

He assured her once again that she would have "warmer friends and a heartier welcome, and a greater triumph in England" than she had had elsewhere. He asked her do her duty and resign herself to the consequences. At the end, he wrote more personally again:

I'm very unselfish in advising you thus; for it appears very improbable to me that we shall meet in England. If I go there at all this year—which is still uncertain—I shall leave here at the beginning of April and remain there only until the beginning of May. And you will hardly be in London before the beginning of May? I had imagined it all so nicely to myself: to show you some of my favorite places and make you acquainted with two of my very special friends there. But if this may not be, we will meet again soon, somewhere or other; and I am confident that we shall meet again unchanged. Please let me soon know how you are, and whether you can place confidence in me and can drive away the anxiety, and bear in remembrance your friend, Felix Mendelssohn Bartholdy.

Two days after Mendelssohn wrote to Lind, while Lewin, Lind, and Louise enjoyed a leisurely carriage ride in the country, Lewin mentioned London. That caused Lind to let forth such a barrage of sharp words that he became mute and had to blink away tears. It was better in the early evening, yet later Lind was so out of sorts that she slapped Louise on the head. Lewin did not mention London to Lind again but urged Lumley to come to Vienna himself to try to persuade the "self-willed girl" to go to England.

The next day *The Times* in London published a letter by Bunn in which he stated that he was getting the best lawyers in Germany and England regarding his suit against Lind.

Lind sang in the last opera of the season at Theater an der Wien on the 25th of March. The next morning Louise began making preparations to leave, although neither she nor Lind knew where they would go. However, later on the same day Lind responded to a letter from Mme. Wichmann by saying that she *had* to go to London. She ended the letter with "God directs everything."

Meanwhile in London Lumley was desperate, as his theater was losing a great deal of money. Therefore on March 28th, the first day of the Easter recess, still in his evening dress, he left the opera house between acts in order to catch the Calais train. Four days later he arrived in Vienna to attempt to persuade Lind to come to London.

He could hardly believe his eyes when Lind met him with a smile and outstretched hands. Louise noted in her diary that day that Jenny was in a "brilliant" mood but failed to note the reason.

The next day, in the best of spirits, Lumley, Lind, and Lewin visited churches and went to Jaegers at noon.

On the same day Lind wrote to Pokorny,

Vienna, 2 April 1847
*Bester, guter Herr Direktor,*
I must again thank you heartily for all your kindness, and tell you that Vienna cost me bitter tears before I finally came, but that they were changed to laughter, for I will never stop thanking God for the rest of my life that all went so well here, and *never* will I forget how much I still have to do to be worthy of such acclaim!
My best thanks, *Herr Direktor! Leben Sie wohl...*and if you ever wish to use me on your stage, and conditions are right, count on your devoted Jenny Lind.

The next evening she and Louise went to Jaegers again, and Lewin and Lumley joined them at ten. Again Lind was in such an exuberant mood that she gave Louise some gulden.

---

Mendelssohn decided to go to England even though Lind would not be singing in his *Elijah*. When Schumann stopped in Leipzig at the end of March to see Mendelssohn, he made note of the fact that he was "struck by Mendelssohn's appearance."

Felix felt the need to talk privately to his brother, Paul, and two weeks before he was to leave for his trip to England, he sent a short note to him: "Since it's not permissible to travel on Palm Sunday but is impossible any other way, I'll come alone on the first train next Sunday and will return on the first train on Tuesday."

That is what he did, and on Good Friday, four days after his return to Leipzig, he conducted his oratorio *Paulus*. Although he had not expected good results, the performance went quite well. On Easter Sunday Cécile's sister Julie sent him a note from her mother-in-law's home in Dresden: "*Paulus* inspired me more than many a sermon—if only the English papers didn't have so much about Lind and you, or we will burst of envy."

The next day Mendelssohn finally found time to compose a long letter to a good friend of his youth, the classics professor Gustav Droysen. His wife had died at the beginning of March at the age of twenty-seven, after a long period of suffering, leaving him with four children under the age of ten:

Leipzig, 5 April 1847
*Mein lieber Freund,*

If, in this difficult time that God has laid on you, you would rather not think about the days of our youth and the like…and you would rather remain undisturbed in your pain…put this letter aside and do not read on. For I have nothing new and comforting to say to you, no one has; what needs to be said has already been said, or you already know it, and it can only hurt you if you hear it repeated by everyone. So I only wanted to remind you of me and my handwriting, and to distract you for a moment, in that I tell you that…I experience with you what you experience, the greatest joys and the greatest sorrows that you have had to suffer now. If, for a few moments, you wish to be distracted from the main thought, read these lines, and think of me, and know that I am thinking of you.

If only the time would soon come when you could really work again, or if you had a profession such as an artisan, doctor or preacher; I have always envied them because they are indispensable to people; they have to help people, no matter how they feel inside, and artisans can always work. But to write a book or a symphony, to go to a lecture or a concert in such times seems so meaningless for so long until the right divine point of view (or basis—*Standpunkt*) returns, in which the blind juggler and Napoleon are not dissimilar. I hope you will soon be able to become immersed in your classics again and lead us onward again, as you have often done. Or if music would bring you joy, and you would be able to have your organist play "*Schmücke Dich, liebe Seele,*" by Sebastian Bach…

How everything which was fresh and young in our youth has disappeared, has become desolate, and become old! But only almost everything, thank God, not everything; and thank God, the best never disappears, but is eternally renewed, even in death.

He said he longed to be with him, not so much to talk as to play for him. He ended the letter, "Forgive all this! It seemed to me as if I was sitting on the sofa with you and shaking your hand."

On the same day, Felix also quickly dashed off a note to Paul to inform him that he would leave for England in three days and that he was traveling alone because it was the "most sensible."

In his diary on that day, Moscheles described his friend's state of mind:

> We were in quite a fix the other night at the pupils' public concert, when four young ladies were to play Czerny's piece for eight hands: *Frl.* Flynn had forgotten her music. Mendelssohn was up in arms at once. "What?" he exclaimed, "forget your music for a public performance, as if it were a mere trifle! This is dreadful. The audience is sitting there and has to wait because you have forgotten your music!" etc. etc.
>
> In this dilemma I fetched the tuner out of the corner where he was waiting. "Sit down," I said, "busy yourself with tuning the two pianos, and don't stop until you see that the messenger who has been dispatched brings Miss Flynn's music."

The tuner did as he was told; Miss Flynn and the other three pianists played, and all was well.

Mendelssohn left for England early on the 8th of April. Unbeknown to him, Jenny Lind left Vienna at four o'clock on the same morning.

---

Cécile had hoped to go to England with Felix again, but because her grandmother was not well—Mme. Jeanrenaud described her as being in an almost childish state—she felt she could not leave her five rambunctious children at the Souchay mansion.

Shortly after Felix left for England, Cécile vented some anger in a letter to Fanny.

> *Liebste* Fanny,
>
> It seems that Felix has blackened my image, so that you all damn me for not coming to Berlin, whereas I was very sorry not to come. But he alone is to blame, for when he saw that it was already too late, he with his hat on his head, I with my hair flying, he suggested it, with the clear intention that I wouldn't accept, so that I wouldn't know what tricks he was up to in Berlin.

Now he has left me again, and I am very deeply sorry that I will miss so much of his music…I tend to my children and don't understand how it is that they go to bed at night with all their limbs whole, because even the little one, who can hardly walk, climbs and crawls and romps around on the floor with her brothers so that it strikes fear into my heart.

On their way to England, Mendelssohn and the young violinist Joseph Joachim stayed at an inn in Frankfurt, but Felix called on Mme. Jeanrenaud.

One day before Mendelssohn arrived in London, his sister Fanny played the piano in the premiere of her trio for piano, violin, and cello at a Sunday matinee at Leipzigerstrasse 3. Some members of the audience declared that it was not only good as a composition "by a woman," but also a lovely, important composition. Little did Felix realize that he would never hear her play it or congratulate her.

He arrived in London on the 12th of April. The next day he fainted on a bridge over the Thames River. Six days later, Cécile received her first letter from her husband and wrote to Fanny that he was "already speaking very much about his return" and that he planned to leave London by the 30th of April.

Three days after his arrival. Mendelssohn conducted the first performance of the revised *Elijah* in Exeter Hall on The Strand. The orchestra was poor, the chorus unruly, and three singers had to share one copy of the score. Some critics wrote negative reviews.

When Mendelssohn called on Mrs. Grote on the day after the London premiere of *Elijah,* she surprised him with the news that Lumley had succeeded in Vienna, that he had accompanied Lind and her companion to Strasbourg and hoped they would arrive at the Grote home that very day.

The two anxiously waited for Lind on the street that afternoon, and she really arrived—with two four-wheeled carriages, at least eight large suitcases, hat boxes and other paraphernalia. She was exhausted from the ten-day journey from Vienna but brightened when she saw Mendelssohn. After they exchanged greetings, Lind retired to her quarters in the Grote home.

In the evening she sat with her hosts in their box in Her Majesty's Theatre to hear Bellini's *I Puritani* with the great basso Luigi Lablache in the leading role. She was, as usual, simply dressed and without jewels, in great contrast to the elegant *toilettes* of many of the women in the audience. At first no one paid any attention to the pale blonde young woman sitting with the Grote couple in the "grand tier." However, after Lumley came to pay his respects and Lablache bowed over her hand in the first intermission, the people in the neighboring boxes realized who she was and began to stare. In the second intermission opera glasses and lorgnettes were focused on Jenny Lind.

She was still living in the Grote home when Mrs. Grote invited Mendelssohn and the portly, tall, and mirthful Lablache to a dinner party. Of course there was music that evening, and of course Mendelssohn accompanied the singers. Lind attempted to sing Mendelssohn's "Auf Flügeln des Gesanges" but broke down completely. Lablache then sang some Neapolitan songs; and after Mendelssohn played again, he went to Lind and, with his warm smile, invited her to sing. With that she let herself go completely in the fiendishly difficult Swedish song "Tanzlied aus Delcarlien" (Dance Song from Delcarlien) to her own piano accompaniment.

Although Jenny Lind was now in London, Lumley had not yet won the battle. As in every other new city to which she went, Lind was consumed by fear that her voice would not fill the opera house. As long as she did not sing, Lumley continued to lose money because almost no one would come to his theater before Jenny Lind appeared. As he waited day by day for her to decide when to appear, he soon complained, "Bringing the Swedish Nightingale was child's play in comparison to persuading her to sing."

Mendelssohn, as well as William Sterndale Bennett, went almost every day to encourage Lind to attend a rehearsal. But she told Mrs. Grote that this time her fears were unconquerable, and she begged her to ask Lumley to release her from her contract.

However, one day, while on a carriage ride, Mrs. Grote bluntly told her about Lumley's financial woes. That evening at a dinner party, Lind informed Lumley that she would come to a rehearsal on the following Monday, the 26th of April. She had chosen to sing *Robert le diable* in the Italian language at her London debut.

Next, another problem surfaced. The sets had been newly painted, new costumes had been made, and a new Italian translation obtained from Paris when the Lord Chamberlain, Lord Spenser, refused to license the opera. "One might as well bring the devil and his horns on the stage at once," he declared.

Thus Lumley made drastic changes in the opera—secular "ladies," not nuns, would attempt to seduce Roberto—and the rehearsals continued.[2] Meyerbeer sent written instructions to Lind from Paris almost every day.

Lumley found a lovely dwelling, Clairville Cottage, in the midst of the Brompton market gardens, near the theater, for Lind and Louise.

Mendelssohn's schedule in England was exceedingly taxing; in two weeks he conducted *Elijah* six times, four times in Exeter Hall in London and once each in Birmingham and Manchester. In addition, he conducted the Philharmonic Society Orchestra and played the piano several times.

When people commented that he outdid himself in the performance of Beethoven's G-major piano concerto, he explained that he had wanted to please "two wonderful ladies in particular, the queen and Jenny Lind." *The Spectator* commented on the performance:

> Mendelssohn's performance [of Beethoven's G-major concerto] was as unique and unrivalled as the work itself; he played it without the music before him, and appeared to have stored it not only in his mind but to have made it his own...John Cramer[3] observed with a sigh, "What a pity it was that Beethoven had never heard his own conception expressed in a way which he could only have dreamed in his imagination."

After the last performance of *Elijah* in Exeter Hall on the last day of April—the same day that Felix had said he would return home—Prince Albert sent him a note in the German language: "Like another Elijah, the noble artist, surrounded by the Baal worship of false art, has succeeded, by means of genius and study, to faithfully fortify [*bewahren*] the service of true art...In grateful remembrance, Albert."

---

In Berlin Fanny lamented that Felix was in England but that she had not "heard a syllable from him."

---

On the first of May Mendelssohn was still not on his way to Frankfurt. That morning he played privately for Queen Victoria for two hours from his composition *Heaven, Earth, and Hell.* He had decided to postpone his departure in order to attend Lind's London debut. On the 4th of May he played the piano in his trio in an all-Mendelssohn matinee concert of the Quartet Society. Mrs. Sarah Austin, a "bluestocking," saw Mendelssohn at this event and was struck by his appearance:

By daylight and in closer contiguity, the spectator was struck by a certain appearance of premature age which his countenance exhibited. He seemed already to have outstretched the natural term of his existence by at least ten years. No one, judging by the lines in his face, would have guessed his age to be only 39 [*sic*], especially noticeable at the *Homage à* Mendelssohn concert by the Beethoven Quartet Society.

---

1. Dirichlet always referred to Albertine, Paul's wife, as the family *Standarte.*

2. In Nils-Olof Franzén's *Jenny Lind—Die schwedische Nachtigall* the author states that the chamberlain had to give in, after it was explained to him that the opera had already been given in its original form in the Italian language.

3. John Cramer, 1771–1858, was the German Johann B. Cramer who came from Mannheim to London as a child. He was a pianist, composer, and music publisher. He had met Beethoven in Vienna at the beginning of the nineteenth century.

# t w e n t y - t w o

ON THE EVENING OF THE 4TH OF MAY, MENDELSSOHN JOINED THE THRONG that eagerly waited to hear the "Swedish Nightingale." From early afternoon there was such a solid line of carriages on the way to Her Majesty's Theatre that pedestrians could not pass through. And when the doors opened at 7:30, the crowd moved with such force that many people were swept off their feet.

The house was filled in a matter of minutes. The pits, with their unreserved seats, were so crowded that some people could not get a glimpse of the stage. The queen and her retinue arrived in the royal box.

In the dressing room, before the performance, Jenny spoke harshly to Louise.

Lind had chosen *Roberto il diabolo* at least in part because her entrance was inconspicuous and she need not sing immediately. On the continent Lind had always had to prove herself before the audience voiced their approval. But as soon as she appeared on stage here, in pilgrim's dress, dragged on by Roberto's men, the audience cheered loudly and waved hats and handkerchiefs. They applauded again after the first few short passages in the first recitative. Then, with Lablache in the lead, they interrupted her first cavatina with thunderous applause.

When she came to the romance "When I Leave Normandy," in the second act, the audience encored each verse separately. Some accounts spoke of bursts of applause lasting twenty minutes. And one critic declared that he thought the roof would split with the continued acclamation at the end of the opera. Lind had to take three curtain calls, and the queen herself threw her beautiful, large bouquet at her feet.

In all previous debuts, in Copenhagen, in Berlin, and in Vienna, critics had said that never before in the annals of those cities had an artist received such adulation. But the London audience outdid them all. Newspapers described wild scenes of evening coats being reduced to rags, of ladies fainting and of gentlemen being carried out senseless, of "delicate" ladies fighting for their places and "frenzied" gentlemen pushing themselves in front of ladies.

*The Times* published a laudatory review of the performance:

> If our expectations were great, we must say that they were fully realized. The delicious quality of the organ—the rich gushing tone—was something entirely new and fresh…the sustained notes, swelling with full richness, and fading down to the softest piano without losing one iota of their quality, being delicious when loud, delicious when whispered, dwelt in the public ear, and reposed in the public heart. The shake, *mezza voce*, with which she concluded the pretty air "When I Leave Normandy," was perfectly wonderful for its rapidity and equality…And the impression she made as an actress was no less profound. There is no conventionality about her, no seizing the strong points of a character and letting the rest drop…Her whole conception is a fine histrionic study, of which every feature is equally good.

A critic opined in the *Illustrated London News* that after hearing Lind, it was as if the audience was able to learn for the first time what singing actually was. J. W. Davison wrote a detailed and subjective account for *The Musical World*. Chorley noticed that Mendelssohn smiled during the opera, this opera that had utterly repulsed him in Paris fifteen years earlier. The critic spoke of Mendelssohn's enjoyment of Mlle. Lind's talent as being unlimited "and his attachment to her genius as a singer, unbounded, and with it, desire for her success."

The day following Lind's debut, Louise wrote in her diary that Jenny was very kind to her, but the harshness of the night before had so upset her that it was difficult to savor the kindness.

On the same day Lind reported to Herr Buettner,

I appeared here yesterday as Alice in *Robert* and everything went *gloriously!* I wasn't able to sleep because of joy last night even though I went to bed at only three o'clock, but—it was too much to bear, and I could not stop thanking my God. *Ach,* Herr Buettner, how lovely it was yesterday! What a reception! The queen and Prince Albert and all the highest *noblesse* in England were there from the beginning, and the handkerchiefs and hats waved as if a spring wind wafted through the hall, and greeted me in a friendly way, "Welcome"…
I think Mr. Lumley has found the prettiest house in all of London for me. The birds sing in my garden and are as happy as I! Ah! how happy I am now. The last struggle is over, and now things will go like water streaming down from the mountains. The theater is so *sonore* that one needs to sing with only *mezza voce,* and my voice has not sounded better in any hall than here.

Lind received even greater acclaim after the second performance, and the same crush occurred in her subsequent appearances at Her Majesty's Theater.

Mendelssohn still did not leave London after Lind's debut. The following day he played a Bach prelude and fugue and improvised on the prelude on the organ in an ancient music concert. Prince Albert had drawn up the program; how could he refuse?

He spent the following morning at art galleries and played the piano at a large party at the Prussian embassy in honor of the outstanding British statesman William Gladstone in the afternoon. After a choir sang the last piece, his *Sei getreu bis in den Tod* (Be faithful until death) from his *Paulus,* he bolted out of the room, saying, "I cannot take farewells. God bless you all." Klingemann was alarmed at his friend's appearance.

At last, after a final visit at Buckingham Palace, Mendelssohn left England on the 8th of May. He had been away from home for more than a month. And he lost more time on his return trip when he was detained by guards at the German border. The authorities were looking for Felix's cousin Arnold Mendelssohn, whom the authorities accused of a politically motivated theft.

On the 12th of May, Felix arrived at the Frankfurt inn where Cécile, the children, their tutor, and their maids anxiously waited for him. On the same day Felix advised Paul that he wanted to rest before proceeding to Switzerland, but that he would wait for him if he came a few days later. He spent some of the intervening time again revising *Elijah.*

Five days later, instead of Paul, a messenger came from Berlin with news that his sister Fanny had died on the 14th of May in the midst of a rehearsal of her brother's cantata, *Walpurgisnacht.* She had attained the age of forty-one.

Immediately after reading the letter, Felix shrieked and fainted and remained motionless for several minutes. Even Cécile lost her normal composure. The only comfort he could find, after he revived, was in the company of his children. He longed for Paul. In his own great pain he wrote to Hensel, "I feel deep, bitter regret that I had not done more to provide her with happiness, that I did not see her more often and spend more time with her. That would, of course, have been my happiness, but she would have been content with that."

It is obvious that he had King David's penitential psalm[1] in mind when he wrote to Fanny's only son, the now seventeen-year-old Sebastian, "There is nothing one can say or do except one thing—pray to God that He give us a pure heart and grant us a new spirit."

Cécile wrote first to Rebecka,

*Meine liebste* Rebecka,

I don't know what to write to you, and yet I must write, that is how I feel towards Felix all day, would like to console him, but cannot. Then we speak of Fanny, and reminisce together, and ask God to help us to bear the heavy blow which He has dealt us, without complaining and sinful thoughts. Next to Hensel you have lost the most.

How often since yesterday I regret that I did not spend more time with you in Berlin, and through my inclination to trivialities have prepared an everlasting reproach for myself. For I too have lost my best friend… God help us all.

Felix began his portion of the letter, "God help us all, God help us all."

Shortly before her death, Fanny had made this diary entry: "What have I done to deserve being among the few happy ones in the world? My inmost heart is full of thankfulness. I am quite overcome by my own happiness." On the morning of her death she had composed the song "Do Not Leave Me Alone in the Sepulchral Kingdom."

---

In England, Lind sang Bellini's *La Sonnambula* (The Sleepwalker) for the first time on May 13. Frederic Chopin attended the performance—after he had called on her, Lind had sent him a ticket for one of the best stalls. Subsequently he wrote to his friend Count Albert Grzymala, "This Swede is an original from head to toe. She doesn't show herself in the ordinary light, but in the magic rays of the aurora borealis. Her singing is infallibly pure and true, but above all, I admire her piano passages, the charm of which is indescribable."

Hans Christian Andersen attended the same performance and described the effect of the sleepwalking scene:

> The maidenliness, the purity, that, as it were, irradiated her, brought something holy to the stage. The way in which she takes the rose from her breast in the sleepwalking scene in the final act, lifts it up and accidentally lets it fall had a grace, a beauty, something so strangely gripping, that one's eyes filled with tears; there was also such applause and jubilations as I have not heard equaled even among the passionate Neapolitans.

---

Felix longed to be with his two remaining siblings; he did not wish to be with strangers—not even with friends—and did not know if he even wanted to go to Switzerland now. To Paul he wrote,

> *Mein liebster Bruder,*
> After I received your letter today, I am counting the hours and days until I can see you. I have nothing to say to other people now, and don't know what to ask them…And so the news that you are coming makes me happy, as much as it can at present, and for a long, long time.
> If possible, don't postpone your trip, and spend a great deal of time with your children; only their faces and their nonchalant words make one feel better.

He said he believed that he would finally only really believe that Fanny was no longer living when he saw and spoke to him.

On the same day he composed a letter to General Emil von Webern, the friend who had written the news about Fanny's death:

It's certainly true that no one who has ever known my sister can ever forget her all his life, but what we siblings have now lost, and I, especially, who felt her presence and her goodness and love every moment, and who could experience no joy without thinking of her rejoicing with me, I believe none of us can yet measure it; I will never, never become accustomed to it.

On the 22nd Rebecka wrote to Cécile, "Who has not felt the loss? But the tears of the world don't sustain us. God alone, who has always been with you, can help us on our way."

The constant noise at the inn aggravated Felix, but he did not want to go to Soden, where he would meet Frankfurt acquaintances. So he and his family traveled south and left word that Paul and his family should meet them at Badenweiler, near Baden.

While he was in Baden, Mendelssohn received an invitation to conduct *Elijah* in Vienna in the fall. The writer suggested that if Jenny Lind were there at the time, perhaps Mendelssohn could arrange for her participation. Mendelssohn replied that he was still too numb to consider accepting. But he emphatically stated that in case he came, he wanted no honorarium or remuneration for the cost of travel and lodgings, as he knew the circumstances of the music society. He did not mention Lind.

In his long letter of condolence to Mendelssohn, Klingemann included news about London:

It seems to me that I should grieve most for you, as if your loss was even deeper than Hensel's. I have always had to think of you, *mein Freund*, and I long to know whether you had the strength to bear the first loss of this kind…We must be prepared to see our parents die, but siblings, contemporaries…that is difficult. And then that it should have been she! Such a gifted being, such a treasure of accomplishments…it is an everlasting misery [*Jammer*]…

If only I had heard from you! You must write to me soon…Tell me what you know and how you feel. Calm me soon in that I hear that you are taking comfort the right way, that is, in those things God has granted you, with what you have left…Don't give up your Switzerland plans…

I have not yet been able to see Lind at her home although I went there early and late…On Sunday I was invited to meet her at Dulckens…She came and sang two of her Swedish songs—to the well known, yet not expected magic…She apologized in the most delightful way about not being at home, but there was no opportunity for further conversations. The jubilation regarding her performances is increasing. *Sonnambula* continually engenders delight. *The Daughter of the Regiment* on Thursday will probably become even stronger…

Isn't it great not to be alone in sad times? I, at least, feel this.

Mendelssohn replied,

Baden Baden, 3 June 1847
*Mein liebster Freund,*

…The blow was so hard and unexpected that I am still walking about almost as if in a dream. With time, God willing, I will again find the right way, but not only a part of my youth is now gone, it is all gone. I have often thought back on those days and remember how little I asked about your deceased sister, that I talked with you about the most inconsequential matters and spoke only a little about the one. I thought I knew what it was like, but I did not know, and have now learned…

God grant that things will prosper, and that I can again resume composing, in order that the insistent, bitter pain will become a gentle, quiet one. Until now I have not been able to think of composing at all without feeling the greatest emptiness and dryness in head and heart. Hopefully it will soon pass…

Fanny wasn't ill and didn't suffer. She was never as well as in the last days of her life. At a rehearsal for her Sunday Music, while they rehearsed "Es lacht der Mai"…and she accompanied, she became unwell, left the room, and when Paul came three-quarters of an hour later, he found her completely unconscious, and four hours later she was no longer alive.

The last morning she had composed a song by Eichendorff, which ends *Gedanken gehn und Lieder bis in das Himmelreich* [Thoughts and songs ascend up to the kingdom of heaven]. Now they have gone there.

As I write, I cannot believe it, and yet it is true, and yet I feel it my task to be content with what God has so generously given me in Cécile and the children, and thus continue to live happily. And I will take pains to succeed. The children are very good, and their happy faces are a comfort to me.

Again he did not mention Lind, nor respond to Klingemann's statement about his feelings about not being alone.

News of Fanny's death reached Rome within a week. Adelaide Sartoris added a note in her husband's letter of condolence to Felix:

> You cannot imagine with what a pang it went to my heart that the only time we spoke together of your poor sister, I should have mentioned her unkindly. Can you forgive me, or will you now hate me forever? You hardly would if you knew how grieved I am at your loss, at the thought that I had ever said a harsh word of one so dear to you. Do write to us, or to Edward at least.

---

1. This is in reference to Psalm 51. Biblical scholars are convinced that King David wrote this psalm after he was confronted by the prophet Nathan about his adulterous relationship with Bathsheba. Mendelssohn knew the psalm well; he himself had chosen it in 1834 for the apostle Paul's prayer in his oratorio *Paulus*.

# twenty-three

THREE WEEKS AFTER FANNY'S DEATH, FELIX WAS STILL UNDECIDED ABOUT WHERE he wanted to spend the summer. He believed he could not experience real pleasure even in Switzerland now.

When the thought of music became less odious to him in Baden, he put the finishing touches on three sacred compositions for the Anglican service, *Magnificat, Nunc Dimitis* (Now Lettest Thou Thy Servant Depart in Peace), and *Benedictus.*

After Paul arrived in Baden with Albertine and their three infants, Felix wrote to Mme. Moscheles that nothing did him and Paul more good than walking in the woods and living quietly and alone and spending much time with the children.

One week after Paul's arrival with his family, Cécile responded to some of her mother's questions:

> You ask if Felix has improved; he has become somewhat more communicative, and his color is better than that of my brother-in-law, whose pallor is striking, pale and yellow. Perhaps Felix will be able to

decide later what to do for the rest of the summer. The children are very happy here. They take long walks with the men. Usually we take the children for a ride in a carriage after dinner.

Together with his birthday wishes for Sebastian, Fanny's only child, Felix wrote,

Whatever area of life or knowledge or work to which you may devote yourself, it is indispensable to *will* (not to wish, but to *will*) something good and solid; but this is enough. In all employments and in all spheres there is now, and always will be, a need for able, honest workmen, and therefore it isn't true when people declare it is more difficult to achieve something now than in former times…a sincere, faithful heart, true love and a courageous, determined will are all necessary, and you will certainly not fail in these, with such a bright and beloved example steadily shining before you.

And even if you follow this and do absolutely everything in your power, still nothing is done, nothing is attained without the fulfillment of one fervent wish—May God be with you! This prayer comprises consolation and strength, and also cheerfulness in days to come.

I often long to spend these days with you and your *Tante* Rebecka…I wish you could come with your father, and we could sketch together from nature…May God bless you.

Ever your Felix Mendelssohn Bartholdy

Sebastian replied, "Nothing can fill the void; the only thing I enjoy is art. Believe me, *lieber Onkel*, I will now become a serious, competent [*tüchtiger*] person and will try to give you pleasure."

In the middle of June, both Mendelssohn families spent a few days in Freiburg, Germany, at the edge of the Black Forest, where Felix and Cécile had spent most of their honeymoon and where an old family friend, law professor Franz von Woringen, lived and worked. Although Felix and Paul still had not recovered completely, some of the old sense of fun occasionally returned. Von Woringen described one such event with Felix to his sister-in-law, Malvine:

How happy I was when here in Freiburg Felix became livelier for the first time since Fanny's death…What an effort I made to help him therein.

One day we were in Badenweiler in glorious weather; I always think about how he was there and what he said! It was all so lovely, everything he said was so fine, but even his jokes were serious.

We were on the tower, and while we were descending, I suddenly called to him that he should catch me; we ran down the winding staircase at such a breakneck speed that we were in danger of falling, and even though I had been ahead of him, I barely got away from him when he laughed as of old and grabbed me and in the merry way of olden times said, "We are children."

Dr. Louis Stromeyer, who was part of the Mendelssohn circle until 1827 and now practiced in Freiburg, described Mendelssohn at this time as "prematurely aged, his face showing traces of severe mental strain, his eyelids, which had always been half closed, more so now, his head thrust forward, his carriage having lost vigor and elasticity."

The large Mendelssohn party proceeded to Switzerland after all in the third week of June, first to Schaffhausen, where Fanny's husband joined them, and gradually to Zurich. There Mendelssohn received a long letter from Harriet Grote:

> Nothing but the deep sympathy with your affliction has kept me so long silent. I should have written at least a fortnight ago to convey to you my wishes, Jenny's wishes, Lumley's wishes; everybody's wishes, in fact. I assure you that our dear Jenny Lind participated in your pain with fervor and sincerity, which rendered her, to my mind, more amiable than ever.

Mrs. Grote also gave an account of the many activities she and Jenny enjoyed and suggested that he and Jenny might give concerts together in Birmingham and Liverpool.

At the end of June the Mendelssohn caravan arrived in Thun, where they had a lovely view of Lake Thun and the Bernese Alps, including the Niederhorn and Jungfrau peaks. While walking in the mountains one day, a melancholy song, "Auf der Wanderschaft," with words by Nikolaus Lenau,[1] came to the grieving composer:

> I wandered away to distant lands; moved, I looked back once more
> And saw that her lips moved and that she waved her hand.

Probably she sent a kind word after me on my sad way,
Yet I did not hear the lovely sound, because the wind carried it away.
I must forego all happiness, you raw, cold wind.


The Mendelssohn party remained in Thun for only a week before moving on to their final destination, Interlaken, between Lake Brienz and Lake Thun. The Aare River flows through Interlaken between the two lakes. There Felix again took out his paintbrushes and completed numerous watercolors. And, often together with Paul, he took long walks in the mountains. There was such deep love and trust between the brothers that Felix was able to express his deepest feelings and thoughts to Paul—who felt unusually fulfilled in his marriage—and the younger man was able to gently admonish his older brother when need be.

While they were in Interlaken, General Emil von Webern enquired for the king of Prussia if Mendelssohn would conduct three benefit concerts in Berlin: two performances of *Elijah,* and one of *Lobgesang,* in October and November. Mendelssohn did not immediately respond.

On a dark stormy day in July, after the two families had enjoyed each other's company for almost seven weeks, Paul and his family and Hensel left for Berlin. A few hours later, Felix wrote to his brother that in every sense the day had been drearier than any they had experienced for many weeks and that he had reflected for two hours on Schiller's chorus in *Die Braut von Messina:* "Tell us, what shall we do now?" En route on the same day, Paul also wrote to Felix.

Later that evening Felix composed a letter to Rebecka in which he said he had enjoyed his walks with Paul the most. Less than a week later he wrote to her again:

Hotel d'Interlaken, 24 July 1847
...In September, God willing, I intend to come to Berlin, and Paul has probably told you how seriously I am considering the idea of spending my life with you, my dear ones, and living with you, abandoning all other considerations. I wish to be with you, and I felt this strongly when the steamboat left for Thun with Paul and his family and Hensel. And strangely enough...it is almost impossible for me to be with strangers at this time.

There is no lack of visitors here, both musical and otherwise; but they all seem to me so empty and indifferent that I, no doubt, must appear at least the same to them. So I heartily wish that we may soon part, and remain apart; and in the midst of all the phrases and inquiries and reports I have only one thought: how short life is…I hope we shall soon be together, and for a long time.

He informed her of his new role after Dr. Klingel left for Germany on the 26th of July:

Now the cold rainy days give me the opportunity to spend the whole day with my three older children; they work at writing, arithmetic and Latin with me, paint landscapes during their free hours or play draughts, and ask a hundred wise questions which no fool can answer (people generally say this in reverse, but this is not so!)…*Lebwohl, liebe Schwester*, until we meet again.
Felix

In August Mendelssohn composed almost the entire first act of *Loreley*. In this final version, Loreley is the beautiful foster daughter of a seaman in Bacharach on the Rhine. She is chosen to lead her playmates in congratulating the couple at the wedding of a Palatinate count. When she recognizes the count as her own beloved who had come to her garbed only in hunter's clothes, she feels betrayed and hurt. As she wanders along the Rhine at night and screams about her desire for revenge, the air and water spirits overhear her and promise her revenge if she will consecrate herself to them forever. That moment constitutes the finale of the first act.

After reading the second act of the libretto, Mendelssohn wrote to Geibel that there were things in the libretto that he did not notice until he began to compose and that he wished to meet him in November.

───────────

Lind and Lablache sang in the premiere of Verdi's *I Masnadieri*, with the composer conducting, at Her Majesty's Theater on the 22nd of July. Chorley described it as a "terrible opera, with a riot in every act"; the audience agreed with his assessment.

In the next month Lind gave concerts throughout many parts of England and made her last appearance in 1847 at Her Majesty's Theater on the 21st of August. Before she left England, she wrote to Hauser after a long silence:

[London] 19 August 1847

Believe me that I have thought of you *much and often* and have not changed my mind about you. *You* are and you will remain—forever—a Mensch whom I love deeply. I always wanted to write, but I have been so dreadfully busy that I could not.

Things have gone well with me since I left Munich and all of you in Germany…I have been successful in bearing the entire theater on my shoulders, and that is the only excuse I can give. I have worked very hard and have also been richly rewarded, as the public here treats me as *its child* and I find the English the most grateful public that exists. I have had luck, particularly with *Sonnambula,* and we could have given only this opera for the whole *saison.*

She did not mention Mendelssohn.

———————————

When Mendelssohn finally responded to the invitation of the Vienna Choral Society to conduct *Elijah,* he said he would be pleased to conduct his oratorio and that it would be absolutely necessary that Staudigl take part; he could hardly imagine the performance without him. He also mentioned that the other three solo voices, especially the soprano, were no less important, but he did not insist that Jenny Lind should sing the soprano part. Nor did he say, as he had said to Mr. Moore in 1846 and again in 1847, that she was a very important person for the success of the performance. In fact, he did not mention her in his letter.

Vesque von Puettlingen[2] replied for the Vienna Choral Society that a female singer described as the second Lind would arrive for an audition soon. In his reply Mendelssohn reiterated his opinion that if the oratorio were to be successful in Vienna, Staudigl must sing the part of the prophet. But he did not mention Lind or any other soprano.

Chorley came to Interlaken at the end of August and found Mendelssohn "sad and stooped, but with the brightest smile and a cordial welcome." The two men frequently walked in the mountains and talked at great length about future operas he might compose, about church music, about his desire to live on the Rhine, and about Vienna. On more than one occasion Mendelssohn interjected, "But I shall not live" or "But I must have peace and quiet, or I shall die" or "But what is the use of planning anything? I shall not live."

The two men discussed politics and politicians, poets and poems, education, good citizenship, sound society, happy homes, duties, and disregard of obligation. There were tears in Mendelssohn's eyes when he spoke of corruption and immorality of those in high places, and he supplied anecdotes and illustrations of unseemly behavior. During the summer the press had made much of King Ludwig of Bavaria's relationship with the Irish dancer and courtesan Eliza Rosanna Gilbert, who paraded as a Spanish dancer named Lola Montez.[3]

On one of their walks, Mendelssohn and Chorley came upon a tiny church in a village on Lake Brienz. It was open, and the composer strode to the simple organ and smiled serenely as he played on it, to the delight of the amazed villagers.

On another occasion, referring to Donizetti's *Daughter of the Regiment*, Mendelssohn told Chorley with a smile, "One can become accustomed to bad music."

Chorley found Mendelssohn to be "too depressed and worn, looking old and walking too heavily," although having bursts of hope and energy, alternating with depression.

While he was still in Interlaken, Mendelssohn heard from William Bartholomew:

London, 1 September 1847
"Barty, have you heard Jenny Lind?" "No, I have not heard her." For two reasons I have not. I could not afford to pay enormously for a comfortable seat, and if I could, the music, with the exception of *Figaro*, that she has sung is not what I care to hear, for I would rather hear fine music less finely sung than shallow trash, even though warbled by Jenny Lind. She has made an enormous hit, and her coming has proved the salvation of Lumley; like Atlas, the whole concern has been put on her shoulders and sustained well thereon.

Bartholomew was not alone in his views. The satirist, parodist, and novelist William Makepeace Thackeray[4] fumed about Lind's operatic performances, "I cannot think why she always prefers to be in bad theater, [and] sing bad music the best—which is odd."

At the beginning of September it was already quite cold, and a thick blanket of snow covered the mountains when Mendelssohn completed a brooding, passionate string quartet. He found it difficult to leave their calm and comfortable life and dreaded the time when he must return to be with people other than his family. Nevertheless, he and his family began their homeward journey by traveling first to Thun and then down the Rhine by steamboat.

The family spent two days in Frankfurt. From there they went directly to Leipzig. Five days later, Felix, Cécile, and their two older sons went to Berlin for one week. Friends described the composer as aged and over-anxious, irritable, and misanthropic.

From Leipzig, Felix wrote to Mme. Jeanrenaud,

> It was so pleasant again in the few days of the last week that as soon as we left, I began to count the days until I could come again. And with this hither and yon, the migratory bird [*Reisevogel*] passes his time and allows himself to be laughed at, even by his mother-in-law; then he becomes angry, and she strews a few cake crumbs in front of him, and he eats out of her hand again.

In a letter to Theo Hildebrandt, the Duesseldorf painter, Mendelssohn made kind comments about Ferdinand Hiller, the old friend from whom he had been estranged for three years.

On the same day, October 1, on Schleinitz's birthday, Felix presented the lawyer with "Nachtlied," a moving new song about death, which ends with the words "Sing, nightingale; and waterfall, sound brightly. We will praise God until morning dawns."

Two days later, after listening to Joachim perform his violin concerto, Mendelssohn rushed out of the Gewandhaus. The Erfurt music director, Helmhold, approached him as he left but returned to report to a friend, "I can't understand why Mendelssohn appeared so strange. He was always so friendly; this time, however, he was very abrupt and repellant towards me."

On the same evening Mendelssohn wrote his last letter to Klingemann:

> Leipzig, 3 October 1847
> I haven't let you hear from me for a long time; forgive me. But now I must gradually begin to put my life and my music back together, with the consciousness that Fanny is no longer here, and that becomes so

bitter to me that I cannot yet attain a proper perspective and objectivity, and that is why my correspondence is in a sorry state.

But I cannot allow Mr. Buxton to leave without a sign of life and love, as he told me that he would be in London on Saturday and asked me if I didn't have something for Klingemann…

I went to the first subscription concert to hear Joachim play my violin concerto, but it didn't go very well…

It was good to be in Switzerland because it did help me get over the first months, but time will tell whether or not life will be more bitter here. The great blessing of our stay was that Cécile and the children look and feel better than they have in a long while. In the two months we spent in Interlaken, Cécile has become "fatted," as she calls it, has painted the loveliest Alpine flowers. I have painted too, and the children have dabbled also, but we were together all the time, and that has given us a sense of physical well-being that we still feel today; people maintain that I have gained weight also. But I have noticed that it will not soon be possible to be with half-friends and acquaintances, of which relationships and socializing actually consist everywhere. Therefore, if at all possible, we will try to have the same kind of life here that we had in Interlaken, except for the few hours at the conservatory.

He expressed his wish to go to Norwich, England, in 1848 to play the splendid cathedral organ. He ended the letter, "I would like to stay at home, enjoy my family, and compose very diligently. All else is no good [Alles andere ist vom Übel]."

In the following days, Mendelssohn spent much time putting all his compositions in order and cleaning out his entire writing desk. He made a new copy of his "Altdeutsches Frühlingslied," the disconsolate song that had been in his head all summer. Although he took part in the students' exams on the 8th of October, he seemed to take little interest in them, as he sketched landscapes the entire time. The next morning he walked to Rosenthal Park with Moscheles, who had come to head the piano department at the conservatory in the previous fall. When Moscheles' wife, Charlotte, asked Mendelssohn how he felt, he replied, "Gray on gray."

He planned to go to Berlin on the 10th of October—on Cécile's birthday—to begin the rehearsals of Elijah the following day. Lind was scheduled to arrive on the same day.

In the afternoon of the 9th of October, he went to Livia Frege's home with seven of his latest songs and a copy of *Elijah*. "No one sings *Elijah* the way she does, and I want to encourage her," he had told Moscheles.[5] He was so moved when she sang his "Nachtlied" that he asked her to repeat it immediately, then said, "*Hu,* that sounds sad, but that's how I feel." Then he asked her to sing all the songs several additional times. Finally he requested that Livia join him in singing the quartet from *Elijah:* "Ho, all ye that thirst, come to the water, come to Him and bend your ear, so shall your soul live." He told her that he had wept at home as he sang and played the trio "Lift thine eyes, O lift thine eyes to the mountains, whence cometh thy help," from the same oratorio.

Afterwards, he suffered an attack of cold, numb hands and feet and a severe headache and left the Frege home before it was completely dark outside. He did not improve at home. The next day he had a violent headache.

Cécile informed Count von Arnim that Felix was too ill to go for the first rehearsal in Berlin but planned to go somewhat later. She believed that her husband's illness was similar to the malady he had suffered five years earlier and wrote to her mother that it was less serious.

For Cécile's birthday Felix had prepared another priceless gift. He had recently worked over the hasty sketches he had made in the common diary that he and Klingemann kept when they toured Scotland in 1829 and had had them bound.

Cécile informed her mother that she was "not very happy" that her husband was indisposed on her birthday and that the doctors applied eels for bloodletting. She opined that he was getting better but would have to cancel his trip to Berlin. She did not mention the album.

On the same day, Devrient informed Mendelssohn that he would go to Berlin to talk to Geibel about improving the libretto of *Loreley.*

Mendelssohn had hoped to present the first printed copy of his revised *Elijah* to King Friedrich Wilhelm IV personally but sent an unbound copy to Paul instead, together with a letter to the king. He instructed his brother to have the score of the oratorio bound and to present both to the monarch.

When Julius Benedict came to call, the men talked for two hours. During their conversation Felix said, "I've had a narrow escape; I'll get well only if I go to Italy" and "Oh, my poor head."

Some time after his attack, Felix told Ferdinand David, "I feel as if someone is lying in wait for me and is saying, 'Halt, no further!'"[6]

Lind gave her last concert in Berlin on the day that the first performance of *Elijah* was to have taken place. Before she left Berlin, King Friedrich Wilhelm IV wrote her a simple note in his own hand, appointing her as his chamber singer. While still in Berlin, she wrote to Herr Buettner, "I would have given a great deal to have been at the meeting with you, Grote, and Mendelssohn. On the 21st I'll leave for my fatherland and am looking forward to it very much."

Lind left Berlin on the 19th of October; she was anxious to return to Sweden before the cold weather set in and looked forward to giving benefit performances for poor students. On the way she sang in *The Daughter of the Regiment* in the port city of Hamburg. The critics noted that she was not in good voice.

---

In a note to her mother on the 20th of October, Cécile again expressed the opinion that her husband was on the way to complete recovery, although still not well enough to leave home.

She instructed Felix not to write any letters, but one day while she was resting, he sent his last book of six songs, *Opus 71*, and his *Morning and Evening Service* to Breitkopf und Haertel for publication. On the same day, October 25, he sent an urgent plea to his brother: "Come as soon as you can, Paul; you are the best medicine." Paul replied that he must be at home for his birthday but would come the following day, on the 31st of the month. He admonished his brother, "Felix, take care of yourself. Remember that you have a wife and five children." Three days before Paul arrived, Felix suffered a severe setback.

On the evening of the 3rd of November, Felix uttered a loud scream, and he was delirious all night. Cécile knelt at her husband's bed and prayed that he could die. Paul stood by his bed as if turned to stone by the pain, and Schleinitz, Ferdinand David, and Moscheles remained nearby.

The next day, Thursday afternoon, the 4th of November, he was unconscious, as if in a deep sleep, but still breathed quickly and regularly. At eight o'clock in the evening, believing the end was near, Paul fetched Cécile, who had lain down for a few hours. Gradually the composer's breathing became slower, and after 9:14 Felix Mendelssohn breathed no more.

Schleinitz wept as he told friends,

I'm not sorry for Mendelssohn, he is with God, but for his wife and for us. Oh, this woman, she knelt at his bed like a saint, calm, and without complaining she kissed his forehead and received his last breath. And when no one else came, she listened for a while, laid her head on his breast and looked at his face with childlike devotion. Then she folded his hands.

The following day Cécile sent a brief letter to her mother:

*Chère maman,*
The good Lord has willed that I lose all my happiness…I had the strength to see him die. I will also have the strength to live for my children… Having lain down a little after dinner, I saw when I got up that all was lost. I never stopped praying to God that He would deliver him from his suffering.
They assure me that he had not been aware of his suffering since Wednesday, but his sad expression and his plaintive voice, when he replied to my questions, will be engraved on my heart forever.
My health is good, thank God, and I'm doing everything to save my strength for my children. My brother-in-law, Paul, is with me. I am surrounded by good friends. Don't worry about me; you yourself know that God gives supernatural strength on such occasions. I am, as always, *Ta devouée* Cécile.
Pray for me.

At age thirty, Cécile was now a widow; her five children ranged in age from two to nine-and-one-half years. She helped to make some decisions about the funeral, but on the advice of her friends and doctor, she did not walk in the long funeral procession nor attend the funeral service on Sunday. At her request, *Frau* Moscheles looked after the children's mourning clothes.

Six friends, all musicians—Ferdinand David, Gade, Hauptmann, Moscheles, Rietz, and Schumann—carried the coffin from the Mendelssohn home at Königstrasse 5 to St. Paul's Church, followed by a great multitude. The streets were lined with people. Only after all the people had left the church after the funeral service did Cécile go alone to pray at the casket.

Paul Mendelssohn, Ferdinand David, and other friends of the composer accompanied the casket on a special night train to Berlin. They were met in Dessau by a choir and finally in Berlin by the Singakademie choir and the Berlin Cathedral Choir, at the cold, dark morning hour of seven o'clock. The choirs sang Bach's motet, "Jesu meine Zuversicht," and "Wie sie so sanft ruhen" (How Gently They Rest), from Bach's *St. Matthew Passion,* at the graveside service.

Felix was buried just before eight o'clock, next to his sister Fanny. At the time of her previous birthday he had promised he would be with her on her next birthday; that was six days hence.

———————

Jenny Lind was on a boat on her way to Stockholm when Mendelssohn died and did not learn of his death until she read an account of it in a Swedish newspaper nine days after his death.

———————

1. Nikolaus Lenau (pseudonym), 1802–1850, was Austria's most important Romantic poet.
2. Puettlingen, an Austrian diplomat from 1838, amateur composer and vice president of the Viennese Gesellschaft der Musikfreunde, was very active in musical matters.
3. Bruce Seymour has written a biography of Lola Montez, 1821–1861. After King Ludwig was driven from the throne, Lola fled to America, later to Australia. Back in the U.S. Lola repented of her past life and became an eloquent speaker, decrying slavery and doing many charitable deeds. After a stroke in 1860 she asked that the Episcopalian clergyman Dr. Hawks minister to her. He has written a moving account of her penitence and death.
4. Thackeray, 1811–1863, was born in India to upper middle class parents but spent most of his life in Britain.
5. Mendelssohn never heard Lind sing one note of *Elijah*. (He had written the soprano arias with her voice in mind.)
6. This term is reminiscent of chapter 38, verse 11, from the book of Job, for which Mendelssohn had a strong predilection.

# twenty-four

After Jenny Lind learned about Mendelssohn's death, she was afraid to open letters from her German friends, lest they mention him. She told Hans Christian Andersen that there was a change in her soul and she would never be the same. For months, again and again, she expressed her grief, first to Mme. Wichmann, six weeks after Mendelssohn's death, and a month later to Mme. Birch-Pfeiffer. In January 1848, she wrote to *Frau* von Jaeger in Vienna,

> *Ach Mutter,* what a blow Mendelssohn's death was for me! That is why I have been silent for such a long time. I could not write a word in the first two months; it felt as if everything was dead. Never was I so happy, never did I feel so exalted as when I spoke with him! And rarely did two people understand each other as well as we two did. How glorious and strange are the Lord's ways! With one hand He gives everything, with the other He takes everything!

Approximately six weeks later she wrote to Ferdinand Hiller,

Stockholm, 3 April 1848

Best Herr Hiller,

…There are no more music festivals for me since Mendelssohn is no longer on this earth! And I could not make myself go to one in Germany when I recall how happy I was when once I was with him at such an occasion! Excuse my openness…It is only my deep friendship and veneration for the departed one that gives rise to these words, and the feeling that I and many others share about the irreplaceable loss which still upsets and unsettles me deeply.

The following week she composed a letter to *Frau* von Kaulbach in Munich,

What did our good Hauser say about that dreadful account of Mendelssohn's death? Oh! my dear *Frau* Kaulbach, that was my first, my greatest loss, and it made the whole winter quite different for me. It seems to me as if the bond of union between me and Germany is entirely destroyed. But God be praised that he no longer lives in such times as these! These terrible revolutions everywhere. It is almost better to have departed.

Most of Europe was restless at this time. The revolutions had begun in France in February of 1848 with the overthrow of King Louis Philippe and the creation of a second French republic.[1]

After riots in the German states, the liberals proposed that Germany become a unified country with a national parliament. The provisional government, however, could not agree on a constitution, and the old order was restored. The Italian states also experienced revolts, causing Pope Pius IX to flee Italy. Giuseppe Mazzini hoped to unify Italy, but the Italian states were protective of their independence. And in the Austrian Empire, nationalistic fervor grew among the various ethnic groups—Croats, Czechs, Germans, Hungarians, Romanians, and Slovaks. In March Fuerst Klemens von Metternich and the Hapsburg emperor were ousted; all the Hungarian lands achieved freedom, and the new constituent assembly freed the peasantry. In Stockholm hundreds of anti-royalty reform-minded students threw stones; the army retaliated, killing twenty men and wounding ten.

Albertine Mendelssohn's brother was killed in a riot in Berlin, Richard

Wagner was involved in riots in Dresden and had to flee to Switzerland, and Felix Mendelssohn's friend Dr. Alfred Becher, amateur composer and journalist, was court-martialed and shot for "revolutionary activities" in Vienna.

---

Lind was now in her fatherland to raise money for the establishment of a school for the training of disadvantaged children in the dramatic arts. To that end she sang in twenty-seven operatic performances at the Royal Swedish Opera from the beginning of December to the middle of April, at greatly heightened prices. All the money she earned went to a fund administered by trustees.

Apparently Hans Christian Andersen still hoped that Jenny Lind would respond favorably to his advances in the early spring of 1848. She encouraged him to never cease hoping for love elsewhere and to look for a good wife. Yet she also wrote, "Believe me, one needs only poetry…or to live in your present world—alone—but therefore not unhappily."

---

In London, the court decided in Bunn's favor, and Lumley paid Bunn £2,500 in damages for Lind's failure to honor her contract. Bunn's book *The Case of Bunn vs. Jenny Lind* became a best seller, and one English paper published a cartoon of a nightingale with a human female head saying, "I like de English ver' much but not their hot cross bun."

---

Fearful that Jenny's phenomenal success would drive a wedge between them, Guenther had written very little to her for three years. But when they often sang together during the winter, some of the old feelings were rekindled in both singers. Because Jenny was planning to leave the stage, Guenther could hope for marriage again. The two singers exchanged rings.

When she left for England by steamer, two weeks after her last performance in Sweden, Lind received the kind of farewell never before given to a private person. After a serenade by chorus and orchestra, a multitude on shore waved and shouted until the vessel was almost out of sight. Her former singing master, Isak Berg, his wife and daughter, and Lind's new companion, Josephina Ahmannson, accompanied her to England.

"On the steamship I had eyes for only one person on the shore. He is dearer to me than all and everything," Lind wrote to her guardian.

She arrived in England on Good Friday, the 21st of April, with strong feelings of gratitude toward Lumley and the English public for her great success in the previous year. Now she wished to help Lumley again. But she refused to sing until May 4, the anniversary of her debut in London. This time she opened with *La Sonnambula*. If anything, her artistic success was greater than it had been in the previous year.

In the summer she met the nineteen-year-old pianist Otto Goldschmidt and invited him to Clairville Cottage. She decided that he was a "very amiable young man who had much talent and much feeling" and invited him to accompany her in one of her more spectacular charity concerts in Brompton at the end of July. He played two of Mendelssohn's *Songs Without Words* at the event. At the time Lind had no inkling of the important role he would soon play in her life.

On one occasion Lind talked to Mrs. Grote about Guenther for a whole hour. And in June she wrote to Munthe, "My greatest wish is that you learn who Julius, of whom I am so fond, really is, and what an unusually lovable character he has, so that it will become clear to you, Herr court magistrate, what an exception he is among the young men of the present. I am not blind—I speak the pure truth."

With her strong religious scruples against the stage, Lind's new companion, Josephina Ahmannson, exerted great influence on Lind. As a result, Lind now said that she wanted to have no actors or singers in her private world when she settled down and had a family. Guenther did not share her scruples, and Isak Berg became concerned about other difficulties that were developing in the singers' relationship. To further complicate matters, Jenny reproached Guenther in one letter about one of his early love interests, a young singer with a sullied reputation.

Because Lind could earn far more money in England than in Sweden, and because she wished to get married, Berg suggested they get married in April of the following year and then go to London together, where she could sing until she had enough resources to be able to live as she liked.

Despite the difficulties in their relationship, Lind continued to inform friends about the prospect of her marriage. Ostensibly to the Frankfurt businessman Herr Buettner she wrote on July 28, "Perhaps I will soon get married…don't be afraid that it will be a *mesalliance*. I have chosen the best, most noble and most faithful heart, the one who has suffered the most in his love for me…I am now ending the great *carrière.*"

Lind was not quite twenty-eight years old.

Several weeks later, after mentioning two "dark letters" she had received from him, she sent a reply to Guenther:

Clairville, 13 August 1848
I am uncertain as to which frame of mind, concerning me, my Julius is in. I almost wonder whether or not you will accept the enclosure, as I fear you have turned your loving heart to another. I am enclosing a picture, a daguerreotype of me. If you don't want it, give it to Dr. Munthe, because he is the only person I would want to have something which was intended for you. But I hope you will keep it, because I wanted to show you my real tenderness in that I am striking the note which has gone through all of my life, and that has made my soul vibrate so often in all the changes and battles.
Your warmly affectionate Jenny

The note that Jenny struck on the piano was G. However, on the following day she confided in her guardian,

It's impossible to get a quick reply and advice from Julius, the only one whom I would gladly have obeyed and followed. Because of this, I have been unwise enough to write things to Julius which made him so angry that now neither he nor I can see daylight. But he ought to know me better, ought to better realize to what unpleasantness I alone am subject, and not be as cruelly sensitive as he is. But of course, this sensitivity is a natural result of the real inner beauty and nobility of his soul. I know this, and would not reproach him with half a word. All the same, his way of reacting so sharply to my words, so unforgiving, has hurt me terribly, and troubles me very much, particularly since I must constantly be prepared to do violence to my own feelings in front of a large audience.

After Her Majesty's Theater opera season ended, Lind began a tour throughout the British Isles on the 24th of August, in accordance with her contract with Lumley. At the beginning of the tour in Newcastle, she met a young English captain of the Indian army named Claudius Harris, a distant relative of Mrs. Grote. He became enamored with Lind and accompanied her and Josephine to Scotland and Ireland. At first she regarded him as a dull young man.

In a letter to Mme. Birch-Pfeiffer, Lind wrote about her feelings but did not name Guenther or any other man:

> I'm glad and grateful from morning to night! I don't feel lonely…and only find the days fly by too dreadfully quickly. I have blitheness in my soul which strains towards heaven. I'm like a bird, I don't feel the least changed, quite the contrary; and the *summa summarum* is that I have won the greatest profit out of both outer and inner misfortune and can thank God that I know what trouble is! All tends at last to good! God does not die.

Somewhat later she explained to Mme. Birch-Pfeiffer that she loved the English character with all her soul and was fond of Harris because he was a typical Englishman.

From Edinburgh, at the end of September, Lind wrote to Munthe, "Please refer no more to the matter of G. and me. Everything that reminds me of it disturbs and desolates my whole being, and I have not had time to grieve yet." And at the beginning of October, from Dublin, she wrote to Josephson, "I won't get married. I don't know where *the one* is."

In October, after having sung in Donizetti's *Daughter of the Regiment,* she made eight exclamation points after the entry of that engagement in her diary and underlined it heavily. That was to signify that she had made the last operatic appearance in her lifetime. The remaining engagements on the tour were to be concerts.

In the second half of November, Lind spent much time with Harris in the area of Bath. He proposed, and she accepted, after insisting that he get his mother's blessing. Their common interests were the devotional life and charitable works. She chose to be married on March 7, the anniversary of the evening in 1837 when she realized that she could succeed as an opera singer.

For some time already Lind and some of Mendelssohn's English friends had planned to set up a Mendelssohn scholarship. Consequently she and Josef Staudigl sang in a performance of *Elijah* in Exeter Hall in London on December 15, 1848—she, for the first time—in order to raise the money. Because *Elijah* is a dramatic work, she could use all of her dramatic gifts in this form, as well as pour out her increased religious fervor. Mendelssohn had written the oratorio with her voice in mind, notably the opening of Part II, *Hear Ye, Israel,* which begins with what he referred to as her "wonderful" high F.

Lind did not add the brilliant ornamentations that audiences had learned to expect from her in operas but sang only the notes that Mendelssohn had written and declaimed the words with the utmost intensity and poignancy. At the time sacred compositions were virtually never interrupted by applause in Britain, but after she sang "Thus saith the Lord, 'Be not afraid,'" the people could no longer restrain themselves and encored it and several arias later.

Afterwards Lind wrote to Mme. Birch-Pfeiffer, "I have begun to sing what has long been the wish of my heart—oratorio. There I can sing the music I love; the words make me feel like a better person. Listen, dear mother, my career in the future will take this direction, and my favorite ideal will be realized."

As soon as Lind completed her contract with Lumley, she sang only for the poor and disadvantaged and for the construction of hospital wings or to found new hospitals in England.

In the winter of 1849 she spoke and wrote often about her upcoming marriage to Harris, thus to the wife of Bishop Stanley of Norwich,

> I want support, I am completely alone, and just when I want help, the finger of God brings me this dear one who can share my feelings about works of charity, just as I do. I could never marry anyone who did not think as I do on this…We want to live quiet and uninterrupted lives somewhere. I want to be near trees and water and a cathedral. I am tired in body and soul, but most in my soul. More my soul than my body.

Meanwhile, in London, Lumley was frantic again; His Majesty's Theater would fail again without Lind. Lumley did not stop pleading until she agreed to sing six operas in concert form.

The wedding date, March 7, came and went. Nevertheless, that month Lind wrote to another English friend, "I'm convinced Harris is the only one. There are not many like him on our earth; I am not *blind*. I only tell the truth, as he possesses every attribute that I had always wished for…so I must praise God and believe I have received the most wonderful reply from Heaven."

Although the first opera in concert form was excellent, the public was not satisfied, and so Lumley pleaded with Lind once more. Now Lind was in a dilemma; Lumley and her colleagues accused her of ingratitude if she deserted the stage, as if it were a disgrace; she believed that either way "all her happiness was now gone forever." Yet Lind gave in again.

In April a lawyer, Nassau W. Senior, came to draw up a formal wedding document, despite the fact that Lind told Mr. Senior that Harris and his mother regarded the theater as a "temple of Satan" and the singers as "priests of the devil."

Harris also wanted Jenny to hand over all her money into his keeping, because he believed it was unscriptural for a woman to control finances. Furthermore, Harris wanted a clause to say that she would never again appear on stage after they were married. The lawyer objected on grounds that it robbed Lind of her freedom. Lind refused both of Harris's demands and gave Mr. Senior permission to tell Harris and his mother that she believed her first duty was to Lumley; if Harris saw sufficient reason in that to break the engagement, then it was better broken.

Mrs. Harris relented, but because of the divergent opinions, the wedding was postponed to May 16. Harris's leave ended four days later, but he would leave the army if he married.

In the first of the six staged operas, Lind sang *Sonnambula* better than ever, and the audience fervor equaled that of her debut. The last, *Roberto il diabolo*, on the 10th of May 1849, her last appearance in a staged opera, was a triumph unmatched by any of her debuts or farewells.

Lind had not informed Munthe about her engagement to Harris until the 27th of April, saying that only she, God, and Josephine knew "what struggles there had been" but that now her mind was made up. She asked Munthe to find a little country house for her and her future husband in an area with lakes and forest near Stockholm. "I have won a really *whole* and *pure* heart, a person whose life I hold in my hands. I can no longer escape—the hour has struck—I shall soon be married."

Mr. Senior and Mrs. Grote left for Paris on the same day that Jenny sang in the sixth opera. Before they left, Senior advised Lind not to give in to the demands of Harris and his mother and to come to Paris if, for some reason, the marriage fell through.

Four days later Lind simply wrote to Munthe, "I am still *myself*; that is, I am not yet married." But now Harris asked for a postponement, and she and Harris agreed on a mutual release. Lind asked Munthe to meet her in Paris, and she left London. On what was to have been her wedding day, Lind burst into Mrs. Grote's hotel room in Paris. A week later she wrote to Emma Flyare, a friend in Stockholm,

Should I of all people marry someone who not only robbed me of all joy in my past career, but positively forbade me ever to appear on the stage again because his principles would be deeply wounded, and after such a confession, he would never be able to look his friends in the face again? I have left the stage—but I cannot allow anyone to tear down what I have built up with so much labor—and what a life for me, to live with someone who took all memories even of my divine life from me...He did nothing but read psalms and go to church, could talk of nothing but the last judgment which was at hand. I would have lost my senses, and was well on the way of doing so.

When she had tried to explain her dilemma to Harris, she continued, he had told her that she was "completely damned." In the same letter she expressed surprise that all of England was rejoicing that she would not marry him. At the end she admitted that he was infinitely pure, loving, and faithful, but that he was *dull*.

As soon as Mme. Arnemann heard about the wedding plans, she rushed first to London, and then to Paris. Jenny sent Josephine back to London to pack and ship her clothes to Stockholm, and she went to Cologne with Munthe and Mme. Arnemann. There Lind consulted a doctor, who ordered six months of rest; he told her that she would probably have a complete breakdown if she began working before then.

From Cologne, Lind and Munthe went on a Rhine cruise, and at the beginning of July she went to Schlangenbad, a mineral baths spa situated in a deep valley of the Taunus mountain range, just north of Wiesbaden. From there she wrote many letters, the first to Mme. Wichmann:

Schlangenbad, 11 July 1849
I have experienced much lately, my dearest Amalia, and long from my innermost being to tell you about it; but not to put it all down on paper...things and experiences touched me and deeply affected my peace of mind. Everything in my innermost heart was undecided for a long time. I didn't know what to write. I was very close to marrying. But again it came to naught; and I believe this was for the best, as there were things that did not please me, and probably I would not have been happy...
O dear! I am myself again; and I feel that I have many other duties, and great duties, to fulfill towards others—although the finest, the most

sacred of all—I mean a mother's love, is forbidden—no! denied me! I
have often wished for the blessing of motherhood, for it would have
given me a much needed focal point for my affections. With it, and
through the varied experiences that accompany it, I could perhaps have
achieved something better than what I have attained until now.

But, dearest soul, I am happy all the same, inexpressibly happy, for has
God not endowed me with much more than I deserve, such as is granted
to few on earth?…My dear guardian came to Paris in order that I might
have someone I could trust near me.

On the same day, at long last, more than twenty months after Mendelssohn's
death, Lind penned her first letter to Cécile Mendelssohn Bartholdy:

Schlangenbad, July 11, 1849
*Sehr geehrte* [highly esteemed] *Frau,*
Because I *may not* possibly assume that you interpret my long silence as
a lack of concern, I will not further burden you with excuses. I only wish
to assure you that not a day has passed in which I have not thought of
you and the children, and have often intended to write to you, but have
always been prevented from doing so by the importunity of the great
masses of people with whom I have to deal.

Now I am sitting here in Schlangenbad, however, enjoying genuine rest
and heavenly air; and since I have the desire and also the need to send
you a few lines, it is a relief to fulfill this obligation, even though it
comes very late; I hope you will kindly read these lines.

It is still difficult for me to speak of your and all our loss, and I certainly
do not wish to chafe the wounds anew, but it is also certain that the
wound must certainly remain fresh with you, as it does with me to some
extent, and thus it can not be *old* or *new* for you to hear of *him*—so I
will speak from the heart somewhat, *geehrte Frau.*

His *Elijah* is divine. It is my opinion that he *never* composed anything
better, and could never have written anything more *sublime*…with what
love everyone still speaks of him! how all of them, the good English
people, understood precisely *this* music. We have celebrated virtual fetes,
and I sing my part in a very special spirit!

When I think back on everything, how lovely it was to have him
accompany me on the piano! And one evening in Leipzig, when you

stood in a window niche and listened to us in such a nice way. *Ach!* You are certainly being forced to endure the greatest trial, but yet you must be grateful when you recall how much and how dearly you were loved and respected by this pure and most gifted being! And even more, the *good fortune,* the *knowledge* that in *you* he had found the *right one, the only one,* and through your gentleness and love was, might I say, carried on the wings of song through this wilderness of the artist's life! This must be the only consolation, *geliebte Frau,* and I am delighted for you that you feel this.

May you remain healthy, so that the children will keep their mother, and may the good Lord keep you in His utmost care.

I will keep the letters[2] which you so kindly sent me, for the rest of my life, and regard them as a treasure. How very, very dearly I would have liked to have been with you at the lovely Wichmann home, in order to have been able to whisper a kind loving thought to you, and how vividly I can experience with you what you must have felt there. *Ja,* perhaps I can say, honored lady, that *not many,* rather only *few* people understood him as I understood him. Don't regard this statement as presumptuous; the best that I have ever felt all lies in this conviction! I hope that we can meet in this world some time, and after a few words we would certainly understand one another quite well.

Some day all three of us will meet! Then things will be better: God be with you, *sehr geehrte und geliebte Frau.* Do not forget her who loves you deeply.

Jenny Lind

---

1. Marx and Engels had published their *Communist Manifesto* in German shortly before the revolution began in France.
2. It has not been possible to identify the letters about which Lind wrote.

# twenty-five

CÉCILE RECEIVED JENNY LIND'S LETTER IN BAD KREUZNACH, A SPA NESTLED ON an island where the Lahn River, an eastern tributary of the Rhine River, leaves the Palatinate mountains and where the vineyards produce grapes for the Mosel and Rhine wines. She replied quickly and just as quickly received another letter from Lind:

Schlangenbad, 20 July 1849
*Sehr geehrte Frau,*
Yesterday I received your dear letter…and am truly grateful that you have kindly let me know that we are so close to one another that we can finally see each other again…
I am looking forward so much to seeing you. It has been my wish to do so for a long time. I will visit you in Kreuznach if you have no objections, as I will be going to Ems[1] from here in six or seven days. What a pleasure it will be for me to see all the children!…*Auf Wiedersehen.* To my last hour I remain your truly devoted Jenny Lind.

Lind visited Cécile in Kreuznach and wrote to her again in August:

*Geehrte Freundinn* [Honored friend],

I call you that because you acted as one, and received me as a friend, and spoke *vertraulich* [intimately] with me, and I will faithfully remember this until my death. I am unable to thank you; I can only assure you that my visit in Kreuznach was extraordinarily pleasant for me, and has *vermildet* [*sic*] many things for me and placed the seal on my love and friendship for *you, liebe Frau,* to the depth of my soul. God will reward you for your hospitality. I, too, found that we actually said very little to one another and we certainly did not share with one another that which filled both our hearts.

First of all, I didn't know how I should conduct myself, especially when I saw the loving concern of your mother, who, naturally, could not know how much I was concerned about her well-being, and because of that, I was fearful of bringing back painful memories. I would gladly have said *more, more,* and it would not have been enough for a long time.

One thing is certain, I love you very much, *geehrte Freundinn,* and I will always regard you as an expression, the expression which clearly enough tells me who you are and what you were to him, as his nicest memorial, and I also recognize his worth, that he really was what I thought he was, and what you saw represented in such purity and nobility.

May I confess that Lilly has made an indescribable impression on me, and that I love her most of all the children? The little thing has something quite irresistible for me, as she has much, much feeling, more than an ordinary child. That child will give you the nicest memories for the longest time and will weld the past and the present together.

At the end of the letter she thanked Cécile for some music and a memorial page, sent greetings to Mme. Jeanrenaud and the children, and assured Cécile that she would remain her faithful and loving friend.

Lind sent Herr Buettner an account of her meeting with Cécile:

It gave me the utmost pleasure to see Mme. Mendelssohn! The lady was warm, good and kind beyond all description, and we did not want to part. It is unbelievable how good it was to be with her, and I have embraced her in my faithful loving heart, to keep it there until it breaks!

She had three children with her; they are very lovely. The older girl resembles her father extremely much, and this made an impression on me!!!

---

Cécile returned to Leipzigerstrasse 3 in Berlin with her children in October in order to spend the winter there. On the second anniversary of her husband's funeral she resumed her correspondence with Sophie Horsley. She mentioned how sad she felt because she was "reminded of earlier times at every turn." And she wrote about her children, "Marie is like Felix only in appearance; she is not nice. I have to talk to her and scold her all day. Carl is strange at home, but very good at school. Paul is terribly lazy, but good and upright. Lilly is a feast for the eyes."

---

Otto Goldschmidt had returned to Hamburg, and there, at the beginning of December, he accompanied Lind in several concerts. He was able to persuade her to sing some Mendelssohn songs for the first time since the composer's death. Thereupon, Lind invited Goldschmidt to a pre-Christmas children's ball in Luebeck and enthusiastically danced with the young pianist.

On January 9, 1850, Lind signed a contract with a representative of the sensational American showman Phineas Barnum, nicknamed King of Humbug, to go to the United States in the following summer. The terms of the contract[2] were on such a grand scale that Wall Street in New York was sure that Barnum would have to declare bankruptcy.

Lind explained to Gusti von Jaeger in Vienna that she accepted the offer in order to "earn a great deal of money" so as to endow a school for poor and lost children in Sweden. She continued by saying that she regarded the invitation to America as a direct answer to prayer and that she prayed that God would guide her there and "graciously forgive [her her] sins and infirmities."

Her aim, she said, was to help widen God's kingdom.

---

In 1850 Felix Mendelssohn still had many admirers. That year, after Hector Berlioz heard Mendelssohn's *Italian Symphony* in London for the first time, he wrote to a friend,

I looked for you the other night at Exeter Hall. I wanted to tell you what you know as well as I do, that symphony of Mendelssohn's is a masterpiece, stamped as gold medals are stamped, in one stroke. There is nothing newer, livelier, or more spirited, more noble, more masterful [*plus savant*] in his *libre* inspiration.

However, in the same year, under a pseudonym, Richard Wagner published a diatribe against Mendelssohn and all Jewish composers:

Jews are ruining German music...Forthrightly repulsed in his efforts at contact with our people, at any rate wholly incapable of grasping the spirit of our race, the cultivated Jew sees himself forced back upon the roots of his own clan...the Jew has never had an art of his own...the Jew approaches German art in an altogether superficial manner...[All Jewish music] strikes a German as alien, cold, strange, indifferent, unnatural and distorted. Jewish musical works produce upon us the same sort of impression as would, for example, the recitation of a poem by Goethe in Jewish jargon...

What phenomenon can make all this clearer to us...than the works of a composer of Jewish origin endowed by nature with a musical talent such as was possessed by few musicians before him? Everything that our study has laid bare concerning the antipathy between the Jewish character and the German character, all the contradictions of his character in itself and toward us...combine to create a wholly tragic conflict in the nature, the life and the artistic works of the late and prematurely deceased Felix Mendelssohn Bartholdy. He has shown us that a Jew can possess the richest abundance of specific talent, the finest and broadest culture, the most intense and sensitive sense of honor, without ever being able once to produce a profound influence upon us, an effect that moves the heart and soul...such as we have felt innumerable times as soon as a stalwart of our own art...merely opens his mouth to address us...Mendelssohn catered to our amusement-hungry imagination, presenting us with a series or a pattern of the subtlest, smoothest figures, as in a kaleidoscope...

Only where the oppressive sense of this incapacity seizes upon the composer and drives him to the expression of weak and melancholic resignation, does Mendelssohn present his characteristic mood...This is a tragic trait.

Wagner also vilified Meyerbeer's music but did not name the composer, because he was still among the living.

---

In 1850 Lind gave several concerts in Berlin and one in Dresden. The brilliant twenty-year-old pianist Hans von Buelow, at the time an enthusiastic admirer of Wagner's music and often harsh critic of Mendelssohn's, heard Lind sing the latter composer's "Auf Flügeln des Gesanges" in Dresden. He subsequently wrote to a friend, "Auf Flügeln" was never tossed off better; the last three notes were the most beautiful I have ever heard. Mendelssohn's song is charming; you know I don't readily rave."[3] And Ludwig Rellstab, music critic for the oldest Berlin paper, *Vossische Zeitung,* opined that no words were adequate to describe the magic of Lind's singing of Mendelssohn's "Suleika."

In Altona, Lind sang Mendelssohn's "Rheinisches Volkslied" at Clara Schumann's concert—with its many high F-sharps the song was a perfect vehicle for Lind's voice. Robert Schumann found the effect indescribable. At this time Clara made a diary entry about her as a person: "What a pure, pure artist's soul; all she says refreshes one, how she always hits upon the right thing and expresses it in few words—in short, never perhaps have I loved and revered a woman as I do her."

From Hamburg, Lind returned to Sweden in May. Eight cannon-shots greeted her at the pier, and the crowd was so enthusiastic that she had difficulty getting into her carriage.

During the seven weeks that Lind spent in Stockholm, she angered her countrymen by refusing to sing on stage and openly declaring that she was shocked at the ungodliness she saw in her fatherland. During this time she was profoundly influenced by two clergymen, Pastors Per Wieselgren and Peter Fjellstedt, and a lay minister, Karl Olof Rosenius.[4] All three men hoped to deepen the faith of Swedish Lutherans. Lind attended their meetings—as did many members of all social classes—often twice a day and sang at their church services. Her participation was the subject of much gossip, some of it vicious and false. The writer of one article claimed that she had become so agitated at a meeting that she went into convulsions.

Some church leaders and some of the intelligentsia despised the teachings of the three men and publicly deplored the fact that Lind had become involved in the movement. One popular theater piece mocked Lind's piety and inferred that she was helping to pave the way for Jesuitism and Roman Catholicism. At the time that was the worst criticism anyone could level at a Lutheran. Because the clergymen advocated abstinence, one establishment named one of their alcoholic drinks "little Wieselgren."

Lind took the clerics' teaching about anti-materialism and worldliness seriously but reasoned that she needed to make money to help needy children.

She sang in Sweden for the last time in the afternoon service at the Clara church on the 25th of June. The satirical *Sondags Bladet* commented on the event with biting ridicule and scorn. They described her as "The Mam'selle who is so concerned about her salvation" and who sang for "poor old women and other such folk."

Two days later Lind left Stockholm without fanfare.

---

For her American tour Lind recruited Julius Benedict as piano accompanist and Vincenzo Belletti, former member of the Stockholm Royal Opera, as baritone soloist.

A few weeks before her departure for America, Lind sent a farewell letter to Cécile. It was impossible for them to meet again, she said, as she had to hurry to England. In her letter she expressed the wish that Cécile would remain healthy and that her children would be a source of pleasure for her. She ended the brief letter thus:

> You will probably never again be able to be really happy. I seriously believe that, but that is *earthly* happiness, very unreliable. Read God's Word as much as possible, my dear one; this is the only remedy I can recommend, for this is the only thing that is faithful and unchanging! Remember me now and then with kindness and friendship, and truly believe that I have deep love and affection for you in my soul. *Auf Wiedersehen*, beloved friend; may we have a happy reunion here or on the other side of the grave.
> Ever your truly devoted Jenny Lind

On August 17, 1850, Lind sang in Handel's *The Messiah* in Liverpool. The critic J. W. Davison termed her performance "inspired" and the aria *I Know That My Redeemer Liveth* as "perfection." Four days later she embarked on the steamer *Atlantic* in Liverpool, and after eleven days at sea she arrived in New York City, population approximately 200,000.

Barnum had paved the way superbly for Lind. Because most Americans were musically unsophisticated at the time, he played up her charitable giving and her modesty. Nathaniel Parker Willis, the most musically sophisticated critic in the United States at the time and one of Lind's greatest champions, wrote about her,

> That God has not made her a wonderful singer and there left her is the curious exception she forms to common human allotment. To give away more money in charity than any other mortal, and still be the first of prima donnas! To be an irreproachably modest girl, and still be the first of the prima donnas! To be humble, simple, genial and unassuming, and still be the first of the prima donnas. To have begun as a beggar girl and risen to receive more adulation than any queen, and still be the first of the prima donnas.

A crowd of thirty thousand people waited for Lind when the steamer docked in New York City.

She sang her first concert on the 11th of September, dressed in a white gown and with white flowers in her hair, in the largest entertainment center in New York City, the 11,000-seat Castle Gardens. She donated the entire proceeds of the concert, almost ten thousand dollars, to various charities in New York City.

She sang at Castle Gardens a total of six times that month—the second also for charity—before she went to the more musically sophisticated Boston. In all, she sang in thirty-seven different centers, including a number of east coast cities in the United States, in Havana, Cuba, and in Toronto, Canada. From Philadelphia, Lind informed Buettner that she was very happy and that she would sing in Havana in January. After she had been in the United States for two months, she sent a second letter to Judge Munthe:

> It's a great joy and gift from God to be able to earn so much money and then help one's fellow human beings with it. That is the greatest joy I desire in life. All else has vanished from my many colored earthly path. Few people realize what an inwardly *beautiful* and quiet life I lead, how infinitely little the world and its vanities have intoxicated my mind! Herring and potatoes, a clean *wooden stool* and ditto *wooden spoon* with which to eat porridge would make me happy as a child and set me dancing with joy.

Wherever Lind went she sang the folk-like spiritual songs of Oscar Ahnfelt,[5] the Swedish "spiritual troubadour" and former member of the Swedish Royal Opera.

While Lind was in the United States, little Felix Mendelssohn Bartholdy, who was not quite eight years old, died in Berlin after a bout with scarlet fever and was buried next to his father in February 1851. Cécile felt that she had lost her best child. She bore the loss characteristically well; to her great-aunt Julie Schunck in Dresden she wrote, "I, like you, believe God has a claim on all our possessions; God has been with me."

While Lind was being warmly embraced in America, *Die Neue Zeitschrift für Musik* published an acerbic article about her by Hans von Buelow in February 1851:

> After the genuine enthusiasm for the ingenious [*geistvoll*] Liszt, only the platitudinous [*geistlos*] Jenny Lind could enrapture the blasé Berliners…Her virtuosity as a singer was there, of course…but now, in order to dazzle the public she had to employ other empty means, such as charlatanism. Now Jenny Lind cannot be reproached for having profited with all her might from this magnet of *Weltnerv,* money. She knew how to dupe the German and Anglo Saxon race…to appear in the most brilliant light; the arch-German cardinal virtue, prudishness, seemed to suit her; Italians and Frenchmen would perhaps have booed her mercilessly.

In the summer of 1851 Julius Benedict returned to England, and Otto Goldschmidt, who had come to the United States in May, became Lind's accompanist. Only a few months later, from Niagara Falls, Lind informed Munthe that she had met the man she had always longed for. She dissembled on one point in the letter:

8 October 1851

...Otto has all of Lindblad's refinement and genius, together with
Guenther's charm and power, only is still more reliable and cultured, and
a young man beyond reproach. And what is still more remarkable, he
exceeds Lindblad, Mendelssohn and Guenther in being fond of me and
thinking well of me and allowing me to influence his soul in the most
uplifting way I can. He is like Guenther, only smaller and much younger.
He is the first person I could confidently and with inner conviction *in
every way* swear before God that I could make happy and am really made
for. But—he is so young—seven years younger than I—though only
outwardly.[6] For his soul can never be more mature. Goldschmidt can
fulfill *all* the needs of my soul. We are made of the same stuff, and one
of us only needs to begin a sentence before the other knows the end of
it...He spent all his youth in love and thought for me, though I never
knew it. He heard me in Leipzig six years ago and since then has been
my warmest friend! Isn't this cruel! Isn't this absolutely desperate! His
family is Jewish, though he is as little Jewish as I. No one *has* ever existed
or can exist with whom I can live so as *one* soul and *one* heart as with
Goldschmidt—but age, age!

In a letter to a certain Mrs. Peirrepont, Lind vigorously defended her choice
of husband. Two days before her wedding, without a hint of jubilation, Lind
informed Jakob Josephson about her engagement. On the 5th of February
1852—and after Goldschmidt's Christian baptism—Jenny Lind and Otto
Goldschmidt exchanged vows in the home of the Boston banker Sam Grey Ward.
The Episcopalian Bishop Wainwright officiated.

At the end of the following month, from their large, elegant, and beautifully
appointed seven-room apartment in the finest hotel in Northampton,
Massachusetts—with silver, not wooden, spoons—Lind sang the praises of her
husband to a Dr. Baird:

I feel most thankful towards my Heavenly Father that in all truth I
can say that I gained the best, most disinterested friend in my beloved
husband—he is so mild and kind hearted that it is only seldom you will
find a similar character. We are both musical souls—and in all matters
we feel the greatest, most perfect sympathy.

The Goldschmidts had been married for three months when they presented their first concert together. The audience was decidedly less enthusiastic about Goldschmidt's piano solos than about his wife's singing.

---

The couple went to England in June, then spent some time in Hamburg and at a spa before they settled in Dresden. And in the summer of the following year, Lind finally realized her fond dream of becoming a mother. But before that blessed event, fearing that she would not survive, she made her will and instructed Munthe to inform Lindblad and his wife that she had loved them to the end and that, next to her child, they were nearest to her heart.

Just before Cécile Mendelssohn Bartholdy died in her aunt's arms in Frankfurt on September 25, 1853, when Walter Goldschmidt was a few weeks old, she held out her arms as if to welcome someone. She was buried in Frankfurt. Subsequently her two sons, aged fifteen and twelve, went to Berlin to live with their uncle Paul Mendelssohn, and her two daughters, aged almost fourteen and eight, remained with their grandmother in Frankfurt. During the summers the boys were reunited with their sisters and grandmother.

---

Lind returned to sing in Vienna for the first time in seven years in the spring of 1854; there the critic for the Viennese *Abendblatt* wrote another panegyric about her:

> The seven years in which we have heard a number of important female artists have only strengthened our view that Jenny Lind not only surpasses every other female singer, but is unique…She reveals to us the absolute beauty of singing itself in an almost mysterious manner. We don't hear what is sung, but listen to the singing. Like the old king, Jenny Lind changes everything she touches into gold.
> She sang an aria from Bellini's *Beatrice de Tenda*. Is that the same music which we regard, with reason, as insipid and mawkish? What we experienced felt like a fragrant breath. The quiet secure tone slowly swells at great length, and then disappears just as slowly, and at great length…
> The warbling in Jenny's mouth in imitation of birdsongs in Taubert's "Ich muss nun einmal singen" became a thing of ravishing beauty, and the height of technical bravura.

When Lind met August Bournonville in Vienna, she declared, "The theater is nothing but lies and deception [*Blendwerk*]." Otto and Bournonville begged to differ, but Lind argued, "If the archbishop of Canterbury says it is a sin, it is a sin." She often shuddered now when she spoke about the times she sang in theaters.

In 1855 Lind returned to Leipzig for the first time since her concert on Easter Sunday eight years earlier and sang some of Mendelssohn's songs in a Gewandhaus concert. Here, too, she was received with acclamation. It was the first time that Otto Goldschmidt returned to the city where, as a young conservatory pupil, he had fallen in love with Lind.

---

After the violinist Joseph Joachim[7] performed with Lind in a benefit concert in Nordeney, he opined that she had found favor, particularly in England, for her piety and her charitable acts. "But," he continued,

> …her peculiar talent lies in *coquetterie* more than deep feeling and understanding—yet she has great skill in *expression*. Added to this, she has a thoughtless, superficial piety—she often invokes God when talking of the most ungodly things, such as money and fame. But she is very clever; she can be extremely charming and she is much more clearheaded than I am. She knows *exactly* what she wants.

Eduard Devrient was also not impressed by Lind. He sent a report about the then thirty-six-year-old Lind to his wife:

> I visited *Frau* Goldschmidt-Lind. She is old, talks intelligently, but I always had the feeling that she didn't voice her own thoughts, or that she concealed much more, so that she utters generalities, albeit of the best kind…They have obviously confused her about Mendelssohn's music; she says it is far too modern, his music labored…She did not edify me. I went from there to Mrs. Ehrhardt; it was like going from a snowy landscape to a fruitful summer.

The often severe Berlin critic Eduard Hanslick, however, had only words of praise for Lind as a singer. He heard her perform the soprano arias in Haydn's *Creation* and a Mendelssohn song at the Lower Rhine Festival in 1855 and opined in a review that the orchestra performed flawlessly and the choirs were imposing, but that Jenny Lind deserved the crown: "This wonderful singer still has the old magic. Although her outward appearance has lost a great deal of its bloom, even appearing sickly, her features are transfigured when she begins to sing, so that she appears to be almost beautiful."

After concert tours in England and Scotland in the spring of 1856, Lind commented to Amalia Wichmann, "I said my farewell to the English public and am thankful to God for all His grace…They are kind to me because there is no kinder public on the face of God's earth than the English—partly because they don't understand a thing, but I would not call that real success."

The Goldschmidts returned to Dresden, and there Lind gave birth to a daughter, Jenny, in 1857. A few months later they moved to England and rented a house in Roehampton, Surrey. The next year they moved to a large three-story home in Wimbledon Common, London. There, four years later, she gave birth to a third and last child, Ernst. When she informed Amalia Wichmann about his birth, she said that the time she spent with her and her family in Berlin in 1845 and 1846 was the happiest and most carefree of her life.

---

Mendelssohn's elder daughter, Marie, had married her mother's English cousin Victor Benecke and now lived with him in England.[8] When they moved to the vicinity of Wimbledon Common, Lind invited them for dinner. After a few meetings she sent a note to Marie:

> I can say that the greatest pleasure for me this year was that I have drawn closer to you, *liebe* Mme. Benecke, and have become friends with you. The old deep love for your parents has again completely surfaced in love for you. And so let us remain true friends, *meine liebe* Mme. Benecke.

To Mme. Wichmann, Lind reported, "We are living near Marie Mendelssohn, her husband is a clod, it feels strange to have Mendelssohn's daughter here."

Although Lind donated untold thousands to charity, she was less charitable toward her former companions, Louise Johansson and Josephina Ahmannson. In January 1868 she wrote to Munthe, "I hope you can soon tell me that my pensioners have wandered homewards. It's dangerous to have these pensioners; they live so terribly long, these pitiable, joyless creatures."[9] Lind became ever more brusque as time went on, especially when she felt she was being imposed upon. Her husband frequently had to smooth things over. Clara and Robert Schumann's daughter, Eugenie, met Lind in Wimbledon and noted that she had a "forbidding manner."

A copy of Eduard Magnus's large oil portrait of Mendelssohn had pride of place in Lind's living room wherever she lived. She often remembered him in her letters to Mme. Wichmann until the latter's death; thus, in December 1872: "Otto constantly reminds me of that friend who departed from us on the 4th of November, twenty-five years ago. O dear Amalia! How full life is of painful and beautiful memories!"

Many years later Lind-Goldschmidt informed Marie Benecke that after her death she should have her large portrait of her father.[10]

In 1876 Lind visited Sweden—incognito—for the last time and was shocked to see Lindblad's large bulbous blue nose. She wrote to Munthe, "Poor Adolph! A genius like he—and besides, so morally pure as he always was. Often those with the purest hearts suffer most in this world."

Although Lind had ended her operatic career at age twenty-nine, she continued to sing for many years. She often performed in oratorios, in particular in *The Creation, The Messiah,* and *Elijah.* Most of the proceeds in England again went for the construction of hospitals or hospital wings or scholarships. Clara Schumann heard Lind sing some Mendelssohn songs at a soirée at the home of Marie Benecke when the singer was fifty years old and declared that she still sang "gloriously."

Lind vacillated in her feelings about England. In the mid-1870s she wrote to Countess Baudissin in Dresden that it would have been better for her children in Germany: that England was a land of luxury and sloth; that "Fashion reigned and few achieved the highest peak of human development." She also believed that her husband's career would have achieved greater heights in Germany, and she blamed England and the English boarding school that her elder son attended for his personality traits of "fearful intensity" and irritability. However, six years later she declared that there was "no place like London, as far as being interesting and intellectually stimulating [*geistig*] goes."

Near her home at Wynd Point, Malvern, at the age of sixty-three, Lind made her last public appearance as soloist at a benefit for railroad workers. But she continued to sing in the Bach choir that her husband founded and directed,[11] and her voice still soared above the other sopranos in that choir.

Lind was in bed on the 2nd of November 1887 when her daughter came in to draw back the curtains. As the sun briefly came out from behind the clouds that morning, Lind hummed a few measures of Schumann's song "Sonnenschein." That was her swan song. She died later that day, two days before the fortieth anniversary of Felix Mendelssohn's death.[12]

Many years after Lind's death, her former singing teacher, Manuel Garcia, recalled, for Goldschmidt, the manner in which Lind sang the soprano solos in *The Messiah* at Exeter Hall in 1847:

The first notes of *Come unto me, all ye that labour* were so full, pure and perfect in intonation that the refrain which preceded them sounded out of tune. To these qualities there was added so much tenderness in the singing of the whole air that one can understand that the irresistible applause that greeted the final shake forced an encore from even the rigid Costa, who was conducting.

Lind is the only female commemorated in Westminster Abbey—next to Handel's statue, with the words "I know that my Redeemer liveth" on the plaque.

1. Ems, approximately fifty miles north of Kreuznach, also on the Lahn River, and about seven miles southeast of Coblenz, is situated at the edge of a volcanic region rich in mineral springs. It is there that the so-called Romantic region of Germany begins.
2. According to the contract, Lind would sing in 150 concerts at $1,000 per concert; she could terminate after 60 or 100 concerts with appropriate penalties. She would not appear in operas and would have no fewer than four numbers in a concert. All travel and living costs for herself, her companion, and servants, as well as the cost of horses and carriages in every city, were covered.
3. Von Buelow was Livia Frege's nephew. Much later he said he had much to make up to Mendelssohn.
4. Wieselgren was a highly educated pastor, a passionate religious-social agitator of great significance in the social and cultural life of Sweden in the 19th century. The satirical *Sondags Bladet* characterized his meetings as a devouring cancer (*Krebs*), spreading disease into the body of society and infusing poison into its bloodstream. Dr. Fjellstedt was also well educated; according to Wieselgren, he could read and write in thirty languages. Rosenius had great influence on Sweden's religious development during the 1800s.

5. Ahnfelt, 1813–1882, composed or arranged the music for Lina Sandell's hymns and traveled throughout Scandinavia singing the hymns while accompanying himself on a ten-stringed guitar. The state church opposed these hymns and, anticipating a royal injunction on them, ordered Ahnfelt to sing them before King Karl XV. After hearing them, the king told Ahnfelt he could sing them as much as he wished in both his kingdoms (Norway and Sweden).

6. Goldschmidt was born in 1829; Lind, in October 1820.

7. Joachim was concertmaster and solo violinist at the court of Hannover at the time.

8. That branch of the Benecke family had left Germany to become factory owners in England.

9. Louise died in 1894 at age 83. Josephine also outlived Lind; she had remained with the family while the children were growing up.

10. Marie Benecke survived Lind by ten years, dying the same year that her brother Carl died in a psychiatric institution shortly after his 59th birthday. Their brother Paul had died in 1880. Lilly was greatly loved by everyone; she died of cancer in 1910.

11. Goldschmidt conducted the first performance of Bach's B-minor mass ever heard in England.

12. Lind died of cancer; she had spent Christmas alone in Cannes, France, in 1886, when her doctor in Cannes informed Goldschmidt that the cancer was progressing. She had always feared that disease, and only after Goldschmidt came to Cannes did Lind learn what she was suffering from.

## ACKNOWLEDGEMENTS

I am deeply indebted to librarians in England, in several countries in Europe, and in the United States.

To Peter Ward Jones, foremost Mendelssohn scholar in the United Kingdom and head of the music library at Oxford University, who was always most helpful even after his retirement.

To the numerous librarians at the Staatsbibliothek Preussischer Kulturbesitz in Berlin.

To the archivist at the Historisches Archiv der Stadt Köln (Cologne).

To the librarians/archivists at the Stadtarchiv, the Leipzig Universitäts Bibliothek and the Leipzig Musikbibliothek in Leipzig.

To the librarians at the New York Public Library and the Pierpont Morgan Library in New York City.

To the librarians at Stanford University.

To the librarians at the libraries or archives in Stockholm, Sweden: the Kungl. Biblioteket; the Statens Musiksamlingar, Svenskt Musikhistoriskt arkiv; Statens musiksamlingar, Musikmuseet; the Statens musiksamlingar, Musikaliska akadiems Bibliotek, and the Stiftelsen Musikkulturens fraemjande.

To Jenny Lind's great granddaughters, Lady Barbara Lind Welby, in Grantham, Lincolnshire, and Mrs. Oliver Woods, Lewes, Sussex, for information about Jenny Lind.

To Dr. Jutta Biedel for her gracious hospitality in Berlin in 2004.

To friends and writers in Winnipeg who cheered me on, especially Agnes Dyck and Sophie Shulman who read the complete third-last and fifth-last versions, respectively, of the manuscript; the members of MCWA, a writers' group in Winnipeg, who heard several parts of *Passion Versus Duty*, and to Dr. Robert Glendinning, who, in the short time since we became acquainted, was helpful with the wording of the comments at the back of the book and the difficult task of choosing the front cover of the book.

Furthermore, to the Board of Conrad Grebel College, University of Waterloo, who granted me time and the financial assistance for some of the more than twenty research trips to England, Europe and the United States for both *Felix Mendelssohn: Out of the Depths of his Heart* and *Passion versus Duty*.

To the staff at WordAlive Press in Winnipeg for their patience and quick responses to my many comments and questions, especially to Gustav Henne, who, unfortunately, departed from this earth just months before *Passion Versus Duty* went to press, and Caroline Schmidt. Also to all those working behind the scenes.

And finally, thanks to Alf Redekopp, archivist at the Mennonite Heritage Centre in Winnipeg, who oversaw the classification of my copious research notes and copies of the thousands of original letters relating to both Mendelssohn books, in both digital and hard copy form, many in the original languages in whole or part.

Thank you. Thank you to all. I can never thank you enough.

# Persons Index